Literacy Instruction *for* English Language Learners

Nancy Cloud
Fred Genesee
Else Hamayan

A Teacher's Guide to Research-Based Practices

HEINEMANN
Portsmouth, NH

Heinemann
361 Hanover Street
Portsmouth, NH 03801–3912
www.heinemann.com

Offices and agents throughout the world

The authors and publisher wish to thank those who have generously given permission to reprint borrowed material:

Chapter 2: "Mini Shared Reading and Collaborative Text Writing" from *Teaching to the Potential: Mini Shared Reading as a Bridge to Proficient Reading in L1 and L2* by Barbara Flores. Presented February 2008 at the Pre-Conference Dual Language Institute at the 37th Annual International Bilingual/Multicultural Education Conference, sponsored by the National Association for Bilingual Education, Tampa, FL. Reproduced by permission of Barbara Flores.

Chapter 6: "Suggestions for Assessment Accommodations for ELLs" from *Designing Comprehensive Course Assessment Prompts, Portfolio Tasks and Exhibition Projects for ELLs* by Deborah Short. Presented December 2007 at the Secondary ESL Institute, Pawtucket, RI. Reproduced by permission of Deborah Short.

Permission for use of student work in Chapters 2 and 5 granted by the Charles N. Fortes Elementary School (a Museum School), Lori Hughes, Principal, Providence, RI.

Library of Congress Cataloging-in-Publication Data
Cloud, Nancy.
Literacy instruction for English language learners : a teacher's guide to research-based practices / Nancy Cloud, Fred Genesee, Else Hamayan.
p. cm.
Includes bibliographical references and index.
ISBN 13: 978-0-325-02264-2
ISBN 10: 0-325-02264-X
1. English language—Study and teaching (Elementary)—Foreign speakers.
2. English language—Study and teaching (Middle school)—Foreign speakers.
3. English language—Study and teaching—Foreign speakers—Research.
I. Genesee, Fred. II. Hamayan, Else V. III. Title.
PE1128.A2C57 2009
428.2'4—dc22 2008043444

Editor: Kate Montgomery
Production: Elizabeth Valway
Cover and interior designs: Lisa Fowler
Composition: Publishers' Design and Production Services, Inc.
Manufacturing: Steve Bernier

Printed in the United States of America on acid-free paper
13 12 11 10 VP 3 4 5

To all English language learners who enrich our schools
and to their teachers who enrich our educational system
with their commitment and hard work.

NC, FG, & EH

Contents

Acknowledgments vii

Introduction 1

Chapter 1: Foundations 7

Big ideas about schooling for ELLs 8
What we know about literacy development 12
What we know about literacy development in ELLs 14
Getting to know your English language learners 20
Summing up and looking ahead 32
Additional resources for teachers 34

Chapter 2: Emergent Literacy in a Second Language 35

Home language literacy first 36
The importance of English 36
Know your students 37
Planning stage-appropriate instruction 40
Teaching initial literacy to ELLs 43
Promoting growth in literacy for beginning ELLs 60
Learning to read in a new cultural context 68
Using literature for cross-cultural learning 69
Curriculum development for ELLs 71
Summing up 73
Additional resources for teachers 74

Chapter 3: Helping English Language Learners Become Biliterate 80

Critical role of the home language 82
Different levels of biliteracy 88
Using the home language to support English 93
Social aspects of biliteracy 104
Implications for all teachers 110

Summing up 112

Additional resources for teachers 113

Chapter 4: Reading and Writing to Learn: Academic Language and Literacy for ELLs 116

Promoting language and literacy across the school day 118

Joining forces for language and literacy development 121

Promoting academic literacy in K–8 classrooms 124

Strategies for teaching literacy and academic content together 133

Extending academic learning 147

Summing up: Learning English while learning content 149

Additional resources for teachers 154

Chaper 5: Connecting Reading and Writing 155

Making the connection between reading and writing a routine in the classroom 156

Strategies for ELLs in the beginning stage of literacy 158

Strategies for beginning and beginning intermediate stages 161

Strategies for intermediate advanced and advanced supported stages 176

Summing up 181

Additional resources for teachers 182

Chapter 6: Assessment 185

What is assessment? 186

Classroom assessment and ELLs 194

Assessment tools 219

Summing up 220

Additional resources for teachers 221

Appendix A: Checking for Quality of Books in Languages Other than English 223

Appendix B: Quick Guide to ELL Literacy Strategies 224

References 231

Index 240

Acknowledgments

We'd like to thank those whose help was invaluable in the creation of this book.

A very special thanks to the talented editors and staff at Heinemann. We particularly appreciate the support, encouragement, and feedback of our lead editor, Kate Montgomery, literacy editor, who understood our vision for this visually explicit research-to-practice teacher resource book and made our concept come to life. Special thanks also go to Olivia MacDonald, editorial coordinator, Elizabeth Valway, production editor, and Doria Turner, promotions coordinator.

We also thank our colleagues Yvonne and David Freeman for their encouragement and support from the very first step of writing this book. Closer to home, we thank Naomi Holobow, whose keen eye and good humor helped clean up our manuscript, and Ludmila Nekola for her perspective as a nine-year-old trilingual. We also thank all the teachers who have taught us and inspired us over the years. We hope our book encourages classroom teachers, ESL teachers, and reading specialists to teach well despite misguided policies that ignore the best interests of children and to continue to nurture and enjoy the diversity that English language learners bring to school.

Introduction

Reading and writing are essential for successful schooling. Students learn to read and write in school, and they use reading and writing in school to acquire new knowledge, skills, and points of view about themselves, their communities, and the world around them. It is not sufficient for students to acquire merely basic reading and writing skills; these will not get them very far. Rather, once they have acquired the basics in the primary grades, they must acquire *academic literacy*—fluency and accuracy in reading and writing—so that they can use these skills to comprehend and express complex and abstract ideas in written form.

Jerome Bruner, a famous child psychologist, said that to acquire literacy skills in school was to extend the capacity of one's cognitive abilities to go beyond the limits of oral language.

Reading and writing are also fundamental life skills. They are critical for day-to-day living, whether for getting a driver's license, looking up schedules for movies or other events, reading signs in stores or on roadways, or navigating the Internet to look for information about their favorite singers or athletes, or simply for pleasure. Functional literacy is the cornerstone of a well-functioning democracy since literacy allows people to follow political debates in the newspapers and to exercise their power to vote at the ballot box. For these reasons, and others, it is in everyone's best interest that English language learners acquire advanced levels of functional literacy so that they can participate fully in school and, later, in society at large.

This book is about teaching students to read and write. Our focus is on students in kindergarten to grade eight who come to school speaking a language other than English and who have no or little proficiency in English. We refer to these students as English language learners (or ELLs for short). These students are a large and growing sector of the United States and other economically developed English-speaking countries around the world, for example, Canada, England, Australia, and New Zealand. Teachers in virtually every urban school in such countries and, increasingly, in most suburban and rural schools as well have ELLs in their classrooms.

Although helping ELLs become proficient in English is typically seen as the responsibility of English-as-a-second-language (ESL) and bilingual specialists, this is not enough. To achieve the goal of proficiency, all teachers must assume responsibility for teaching literacy skills to ELLs at the same time as they teach students the core curriculum. Teaching reading and writing skills cannot be done successfully if it is restricted to certain times of the day or to certain teachers, nor can it be isolated from the rest of the curriculum. All teachers need to be competent in teaching reading and writing to ELLs. In this book, our goal is to enhance all teachers' effectiveness in facing this challenge.

The primary audience for this book is practicing teachers who teach reading and writing to ELLs in kindergarten to grade eight. The book will also be of interest to reading specialists, ESL teachers, bilingual teachers, administrators, coaches, mentors who provide support to new or struggling teachers, and any other teaching specialists working with ELLs. This book should be of interest to educators in any country (e.g., the United States, Canada, England, Australia, and New Zealand) or school with a population of ELLs where English is the primary language of instruction. In fact, educators in any country with a significant immigrant or refugee population face the same challenges, regardless of the language of the host country. The book will also appeal to teachers in international schools all over the world that have large ESL populations.

Wherever possible, the guidance we provide in this book is based on relevant research.

NOTE

Special points that are addressed to specific groups, like administrators, special education teachers, or policy makers, are presented in separate sidebars like this one throughout the book.

WE EMPHASIZE A RESEARCH-BASED APPROACH FOR SEVERAL REASONS:

1. School personnel are under increased pressure to show that their practices are evidence-based.
2. By linking practice with research and theory, we, the authors, can better explain to teachers *why* certain teaching strategies and approaches are more appropriate than others.
3. Highlighting research evidence allows teachers who use those practices and approaches to feel confident in what they are doing. In particular, many "best practices" require sustained implementation for real benefits to be realized. Understanding the research basis for these practices can give teachers the confidence they need to continue even when the short-term gains of the approach they are using seem modest.
4. A research-based approach provides administrators with the evidence they need to justify their educational practices and policies when they are challenged by board members, politicians, or parents.
5. Linking research to practice helps identify gaps in research evidence, which in turn helps establish a research agenda for professional researchers so that they can help fill these holes in our educational knowledge.
6. Basing their practices on research encourages teachers and school-based educators to undertake action research in their classrooms, especially when evidence is not available from professional researchers.
7. A research-based approach encourages school personnel to look for the *why* of what they are doing, leading to improved teaching.

Research Question

ELLs are quiet in class because they lack well-developed proficiency in English to respond. However, they might become more engaged if you have them work in subgroups with other students who share the same language. Try doing a brief experiment in your class in which you ask students to describe what they most like about school (or a question related to a topic in one of your subjects, like science). First of all, ask all the students to do this only in English, and then group the ELLs into groups that speak the same language and tell them they can formulate an answer among themselves using their home language. They should work together to prepare a response to the whole class in English. See which method results in a higher rate of engagement among your ELL students.

Although much research has been undertaken during the past two decades on literacy development in ELLs, some significant areas, such as the acquisition of writing skills by ELLs, have not been explored in depth. There is also little research on ELLs who begin school beyond the primary grades and have had limited prior schooling and literacy instruction. Research on sociocultural factors and even on instructional issues is available but somewhat fragmented and often lacking focus. Some research is so specific that it is difficult to generalize to other contexts or classrooms. We believe that classroom teachers and school-based educators in general should be continuously evaluating their own practices and theories to validate and improve them in order to enhance student performance. Thus, we encourage classroom-based research, especially when issues have not been explored adequately by professional researchers. We pose Research Questions, identified by a magnifying glass in the margins of the book, to draw your attention to questions that you could investigate in your own classroom, like the one on this page.

When we discuss issues that lack a strong research base, we are necessarily more speculative in our suggestions. In these cases, we draw on what we believe to be best or reasonable practice given what we know from our reading of research on language teaching, learning, and education in general. A great deal of professional wisdom has shown itself to be valid over the years (Ayers 1988, Clandinin 1986, Schon 1983, Wein 1995); we draw on that wisdom when needed. Of course, by doing your own classroom-based action research, you, too, will acquire the same wisdom over time.

To facilitate your understanding of the research base for planning literacy instruction for ELLs, we summarize research findings relevant to the issues we are discussing in the main text on file cards marked *Research Finding* alongside the relevant text—like the one about reflective teachers.

We also use quotation bubbles to present direct quotes from research studies to back up our claims and recommendations; see the quotation from Reese and her colleagues about

Research Finding

Research shows that one of the hallmarks of effective schools is reflective teachers and administrators who examine the effectiveness of their work (DuFour & Eaker 1998, Freeman 1998).

the role of ELLs' home language in the acquisition of reading skills in English.

"... early literacy experiences support subsequent literacy development, regardless of language, and time spent on literacy activities in the native language whether it takes place at home or in school is not time lost with respect to English reading acquisition. ..."

(Reese et al. 2000, 633)

As well, we use shaded boxes in the text to emphasize particularly important information in point form for your attention.

Although we link educational practice with research throughout the book, this is first and foremost a practical guide for educators. We have avoided highly technical terms, and, on occasion, we isolate technical descriptions in sidebars; we also use lots of classroom examples to illustrate our main ideas and provide additional practical references for those who want to extend their understanding of specific issues. These appear at the end of each chapter under the heading Additional Resources for Teachers (see sample on page 6).

You will become familiar with all of these icons and other special features of the book as you continue reading.

Additional Resources for Teachers (A Sampling from Forthcoming Chapters)

- National Clearinghouse for English Language Acquisition and Language Instruction Educational Programs: www.ncela.gwu.edu/

  This website provides a wealth of information on English language learners including information on demographics and federal policies.

- http://nancykeane.com/rl/317.htm

  This website lists 135 wordless or almost wordless picture books that can be used with ELLs with no or only emergent literacy skills.

- A list of selected multicultural book publishers that offer folktales and fables that are useful for young ELLs follows:

  Culture for Kids (www.cultureforkids.com)

  Asia for Kids (www.afk.com)

  Bilingual Books for Kids (www.bilingualbooks.com)

  Shen's Books (www.shens.com)

Learning in two languages: Questions parents ask (in Spanish/English)

- A PBS Parents' Website: Because educating multilingual children offers unique opportunities and challenges, parents may have questions as to what to do at home in each language. This article provides answers to many of these questions and useful advice that parents can use to support language development and reading at home. The website, which supports the use of native languages to promote language and literacy development in bilingual children, is organized into three sections: 1) Talking with Children, 2) Reading to Children, 3) Other Questions Parents Ask.

  www.pbs.org/parents/readinglanguage/spanish/articles/multifamilies/main.html

CHAPTER

1

Foundations

Big ideas about schooling for ELLs 8

What we know about literacy development 12

What we know about literacy development in ELLs 14

Getting to know your English language learners 20

Summing up and looking ahead 32

Additional resources for teachers 34

This book is for mainstream teachers and reading specialists who work with English language learners (ELLs)—students whose first language is other than English or who have not fully mastered oral English. It is also for English-as-a-second-language (ESL) teachers whose primary responsibility is to promote these students' proficiency in English so that they can succeed in school. There is a growing number of such students in all schools: urban, suburban, and rural.

Our goal is to provide guidance to mainstream teachers, reading specialists, and ESL teachers on how to teach literacy in English to ELLs so that they become fluent readers and writers and successful in school. In this chapter, we lay the foundations for you to help ELLs become literate in English, their second language. We begin with general ideas about schooling for ELLs. Then, we discuss specific ideas about reading and writing for ELLs and describe what we know from research about literacy development in a second language. We end the chapter by describing what is important for teachers to know about their ELLs.

Big Ideas About Schooling for ELLs

We begin this chapter with some big ideas that have emerged from research on language and literacy development in ELLs. These ideas have also emerged from our work with ELLs, their teachers, and other educators. We return to these big ideas in more detail throughout the book as we talk about how best to teach reading and writing to ELLs. These are ideas that can guide your thinking, instructional planning and delivery, and assessment with ELLs.

BIG IDEAS ABOUT SCHOOLING FOR ELLS

- ❑ Learning takes time.
- ❑ ELLs are resourceful learners.
- ❑ It is easier to learn something new when it stems from something familiar.
- ❑ Language learning is culture learning.
- ❑ Classroom-based assessment is essential.

Learning Takes Time

Learning in school takes time, and it takes extra time for ELLs who must learn a new language, acquire new academic skills and knowledge in a cultural context that may be unfamiliar to them, and figure out how to fit in socially with their peers. We know this from common sense, and research has also shown the real outcomes of instruction often can take months or even years to be seen.

"... research studies conducted in several countries show that second language learners usually need at least five years to catch up to native English speakers in academic English. Sometimes the catch-up period is much longer."

(Cummins 2006, 60)

For example, numerous studies on bilingual education for ELLs have shown that they often score below grade level on standardized English tests in the primary grades of the program. However, by grades four, five, and certainly six, they score not only at grade level in English but often above grade level (Lindholm-Leary & Borsato 2006).

ELLs Are Resourceful Learners

ELLs are very resourceful. They use whatever language, cultural, and other background resources they have in order to do well in school. In particular, they use a lot of what they know about their home language when learning to read and write in English. This strategy is referred to by researchers as "bootstrapping," because when ELLs use their home language to help them learn English it is like children using the straps on snow boots to pull on their boots—it is much easier than if you just tug away at the boots themselves (see Figure 1.1). They also draw on experiences they have had before joining your classroom to make sense of what is going on in school, to interpret stories they are reading in class, to figure out how to make friends, and so on. Sometimes the connections they make from their home language and their family experiences are entirely appropriate, and sometimes they differ from what a native English speaker would do. When ELLs make connections between their home language and English, it is important to understand that this indicates that they are actively trying to break into English by using whatever resources they have. We should not penalize them during assessment activities for drawing on the home language and culture when they have not yet mastered English, even if this strategy results in a mistake. Rather, we should plan instructional activities that encourage students to make connections with the home language and culture; this can be done even when you, the teacher, do not know the student's home language.

It Is Easier to Learn Something New When It Stems from Something Familiar

Relating instruction for ELLs to what is familiar to them allows them to make sense of it and to acquire new skills and knowledge more quickly. Try reading something that is totally unfamiliar to you in English or your second language. You will find it extremely slow to read, difficult to understand, and almost impossible to remember. Now read something that is related to a topic that you are familiar with—you will not only read the text faster but you will understand the new parts more easily and remember the content better. ELLs are the same: They can understand a lot of what is being taught even before they master English if you begin with the familiar. Mainstream teachers and reading specialists can be challenged to know what is familiar to their ELLs because their backgrounds differ so much from their teachers. This means that mainstream teachers need to make special efforts to understand their ELL students and their backgrounds better, a topic that we address in the last section of this chapter. Throughout this book, you will read about strategies for gathering valuable information about ELLs and for building on their past experiences and knowledge when teaching them literacy skills in English.

Language Learning Is Culture Learning

When ELLs learn English, they learn more than the sounds, words, and grammatical patterns that make up English. They also learn how to use English in socially appropriate and effective ways. Most important,

Figure 1.1 Using the Home Language to *Bootstrap* into English

they are also learning how to be fully functioning and valued members of their peer group. Therefore, it is important to remember that when ELLs are struggling with English, it may be because they have a lot to learn—culture as well as language and new academic material. For older ELLs who start schooling in English in the higher grades, the challenge is even greater.

"The beliefs, attitudes, and values that each of us holds not only shape our perceptions of the world around us, they also make it easier or more difficult for us to build new knowledge."

(Hamayan, Marler, Sanchez-Lopez, & Damico 2007, 185)

It is important to make an extra effort to provide cultural scaffolding to help ELLs comprehend English and use it effectively. We describe ways of incorporating cultural scaffolding into everyday activities in the classroom and school throughout the book.

NOTE FOR ADMINISTRATORS

It is not only ELLs who are learning culture in your school! The English-speaking students from the mainstream culture have the opportunity to learn about all the other cultures represented among their classmates. Take advantage of the fact that you have a tremendous possibility for cultural enrichment for all students.

Classroom-Based Assessment Is Essential: Looking for the Best in Performance

Assessment is integral to effective teaching. Teachers use formal and informal methods of assessment to see if students are learning what they are taught and to judge the effectiveness of their instructional efforts. We discuss classroom-based assessment in detail in Chapter 6.

Teachers use formal assessment when they administer district- and state-mandated tests or even classroom tests. However, the most useful assessment activities in school are informal. They occur during day-to-day teaching, and they inform teachers whether their students are on track, if they have learned what they are being taught, and whether students who are getting additional support are progressing. It is critically important when you assess and when you interpret the results of your assessments that you look for the best in your students. This is especially true for ELLs because they will often demonstrate what they have learned and know in ways that differ from your mainstream students and

Research Finding

Many studies have pointed out the importance of using student-achievement data to shape and/or monitor program effectiveness (August & Hakuta 1997; Corallo & McDonald 2002; Reyes, Scribner, & Paredes Scribner 1999; Lindholm-Leary & Borsato 2006; Slavin & Calderón 2001). More specifically, effective schools use assessment measures that are aligned with the school's vision and goals, with the school's curriculum, and with related standards (Lindholm-Leary & Molina 2000, Montecel & Cortez 2002).

even from your own expectations, for example, when ELLs use words from Spanish to express an idea in English because they do not know the appropriate English words yet. Assess for the best: Be sure to look for what your students know, and understand that there is often evidence of growth and learning even in their "mistakes." When students say or do something that looks "wrong," think harder—there is probably a good reason why the student did what he did.

What We Know About Literacy Development

We all understand that literacy is the ability to read and write fluently and accurately. When we think of reading and writing in this way we think of skills that are linked directly with written language—word decoding, punctuation, paragraphing, and knowledge of text genres (expository versus narrative). All children need to be taught these kinds of skills and knowledge because they are not usually acquired naturally in the course of learning language. Children do not acquire literacy skills without some form of instruction, be it formal instruction in school or informal instruction when parents read to children at home or engage them in conversations about stories they have heard. Many English-speaking children may have acquired some of these skills before coming to school because they have had prior experiences with print or oral forms of literacy. However, there is a great deal of variation in how much even mainstream children acquire these print-related skills at home. Some ELLs will also have had print-related experiences in their home language before joining your class. Students, mainstream or ELL, who have had print-related experiences before coming to school are prepared for literacy instruction in school. However, some ELLs will not have had experiences with written language at home; they may speak a language at home that is not written, or their parents may be too busy working to read to them. Even those ELLs who have had print-related experiences in the home language may have had experiences with a written language that uses a different script (e.g., Chinese or Arabic) or that is organized differently, such as from right to left (e.g., Hebrew) and not from left to right as English is. Mainstream teachers and reading specialists need to consider these points when they plan literacy instruction for ELLs.

A definition of literacy that focuses only on written forms of language is an over simplification of what students need to know in order to read and write well. A host of different kinds of skills and knowledge are involved in reading and writing that are not linked exclusively to written language. For example, if students are asked to read a story about a visit to the dentist, they must have certain background knowledge: what a dentist is, what she does, and why children go to dentists. Some ELLs may not have had experience with a dentist, and, as a result, they will have trouble making sense of the story. In order to understand this story, students also need to know how verb tense and adverbs are used in English to sequence events: "*Jason had a toothache so his father took him to see the dentist. When Jason was in the dentist's office, the dentist gave him a coloring book so he wouldn't be scared. After he played with the coloring book in the waiting room for a few minutes, Jason went into the dentist's office.*" Many native English-speaking children will be familiar with how English is used to sequence events because they have been using English all their lives; many ELLs will not be familiar with these aspects of English. Of course, to understand the story, students must also know the meanings of specific words—*dentist, appointment, toothache, cavity, filling,* and so on. Most mainstream students, although not all, will know these words already simply as a result of being proficient in English; some ELLs will not.

Many of these skills are part of language competence in general, rather than competence with written forms of language per se. We know that the foundations of literacy lie in children's general language competence—the breadth of their vocabulary and their comprehension and production of complex language to explain, analyze, critique, and narrate. We refer to these as *underlying language competencies.* Acquisition of these kinds of language competencies requires experiences in which things are explained, people tell stories, or someone critiques something. These experiences can take place in the home or in school.

In case we give the impression that the diverse components of literacy development that we have just described exist in isolation and, therefore, can be taught in isolation, it is crucial to emphasize that literacy development is an integrated process. Figure 1.2 is a good graphic representation of how all of the components of reading fit together. As this figure illustrates, literacy involves bidirectional processes that include bottom-up and top-down processes. The bottom-up processes include foundational skills—related to letter-sound knowledge, decoding, and spelling—that are related to reading and writing individual words or sentences. The top-down processes include larger or higher-order skills that allow readers to link text to meaning and the world at large. Top-down processes include comprehension of text, inferencing, and analysis and criticism of written text in relation to what students know, among others. ELLs often have the knowledge needed to engage in top-down processes—knowledge of the world, story structure, knowledge of the meaning of individual words and common phrases—but they do not necessarily know how to apply this knowledge and these skills to written English. Nevertheless, this knowledge is a starting point that allows them to link written language to meaning, even before they can decode or encode words in English using processes represented at the bottom of the model (sounds, letters and numerals, punctuation marks, etc.).

ELLs who are learning to read and write English have all of the challenges that mainstream English-speaking children face, and, in addition, they must acquire proficiency in English for both social and academic purposes; they must acquire background knowledge that is the foundation of the school curriculum; they must acquire enough knowledge of mainstream culture to integrate and function effectively in school and with their schoolmates; and they must keep up with the academic curriculum. The multiple demands of schooling on ELLs need to be addressed all at the same time. This is a challenge for mainstream teachers who are also working with English-speaking students.

What We Know About Literacy Development in ELLs

A great deal of research has been done during the last two decades on reading acquisition. The lion's share of attention has focused on the acquisition of literacy skills in English as a first language. However, there

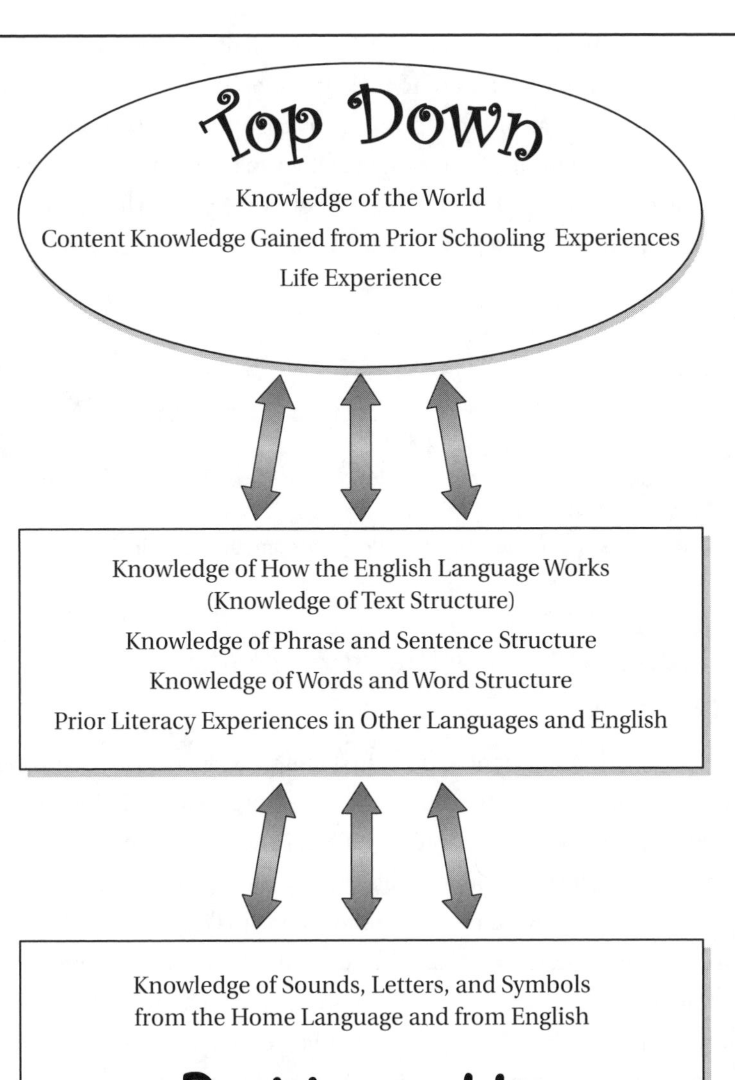

Figure 1.2 Top-Down/Bottom-Up

is also a growing body of research on the acquisition of reading and writing skills in English as a second language. The National Literacy Panel on Language-Minority Children and Youth (August & Shanahan 2006) and the Center for Research on Education, Diversity and Excellence (Genesee et al. 2006) published reviews of that research.

The findings from these two panels have guided the preparation of this book. In this section, we want to review for you the main findings from those reviews. These findings form the basis for the strategies and activities that we describe for teaching literacy to ELLs, so we will be returning to them throughout the remainder of the book. The main findings from those two panels that we think are particularly important follow:

1. Second-language literacy development is complex.
2. Second- and native-language literacy development are similar in some important ways.
3. Second-language literacy development differs from native-language literacy development.
4. What matters depends on the learner's stage of development.

1. Second-Language Literacy Development Is Complex

Like literacy development in one's first language, learning to read and write in a second language includes several interrelated skills and the use of diverse kinds of knowledge (cultural and real world) at the same time. Some of the component skills involved in reading and writing (like phonological awareness, decoding, and spelling) are building blocks for other skills, such as reading comprehension and complex writing. Difficulty with these building-block skills can impede students from achieving fluent and accurate reading comprehension and writing skills later on when more complex forms of written language are involved.

Meaning and interest in reading are also important components of literacy development; in fact, they are so important that they are crucial at all stages of learning to read and write. For reading and writing to be meaningful and interesting, ELLs must be able to relate what they are reading and writing about to their lives and to things in the world around them. Thus, background knowledge is yet another important component of developing literacy skills. If ELLs do not find the literacy activities in the classroom meaningful and interesting, they will not be engaged in the learning process. Engagement is important if ELLs are to sustain their efforts in learning to read and write from grade to grade. The more students read and write with interest and enthusiasm, the more proficient readers and writers they become. ELLs need to see that reading and writing are meaningful, useful, and relevant to their lives.

2. Second- and Native-Language Literacy Development Are Similar in Some Important Ways

Many of the same skills and abilities play an important role in learning to read and write in English as a second language and learning to read and write in English as a first language. For example:

- Print-based experiences and abilities, such as knowledge of letter-sound relationships and concepts of print, are important in early stages of learning to read.
- Phonological awareness is important in learning to decode and spell words; phonological awareness is what allows students to map oral language to written symbols.
- Complex language skills are important in comprehending and writing text.
- Background and cultural knowledge are important, whether reading or writing individual words or connected text; background knowledge makes reading meaningful.

3. Second-Language Literacy Development Differs from Native-Language Literacy Development

ELLs and native English-speaking students differ from one another in how advanced their competence in English is and in the kinds of background knowledge they possess. ELLs have lots of background knowledge, but it often differs from that of mainstream students. Another major difference between second- and native-language literacy development is that second-language learners draw on first-language skills and experiences, particularly in the early stages of second-language literacy development, to break into English. All the abilities and skills listed in the preceding section that are common to first- and second-language literacy development can be applied to learning to read and write a second language if they have been acquired in the first language. For example, Spanish-speaking ELLs who know the names or sounds of the alphabet in Spanish can and often will use those names and sounds to identify letters in English, until they learn the differences. This is particularly likely and useful during the early stages of second-language literacy development when ELLs have not yet acquired full mastery of English. As their proficiency in English increases, they have less need to draw on their home-language skills. However, they will continue to draw on the home language when they need to, even at advanced stages of literacy development. ELLs' use of home-language skills is a way for them to bootstrap into English reading and writing—it facilitates learning to read and write in English. The best example of this is seen in ELLs who can already read and write in their home language. They acquire literacy skills in English relatively quickly in comparison to ELLs who have no reading and writing skills in the home language.

"The studies reviewed . . . provide ample research evidence that certain aspects of second-language literacy development are related to performance on similar constructs in the first language; this suggests that common underlying abilities play a significant role in both first- and second-language development; that certain error types can be understood in terms of differences between the first and second languages; that well-developed literacy skills in the first language can facilitate second-language literacy development. . . .")

(August & Shanahan 2008, 7–8)

4. *What Matters Depends on the Learner's Stage of Development*

Some things are important at all stages of learning to read and write. Meaning and engagement are always important. Meaningful and interesting classroom activities provide engaging contexts for ELLs to acquire the diverse skills that are necessary to become fluent readers and writers. At the same time, some skills are especially important during particular stages of literacy development. Skills and knowledge that are related to small units of written language, such as the sounds of letters, mapping sounds to letters, and phonological awareness, are particularly important early on. However, because these small units of language are likely to be devoid of meaning, it can be a challenge to teach them in a way that is meaningful and interesting to the students. Students usually find learning these small units boring and useless unless they are embedded in meaningful activities; we talk more about this in Chapter 2. The small units of language are important early on because they are the building blocks of word-level skills, which in turn are the building blocks of higher-level reading and writing skills, such as sentence and text comprehension. Students who struggle with decoding words and sentences have trouble attending to meaning. Conversely, however, students can decode fluently but lack the skills needed to comprehend text—for example, knowledge of complex grammar and background knowledge related to academic text. Therefore, it is important to begin to build students' language competence and background knowledge during the early grades so they can draw on that competence and knowledge in higher grades when reading and writing text-length material becomes the focus of attention.

Certain genres of language are particularly important in the early stages, while other genres become more important in later stages. Narrative is particularly important in the early stages because all students are familiar with narratives and can relate to and become engaged in narratives. Expository and scientific genres of written language become more important in later stages when students read and write decontextualized academic material.

You can probably start to see that, if students are to acquire all of these interrelated skills, it is critical to plan instructional activities that integrate multiple skills at the same time—for example, by integrating instruction about letter-sound relationships with vocabulary development and with ELLs' understanding of content related to the academic curriculum. You do not have the luxury of teaching only one set of skills at a time; instruction must be multifaceted. This is true when teaching mainstream students as well; but, it is particularly important when teaching ELLs whose social and cultural backgrounds and levels of English language competence are also considerations.

Getting to Know Your English Language Learners

In order to translate what we know about literacy development into effective practice, it is critical to know your students well. This section describes what is most important to know about ELLs and offers suggestions on how to get to know them. Like all students, ELLs are highly individual. However, it is probably not an exaggeration to say that there are even greater individual differences among ELLs than among mainstream students. By definition, mainstream students have been exposed to mainstream culture and this can have a somewhat homogenizing effect on what they know, what they can do, and how they learn; for example, at the moment, all students in mainstream America know who Harry Potter is. ELLs who have just joined your class and have come from another country might not. It is critically important that you get to know your ELLs as individuals so that you can plan instruction that takes their learning resources and backgrounds into account. In the same way that we strongly believe that mainstream educators should start with what mainstream students already know and can do as a foundation for expanding their competencies, we should do the same for ELLs. Here are some important characteristics of ELLs that are worth thinking about because they might influence how your students learn and, therefore, how you might teach them.

IMPORTANT CHARACTERISTICS OF ELLS

1. Level of proficiency in English upon entry to your school
2. Prior literacy skills and training
3. Prior schooling
4. Grade level
5. Family background
6. Similarity of the home language and culture to that of the mainstream

In the sections that follow, we expand on each of these points and suggest how they might be important for literacy instruction and learning; we provide more detail in the chapters that follow.

Important Characteristics of ELLs

1. Level of proficiency in English upon entry to your school

Obviously, it is important to determine each student's proficiency in English when they join your classroom. This is essential so that you know what level of English you can use with them and where to begin when planning instruction that will advance their proficiency in English. ELLs with no or limited English will need more accelerated English instruction and support than ELLs who have some proficiency in English. It is important to determine ELLs' competence in *social language* as well as *academic language.*

Research Finding

Social language includes language linked to life in and outside the classroom, such as talking with classmates about interests and activities outside school, borrowing a pencil from a classmate, or asking for help. Academic language is linked to academic subjects and instruction, such as following instructions, knowing the names of concepts and objects used in a science or social studies class, describing events or phenomenon that are being taught in class, and describing or explaining events or phenomena in a science or social studies lesson (Chamot & O'Malley 1994, Cummins 2006).

Your school may have administered a standardized test to measure your ELL students' English language proficiency at intake. It is important to remember that the norms for standardized tests that are based on native speakers of English are not appropriate for interpreting test scores of ELLs. Moreover, standardized tests are not adequate by themselves because they assess ELLs in formal testing situations that may be unfamiliar to them and may even be culturally inappropriate or threatening. Be sure to use other informal forms of assessments as well—we provide case studies and lots of details about carrying out assessment of oral language and literacy skills with ELLs in Chapter 6. See the following suggestions for ways of thinking about how to describe ELLs' proficiency in English as a second language.

Ways of describing proficiency in English as a second language

1. Teachers of English to Speakers of Other Languages has published ESL standards for both social and academic language (TESOL 2006). These standards can be useful if your school district has not developed its own framework.

2. In addition to formal frameworks, you can also make a list of the kinds of social language you use with your students to organize them and guide their behavior through the day. You can use these informally to see how well ELLs in your class can use and comprehend such language.
3. With respect to academic language, you can analyze what you are currently teaching and make a list of basic vocabulary and functional language that is needed to comprehend, talk, and read about the subjects you teach. We give an example of this based on an analysis of a content unit in Chapter 4.

2. Prior literacy skills and training

Of course, it is also important to know about your ELLs' stage of literacy development and their prior literacy training, whether in English or in their home language. We talk in detail about how to assess the literacy skills of ELLs in Chapter 6. ELLs with some literacy skills in English have a head start; ELLs with some literacy skills in the home language also have a head start because they can transfer many of these skills to learning to read and write in English. When assessing ELLs' literacy skills, it is useful to refer to a model of literacy development. Alternative models of the development of literacy skills in English as a second language have been proposed. Your school, district, or state may have its own model of literacy development, which provides the basis for instructional planning and assessment in your school. Each model has its own way of labeling and describing the stages of development. Figure 1.3 includes a synopsis of some models and the labels that have been used to identify the stages ELLs go thorough in acquiring literacy skills in English. This list is not complete, but it gives you an idea of how varied and, at the same time, similar the labels are that different models use to describe the stages of ESL literacy development.

Research Finding

Research tells us that students who already know how to read and write in one language can learn to read and write English more quickly and easily than students with no prior literacy training. We also know that ELLs who have preliteracy or literacy skills in the home language will use those skills to break into English reading and writing (August & Shanahan 2006, Riches & Genesee 2006).

We present our own developmental framework for

Models of Literacy Development

READING							
Walker (1992; p. 33)	Emergent	Grounded	Expanding	Strategic	Reflective		
Bear et al. (2007; p. 10)	Emergent	Beginning	Transitional	Intermediate	Advanced		
WIDA (State of Wisconsin 2004)	Entering	Beginning	Developing	Expanding	Bridging	Reaching	
Boyd-Batstone (2006; p. 13)	Beginning	Early Intermediate	Intermediate	Early Advanced	Advanced		
WRITING							
Law & Eckes (2007, 89–98)	Drawing	Scribbling	Use of Letter-Like Forms	Copying	Inventive Spelling (parts of words to full words)	Standard English Spelling	
O'Malley & Valdez Pierce (1996)	Pre-Emergent	Emergent	Dependent	Developing	Independent	Fluent	Proficient
Bear et al. (Spelling) (2007; p. 10)	Emergent	Beginning (Letter-Name Alphabetic)	Transitional (Within-Word Pattern)	Intermediate (Syllables and Affixes)	Advanced (Derivational Relations)		

Figure 1.3 Models of Literacy Development

describing the literacy development of ELLs in Chart 1.1 to illustrate what such a framework might look like. We use this framework elsewhere in the book so that we have a common frame of reference. Our framework consists of four levels of proficiency: *beginning, beginning intermediate, intermediate advanced,* and *advanced supported.* Expectations for reading and writing development are described separately, but this is artificial because reading and writing development occur in tandem. In fact, we talk extensively about teaching reading and writing skills in an integrated fashion throughout the book—see especially Chapter 5. You will also notice that our framework includes different kinds of skills, knowledge, and predispositions, in keeping with research findings that we discussed earlier indicating that literacy development is complex and multicomponential. Some of the components of literacy we refer in Chart 1.1 are linked directly to written language; some are part of students' underlying language competencies; and some involve attitudes, motivation, and predispositions with respect

Literacy Development Framework

READING			
BEGINNING	BEGINNING INTERMEDIATE	INTERMEDIATE ADVANCED	ADVANCED SUPPORTED
• demonstrates knowledge of concepts of print and how print and books are organized • demonstrates interest in oral reading • shows interest in choosing books from class or school library • enjoys "reading" books alone or with others during book time • uses pictures and text features (bolding, italics) to support decoding attempts	• selects books of appropriate level and content, with teacher support • uses a variety of strategies to comprehend text • enjoys reading for pleasure • reads predictable text without assistance • can read different genres but may need some assistance	• independently selects books of appropriate level and content • reads with focus and purpose • chooses books of appropriate difficulty, both narrative and expository	• can listen to, read, discuss & analyze familiar & conceptually challenging text at grade level • understands and can identify features of different genres • can identify, use, and reproduce features of different genres • can compare main features of different genres of text
• uses knowledge of letter-sound correspondences to read words • can read and understand simple high-frequency words (sight words) • recognizes letters, words, and their parts • recognizes commonly used phrases (*thank you, the end, once upon a time*) • uses home language to decode unfamiliar words	• can read many words fluently • knows many of the highest-frequency sight words • uses a variety of strategies to read and understand new words: context, pictures, home language • can define/describe the meaning of familiar words, with assistance • can relate new words to existing vocabulary • understands word classes: nouns, verbs, prepositions, adverbs, etc. • can identify cognate words in English and home language with support	• can read many infrequent or uncommon words accurately (technical and academic words) • uses word parts (prefixes and affixes) and sentence context to understand new words • uses spelling patterns • recognizes and understands root words (nation/national) • can predict upcoming words based on context	• can identify "shades" of meaning in related words and identify alternative meanings of the same word • uses context cues to determine meanings of new words • can determine the correct/appropriate meaning of words with multiple meanings in context
• uses pictures and background knowledge to identify themes and characters in books (in English or home language) • can provide simple description of story theme with support • uses picture cards to describe major story events or a process • uses pictures as an aid to sequencing story events or a process (e.g., how to make tortillas; how foods get from the producer to the consumer) • can predict events in read-alouds (using home language or English) with prompting • can relate oral stories and expository text to personal life (using home language or English)	• can answer literal, inferential, and evaluative questions about text; may need scaffolding • can identify and describe not only main ideas but essential details of text • can critique text for truthfulness, relevance, meaningfulness, creativity • seeks assistance in understanding difficult text • monitors comprehension and uses variety of strategies to comprehend difficult text	• understands structure and purpose of different genres of text: narrative, expository • can answer literal, inferential, and evaluative questions about text with minimal scaffolding • uses text structure and transition words as an aid to comprehension • can identify implications of actions in text • can generalize meanings from texts to new contexts	• can identify the main idea or essential purpose in grade-level text and demonstrates this ability by paraphrasing, summarizing, and locating relevant details • monitors comprehension and uses a variety of strategies to repair comprehension of grade-appropriate text • expresses understanding of main idea or essential purpose of text in an organized, coherent, and appropriate fashion in oral or written form • can analyze and evaluate structure and content of different text genres • draws inferences from what is given in the text and is able to explain and defend the inferences made

Chart 1.1 Literacy Development Framework

WRITING			
BEGINNING	**BEGINNING INTERMEDIATE**	**INTERMEDIATE ADVANCED**	**ADVANCED SUPPORTED**
• knows basic concepts of writing: how to hold a pencil, organize letters from left to right, etc.	• handwriting is legible and age appropriate • appropriate spacing, letter formation, indenting, and use of symbols (. ? " ", ')	• fluent, legible handwriting	• writing is fluent, legible, and organized • enjoys writing for personal purposes
• can write letters, words, and common phrases independently or copy from models • knows the names of letters • sometimes uses names/sounds from home language • uses invented spelling to write words • sometimes uses sounds from home language to spell English words	• writes simple sentences (with some mistakes) and sequences of sentence • spells familiar words correctly • spells irregular and unfamiliar words using invented spelling, home language, or similarity to known words • uses word endings and prefixes appropriately, although not always accurately • some spelling and grammar errors in low-frequency words and complex grammar	• spelling of familiar words is conventional, with few mistakes • can write simple paragraph • sentence grammar is growing in complexity and accuracy • understands and uses appropriate punctuation, paragraphing, headings, etc., in accord with purpose of text • expanded use of vocabulary in appropriate ways	• spelling, grammar, punctuation, and paragraphing are used correctly (for the most part), appropriately, and skillfully for purpose of text • uses topic-appropriate vocabulary and includes new words appropriately • appropriate use of technical terms that are appropriate to subject matter
• can create oral narratives and write them using simple vocabulary and grammar • communicates message at a word and phrase level • participates willingly in group writing using simple sentences and high-frequency words • can tell story or recount story in logical order • can use pictures to sequence events presented during oral story read • uses templates and writing frames as supports for writing	• can retell and analyze simple stories fluently (in English or home language) • with assistance, can predict events and infer consequences from narratives • uses variety of vocabulary and sentence patterns to write • some use of connectors and verb tense to create cohesion in writing	• can express self in writing on a range of topics using basic vocabulary and grammatical patterns • ideas in written text are organized logically according to genre • uses varied sentence patterns; may need assistance • uses appropriate connectors and verb tenses to create coherence • can edit writing, with prompting • can prepare a draft with assistance	• can write appropriately for a variety of purposes, both academic and personal • text is appropriately organized for specific purpose • can make connections between different academic subjects and school and personal/home life • sentence grammar, including tense, is used to create cohesion and relate information in a logical and meaningful way • edits text when given feedback; critiques own writing to revise it • takes chances and is creative writing personal or narrative text

Chart 1.1 Continued

to reading and writing. Our framework is quite simple; other frameworks are much more detailed and complex. This simplified version is adequate for purposes of this book; however, you should be sure to familiarize yourself with your school or district's framework. Some suggestions for getting a sense of your ELLs' prior literacy experiences follow:

To get a sense of your ELL students' prior literacy experiences

- Examine their past school records, if they are available.
- Gather information about their backgrounds by talking with family members or by visiting their homes or neighborhoods.
- Have students write brief descriptions about themselves or their families in English or the home language; even writing samples in the home language can give you a rough idea of whether they have some skills in literacy.
- Use teaching strategies that allow you to get to know your students better, such as dialogue journals, described in detail in Chapters 5 and 6.

3. Prior schooling

It is also important to find out how much and what kind of prior schooling experiences your ELL students have had. ELLs who have had prior schooling before they join your class might be familiar and comfortable with your routines, especially if their prior schooling has been in an English-language setting. However, students who have had prior schooling in other countries may have learned different classroom routines and norms. For example, students coming from many parts of Asia, Africa, and South America may be used to teacher-fronted classrooms where a considerable amount of group or lockstep learning takes place. Classrooms that are student-centered and individualized may be unfamiliar to them, and they may need extra time and assistance to figure out what to do in your classroom. Students with prior schooling may also have learned basic math, reading, and study skills, which they can use to get going in your classroom.

Do not assume that students with prior schooling necessarily know how your classroom functions or that they would be at the same level as your students. They may be more or less advanced in their academic studies than your students. We often think that developing countries, for example, have less sophisticated educational systems than our own. However, in some cases, schools in these countries have more rigorous academic programs. Here are some ways to learn how much and what kind of prior schooling your ELLs have had:

NOTE FOR TEACHERS OF STUDENTS WITH LIMITED FORMAL SCHOOLING

Students who have limited formal schooling (LFS) require special attention because their needs are dramatically different from other ELLs who have been to school already, especially if their limited prior schooling is not like that of the United States or Canada.

Getting information about prior schooling

- Examine students' past school records, if available, to get a sense of not only how the student performed but what was taught.
- Gather as much information about the student's history before getting to your school by asking family members and the students themselves.
- Investigate the educational and social situations in the students' countries of origin.

4. Grade level

The linguistic and academic demands of schooling get progressively more challenging the higher the grade level. The subject matter and skills that students must learn become more complex and abstract, and language becomes more important as a tool for teaching and learning content in higher grades; competence in reading and writing become particularly important at this stage of schooling. The learning curve for ELLs must be steeper than that for mainstream students because ELLs must acquire proficiency in English at the same time as they master new academic content. In the case of students with limited formal schooling, they have to make up for the time when they were not in school. Thus,

Research Finding

Sheltered instruction is a research-based approach that helps ELLs develop oral language proficiency while building literacy skills and content area knowledge. Teachers prepare students for a lesson by building background knowledge; they teach the lesson using strategies that make language comprehensible; they provide opportunities for interaction and practice; and they assess and review (Echevarria, Short, & Vogt 2004).

the grade level you teach will have a fundamental and critical influence on how you organize the learning environment for ELLs. ELLs in the higher elementary grades need extensive use of sheltered instruction to cope with academic subjects and lots of scaffolding and differentiation if they are to learn English at the same time as they learn new academic material. If ELLs are to close the gap with their English-speaking peers, they must have accelerated instruction in English literacy; this becomes even more important the higher the grade level.

5. Family background

ELLs, like many mainstream students, begin to acquire the foundations of literacy and even some beginning literacy skills in their families and communities. Therefore, knowing how language is used, and especially written forms of language, in your ELLs' families and communities can help you plan instruction that builds on what they already know or are familiar with. For example, ELLs in some families may be used to being read to or being told oral stories in their home language. Knowing this, you can create a learning environment that provides continuity with their family experiences and supports them as they learn to read and write in English. Other ELLs may come from families where the parents work at several jobs and do not have time for telling stories or reading to their children; or they may have limited education and literacy skills. Teachers will need to provide these students with the foundations of literacy in school. This does not mean that parents have no role to play; they can serve as "audience" as their children read to them in English or tell them stories. In short, in order to promote literacy development, teachers should link what they are teaching to the literacy-related experiences and skills that ELLs have acquired outside school.

For example, ELLs from some families may be used to working, playing, and doing homework in groups rather than individually. Knowing this, you can provide a learning environment that provides continuity with ELLs' past and supports

Research Finding

Luis Moll and his colleagues talk about the funds of knowledge that students have about life at home and in the community. Funds of knowledge are students' understandings of household activities and customs and ways of doing things at home and in the community; they also include students' knowledge about cultural habits, values, and activities. When teachers use students' funds of knowledge as a cultural resource and a basis for curriculum and lesson development, ELLs can relate to school in a way that they had previously been unable to (Moll 2000; Gonzalez, Moll, & Amanti 2005).

them as they learn new skills and subject matter. The parents of some ELLs are expert farmers, and, as a result, their children may have access to community gardens where they grow their own fruits and vegetables. Others may be doctors who have been trained in Eastern medicine, for example, and may have knowledge about medicinal plants and herbs. Knowing this provides you with knowledge about learning resources that you can draw on to build your ELLs' competence in English literacy and in academic domains. This can be done by linking what you are teaching to what your ELLs already know and can do outside school—for example, create a community garden in the classroom or school playground that permits ELLs with this kind of background to express their competencies. This could also be a terrific context for science or math teaching as well as for including parents in school activities.

6. Similarity of the home language and culture to that of the mainstream

As we have noted a number of times, ELLs are very resourceful. They use all the skills, knowledge, and experiences they have to help them learn in school. The most obvious and powerful resource they have is their home language. ELLs are most likely to draw on resources in the home language in the early stages of acquiring English; this is especially true when they are learning to read and write English, but it is also evident when they speak.

"ELLs with initial L1 literacy experiences, such as emergent and family literacy, as well as those with well-developed L1 literacy skills, progress more quickly and successfully in L2 literacy development."

(Riches & Genesee 2006, 83)

Using the home language to figure out English is sometimes referred to as *transfer*. When students transfer knowledge from the home language that is the same in English, we see this as progress because they are using the appropriate form for English. However, when the home language differs from English, this can result in "mistakes." For example, a Spanish-speaking ELL might not use a pronoun or noun in a sentence where most English speakers would, or she might put the adjective after the noun instead of before it; a Chinese-speaking ELL might not use *s* markings on plural nouns or may not insert endings on verbs in English to mark number and tense (e.g., "two cat" or "he go"). In every case, these students are doing this because this is the way their home language works.

"These L1 and L2 abilities appear to contribute to the development of a common bilingual reservoir that serves both L1 and L2 literacy and create an awareness of systematic relationships between languages, allowing ELLs to draw on existing L1 knowledge in the service of L2 literacy. Furthermore, it appears that L2 literacy is more than the sum of its parts, as ELLs appear to have unique abilities that result from their bilingual status."

(Riches & Genesee 2006, 82)

We notice examples of negative transfer and often interpret them as "mistakes" because they result in a form that is not expected in English or is wrong. We do not notice cases of positive transfer because these forms look like correct English. But it is wrong to view transfer that results in unusual English forms as mistakes. Rather it is more appropriate to recognize that the students are showing resourcefulness by using forms from their home language because they do not yet know the appropriate forms in English. By knowing something about your ELLs' home languages, at least the most common ones (like Spanish, Vietnamese, and Cantonese), you can better understand their efforts to learn English and you can be more confident that they are making progress even when they are using forms that differ from English. You can also use these cases of negative transfer to illustrate to your students how languages differ; this kind of metalinguistic knowledge is helpful when it comes to reading and writing.

ELLs might also use the cultural norms of their families and communities when they relate to other students and their teacher—as a kind of cultural transfer. In some cases, their home culture may have norms that are distinct from the norms used in the classroom; for example, children from some families may be reluctant to volunteer in class activities because they are taught to follow their teacher's directions and not to speak unless the teacher explicitly requests them to speak. In contrast, many literacy activities in mainstream U.S. classrooms rely on volunteer participation and volunteering is viewed as an indicator of motivational level or level of comprehension. If ELLs do not behave like mainstream students, it is important not to interpret their behavior as lack of interest or attention or as signs of difficulty. Rather, ELLs are doing what they know best and think is appropriate. Understanding the norms of ELLs' families and communities can help you better understand their behavior in class.

Here are some suggestions to help you find out about your students' home languages and cultures:

Learning about your ELL students' home languages and cultures

- Consult a member of the student's home culture about norms in their group.
- Ask fluent or near-fluent speakers of the student's language about cultural aspects of language use that are relevant to the classroom—physical distance between speakers, eye gaze, turn-taking, initiating talk. All of these can differ from the way English works. When you ask family members about their ways of doing things, be careful not to evaluate or judge their social norms using your own as a yardstick; this will minimize prejudicial views of the cultural norms and values of your students.
- Read about the various languages and different cultural norms and customs of ELLs in your classroom; see Additional Resources at the end of this chapter for some suggestions.

You can learn more about ELLs' home languages in Chapter 3.

Special Needs

Learning takes time, whether it is learning to read and write, learning new math skills, or learning how to fit in socially. Children show enormous differences in how quickly they learn. Sometimes when ELLs take a long time to learn to read and write or to understand math or science, we think that they have a learning disability or are language impaired. However, there is no reason to believe that learning a second language or being bilingual are risk factors for learning disability.

Research Finding

Although there is an over-representation of ELLs in special-education programs in the United States, it is not bilingualism that leads to academic difficulties. Rather, the problem lies in assessment procedures, the use of a medical model of special needs, and the use of categorical funding in the school system (Cummins 2000; Genesee, Paradis, & Crago 2004; Hamayan et al. 2007).

Children can acquire two languages simultaneously in essentially the same way and time as children who learn only one language, if they are given an adequate learning environment (see Genesee, Paradis, & Crago [2004] for an overview of relevant research).

Generally, children who learn a second language after their first language do not have difficulty if they are given adequate time and input. At the same time, some ELLs, like some English speakers, may have genuine learning disabilities and require additional support. The challenge for educators is to identify specific difficulties that ELLs are encountering and provide them with interventions that help them overcome their difficulties. In trying to provide ELLs with learning difficulties with a continuum of support, extensive information about their school and home life must be gathered and used as a context for instruction (see, for example, the process described in Hamayan et al. 2007). Some ELLs may need to go through a full formal assessment, and because of the way funding is set up in some countries, including the United States, they may need to be formally identified as having a special-education need.

> "There is no scientific evidence that infants' language learning ability is limited to one language. On the contrary, research on infants with . . . dual language exposure indicates that they have the innate capacity to acquire two languages without significant costs to the development of either language. Simultaneous dual language children generally experience the same milestones at approximately the same age as monolingual children, in both the early months and later on . . ."
>
> (Genesee, Paradis, & Crago 2004, 84)

Summing Up and Looking Ahead

In this chapter, we talked about some big ideas concerning teaching and learning in school in general. While these apply to mainstream students as well as ELLs, we focused on how they apply and what they mean for teaching literacy to ELLs who come from diverse language and cultural backgrounds. We then reviewed briefly what research tells us about learning to read and write in a second language. These research findings motivated a great deal of the guidance we provide in the remaining chapters; we consider the implications of these findings for teaching literacy to ELLs in greater detail in the coming chapters. Finally, we talked about how important it is to get to know your ELLs and suggested some ways in which you can do that.

This chapter sets the stage for the remaining chapters. In Chapter 2, we focus on the emergent literacy stage of development; we devote a whole chapter to this topic since this stage is so critical for ELLs and because a large proportion of ELLs start school in English at the lower grade levels when literacy is still in the early stages of development. In Chapter 3, we go on to discuss how you can assist ELLs reach their full potential as readers and writers; here we emphasize your role in helping ELLs become biliterate—in English and their home language. This is not only a desirable goal but also a realistic one if you expand your conceptualization of how you can help students learn to read and write to include community and other resources to support ELLs' home language. The development of academic language and literacy in a second language is the topic of Chapter 4. While the first chapters were about learning to read, Chapter 4 is about reading to learn. In Chapter 5, we discuss ways of connecting reading and writing so that each is promoted. We describe teaching strategies where reading is used to promote writing and where student writing is used as individual or as class text to promote reading. Finally, in Chapter 6, we discuss assessment. Here we emphasize the value and importance of classroom-based assessment as a tool for instructional planning. We provide lots of examples of what kinds of assessment tools to use and how to use them with ELLs.

NOTE FOR ADMINISTRATORS

Given requirements in U.S. schools, as well as in other countries, it is usually difficult to avoid formally classifying ELLs with special academic difficulties for "special education." If you test these students, it is likely that they will appear to have a special-education needs, even if they do not in reality have a learning, language, or reading disorder. However, with growing recognition of the value of Response to Intervention (RTI) protocols for identifying students' learning needs, doors are opening to allow you to set up systems in your school to provide such students with support before formal assessment is completed. See the procedures described in Hamayan et al. (2007) for suggestions on how to do this. See also the special issue of *Learning Disabilities Quarterly* (Vol. 30, Number 2, Summer 2007), which is dedicated to using RTI with ELLs.

Additional Resources for Teachers

Getting current information on English language learners

- National Clearinghouse for English Language Acquisition and Language Instruction Educational Programs: www.ncela.gwu.edu

  This website provides a wealth of information on English language learners including information on demographics and federal policies.

- Migration Policy Institute: www.migrationpolicy.org/

  This website provides research on immigrants and migrants; for example, see Spotlight on Limited English Proficient Students in the United States *(2006) by Jeanne Batalova: www.migrationinformation.org/USfocus/display.cfm?ID=373.*

- US Census Bureau: http://factfinder.census.gov

  This site provides national and statewide data on persons who speak languages other than English at home. It also provides self-report data on persons who speak English at less than proficient levels.

Information about other languages and cultures

- www.ethnologue.com/web.asp

  This website contains a catalogue of more than 6,700 languages spoken in 228 countries.

- www.ipl.org/div/kidspace/browse/owd3000

  This website provides information about the languages, cultures, religions, and geography of many countries around the world.

- Flaitz, J. 2006. *Understanding Your Refugee and Immigrant Students: An Educational, Cultural and Linguistic Guide.* Ann Arbor, MI: The University of Michigan Press.

  This book will help teachers understand the types of classroom experiences students may have had in their home countries. It covers common countries of origin from Central and South America, the Caribbean, Eastern Europe, the Near East, Asia, and Sub-Saharan Africa. It talks about classroom life, teacher status, teacher-student relationships, teaching practices, discipline and classroom management, student-student relationships, and the like. It also identifies potential adjustment challenges and solutions.

- Haghighat, C. 2003. *Language Profiles.* Vols. I–III. Toronto: World Languages Publishing House.

  This book provides linguistic and cultural background information for sixty-seven languages.

Emergent Literacy in a Second Language

CHAPTER 2

In this chapter, we describe the process that second-language learners go through when developing literacy skills for the first time in a new language. This occurs most naturally when learners first come to school and are placed in an early grade (K–2). But it can also occur at later ages if students have atypical schooling backgrounds. We discuss how to devise instruction that respects and promotes growth through the stages second-language learners go through in second-language literacy, concentrating on the beginning or emergent stage.

Home language literacy first *36*

The importance of English *36*

Know your students *37*

Planning stage-appropriate instruction *40*

Teaching initial literacy to ELLs *43*

Promoting growth in literacy for beginning ELLs *60*

Learning to read in a new cultural context *68*

Using literature for cross-cultural learning *69*

Curriculum development for ELLs *71*

Summing up *73*

Additional resources for teachers *74*

We focus on how to provide instruction to initiate reading and writing. Since we know that language learning is deeply connected with cultural learning, we also describe ways to support learners by providing culturally responsive instruction in the early stages and ways to expand their horizons by building background knowledge and promoting cross-cultural learning. Finally, we discuss ways to plan the literacy block and construct the reading/writing curriculum and to select materials so that the emergent literacy program is as supportive as possible.

 Home Language Literacy First

In case placing this chapter early in the book leads the reader to believe that the preferred way to develop literacy is in English only, we wish to begin this chapter by clarifying our position regarding initial literacy instruction. In our approach to initial literacy development, we favor introducing literacy in the home language first. We believe it is best if students learn to read text that they understand orally so that they do not have to struggle with meaning as well as reading. If students are given text in a language they do not understand, then reading the text involves a double load: decoding written language for the first time and connecting it to a language they have not yet mastered. If the meaning of the text is already known to the reader because it is delivered in a comprehensible language, then half the job is done. When students are introduced to reading through the use of highly predictable texts in their home language, they can master the initial steps of literacy more easily and begin to feel comfortable with written language. Because introducing literacy in the home language is the preferred way to teach ELLs, we devote the next chapter entirely to that topic.

 The Importance of English

We put the chapter on emergent literacy in English first because we recognize that there are more English-as-a-second-language (ESL) than bilingual programs in operation; moreover, all ELLs must learn to read and write in their second language. Special circumstances also make it necessary to introduce literacy to ELLs exclusively in English; the most common reasons follow:

- Students may be young and they may not have acquired literacy skills in the home language, but they may have had extensive exposure to English. As a result, English is their preferred and dominant language when they enter school, despite the language backgrounds of their parents or guardians.
- Students may have acquired literacy skills but in low-incidence languages that the school cannot continue to develop because it lacks the human and material resources to do so. Therefore, it may be necessary to develop literacy only in English, even though this is less than ideal.
- Parents may object to the development of literacy in the home language, preferring that their child be instructed exclusively in English. According to U.S. federal statutes, parental preferences must be respected. However, educators should take care to inform parents about the advantages of biliteracy before accepting parental preferences. The points in favor of use of the home language that should be shared with parents are presented in Chapter 3. Certainly, we always want to give the best guidance to parents concerning their child's literacy development, and the following sections are designed to help classroom teachers and reading specialists do just that. But in cases where the parents insist on instruction in the second language only, literacy instruction will necessarily be initiated exclusively in English.

We also started with this chapter to tackle the more difficult situation first—that of developing literacy simultaneously as we develop ELLs' oral language proficiency in English, a very demanding process, indeed.

Know Your Students

To get to know your students, collect as much background information about them as you can so that you can understand and capitalize on what they bring to the task of learning to read and write in English. With respect to the assessment of reading and writing skills, we have devoted a chapter to this—Chapter 6. However, you will certainly want to investigate all of the following:

IMPORTANT BACKGROUND CHARACTERISTICS OF LEARNERS

1. Previous schooling experiences and whether they were in English or the primary language, or both (e.g., day care, preschool, early grade educational experiences)
2. Extent of literacy skills in the home language(s)
3. Extent of oral language proficiency and literacy in English
4. Literacy skills of the parents and the languages in which they are literate
5. Literacy environment in the home (access to print in any form and language, range of materials found in the home)
6. Literacy practices in the home and community (purposes for which people read and write; literary experiences such as oral storytelling and sharing of other oral traditions, such as well-known poems, sayings, rhymes, tales, and the like)
7. Home language literacy instruction provided in institutions other than school (e.g., church, community centers, private programs, or tutoring programs)

Investigate Your Students' Home Language Skills

Research Finding

The level of family literacy influences children's overall achievement and therefore this is an important variable to understand and account for in our programming (Reese et al. 2000).

It is critical that teachers try to determine the nature and extent of their ELL students' home language skills prior to planning instruction for them in English. We know that there are considerable cross-linguistic and cross-modal interactions between the home language and learning to read and write in English: Metalinguistic awareness, initial reading skills, vocabulary (cognates), awareness of print and reading, comprehension strategies, and sound-symbol correspondence all transfer from the home language to English (Genesee & Geva 2006). Learners use what they know about their home language to tackle what they don't know about English. We know that ELLs will draw on skills developed in their home language to break into literacy in English. For example, students who have been told stories in their home language understand story structure; students who know how to write their names in the letters of the home language have an understanding of sound-symbol correspondence and that print communicates something meaningful.

Students with foundational literacy skills developed in their home language have a reservoir of skills and knowledge to draw on to learn to read and write in English. This reservoir is made up of home- and second-language skills as well as world knowledge gained through the home and second languages (August & Shanahan 2006). Therefore, you will want to know what literacy-related skills and experiences your ELL students have in the home language so that you can help them use this important resource when learning to read and write in English. This is discussed in greater detail in Chapter 3.

Research Finding

We know that certain kinds of L1 skills and knowledge facilitate learning to read English as a second language, including phonological awareness, knowledge of cognate vocabulary, reading comprehension strategies, and emergent literacy skills (knowledge of print, letter names, and letter-sound correspondences); see Riches and Genesee (2006) and Genesee and Geva (2006) for more details.

Students who see connections between L1 and L2 learn to read more easily and better; see Jimenez, Garcia, and Pearson (1996).

After an extensive review of research on L2 reading research, Riches and Genesee (2006) found that successful ELL readers use many of the same strategies as successful native English-speaking readers; in addition, successful ELL readers draw on knowledge and strategies linked to the home language, including knowledge of cognate vocabulary, translation, and background knowledge acquired in the home language. They conclude that successful ELL readers have a unique bilingual reservoir of skills and knowledge to draw on to break into English reading and writing.

Investigating Literacy Practices of Families and Communities

You will also want to know about the language and literacy experiences of your students outside of school. Investigate their opportunities to read, to talk extensively, and to witness literate behaviors by important adults in their lives. Find out about the literacy practices in different ELL communities so that you can better understand your ELL students' literacy experiences. Specifically, how have your ELLs been using literacy before they came to your school? What practices are common in their homes

"… writing is a developmental process, whether writing in the native or nonnative language. It is common to find influences from the L1 in ELLs' writing, and instead of interpreting this phenomenon negatively, we need to view it as something to celebrate, as it indicates that students are active learners."

(Samway 2006, 58)

and communities? The answers to these questions might reveal to you that your ELLs have been engaged in more early literacy experiences than you would have imagined if you had just asked them whether they are read to at home and own any books (see Valuable Early Literacy Practices for some ideas of literacy practices that may be occurring). Being read to and having books at home may be common among children who come from middle-class mainstream homes, but these may not be a valid gauge of early literacy experiences in culturally and linguistically diverse families.

VALUABLE EARLY LITERACY PRACTICES

- ❑ Storytelling
- ❑ Sharing traditional nursery rhymes and/or finger plays
- ❑ Sharing traditional sayings (*dichos*) used for teaching purposes (i.e., *Dime con quien andas, y te diré quien eres;* tell me who your friends are and I'll tell you who you are)
- ❑ Singing
- ❑ Reciting poetry or listening to recited poetry that expresses important cultural values (love of country, of mother, importance of teachers)
- ❑ Reading religious books, reciting prayers, singing hymns
- ❑ Writing letters (or email) to relatives, reading letters from relatives
- ❑ Writing lists for shopping or other family purposes

Planning Stage-Appropriate Instruction

While we saw in Chapter 1 that there may not be complete agreement on what to call each stage in literacy development, there is agreement that teaching, including the reading materials that are used, should match each individual learner's particular stage of development. For this reason, a good starting point for planning instruction is to identify each student's current level of reading and writing ability and then select teaching methods and texts that are appropriate for that level. This is especially important at the beginning stage. You can do this by collecting language proficiency information from formal testing conducted by your district or by informal means, such as seeing which set of behaviors best represents your student's functioning on proficiency frameworks, such as the one we suggested in Chapter 1. The main point here is that teachers address all the component literacy skills but in stage-appropriate ways.

Component Literacy Skills

Focus attention on the following foundational skills when working with students during the emergent stage of literacy development:

1. Getting meaning out of texts (understanding that a book is about something meaningful—a story or a subject; using pictures and text features to make sense of texts)
2. Recognizing letters, words (and their parts), and phrases
3. Phonological awareness—breaking spoken words into their component sounds and blending sounds to make words
4. Forming letters (handwriting) and writing words and phrases
5. Receiving and communicating messages at the word level (initial decoding and encoding)

Later you will be able to build more sophisticated skills with your learners.

As noted in Chapter 1, these skills do not exist or develop in isolation. As Figure 1.2 in Chapter 1 illustrates (page 15), literacy is a bidirectional process that includes bottom-up and top-down processes. One way to engage ELLs in top-down processes related to reading before they can actually read is to read to them and ask them to interpret what is being read, infer the consequences of what is being read, and provide alternative interpretations of what can or should happen next in the story. Even though this activity is oral, it builds students' top-down processing skills in ways

Research Finding

The National Reading Panel (2000) identified the following skills as critical components in learning to read English as a first language:

- Phonemic awareness
- Decoding/encoding abilities
- Vocabulary
- Fluency
- Comprehension

The National Literacy Panel on Language-Minority Children and Youth (see August & Shanahan 2006) found similar results for ELLs.

We have noticed a tendency to think that these elements have to be taught in the above order. With ELLs, we suggest, however, that comprehension be given priority to ensure that they see reading and writing as meaningful and functional activities. Thus, in ranking of importance in facilitating learning, we suggest the following order: comprehension, vocabulary, phonemic awareness, decoding/encoding, and, finally, fluency.

Research Finding

The National Literacy Panel found that ELLs often perform at the same level as native English speakers when it comes to word reading and spelling but perform significantly less well on reading comprehension (Lesaux & Geva 2006). Lesaux and Geva go on to note that whereas phonological awareness and working memory are significant predictors of word reading, oral language proficiency in English is not. In contrast, when reading comprehension is examined, oral proficiency in English is a significant predictor. More specifically, English vocabulary knowledge, listening comprehension, syntactic skills, and metalinguistic aspects of language are significantly related to reading comprehension in English.

that they can apply to reading. As you teach ELL students foundational skills related to word reading, you will also want to model and draw on top-down skills that make written language meaningful and useful—inferencing, identifying main ideas, explaining, and so on. ELLs have particular difficulty with reading comprehension, more so than with word decoding. Therefore, it is critical that you are always infusing literacy instruction with the transmission and comprehension of meaning.

Teaching the foundational skills in the context of building and using background knowledge to make sense of text is important because it motivates ELLs. Moreover, it draws on and strengthens ELLs' oral language skills, and this, in turn, supports the entire process of learning to read and write. In short, it is critical to embed literacy instruction in meaningful and functional activities in order to prepare ELLs for the challenge of producing and comprehending complex text later on in their development as readers and writers.

Research Question

Research on the importance of learning letter-sound correspondences and phonological awareness has tended to look at teaching these skills in isolation. Teachers could do their own in-class research to gauge the effectiveness of teaching word-level skills in isolation in contrast to teaching them in the context of a science or social studies lesson or as part of an activity related to the students' own experiences; for example, name all the animals that live in your home country or in your neighborhood whose names start with the letter *b*.

One way of linking bottom-up processes with top-down processes is through the use of themes or topics linked to the academic curriculum. Teaching foundational skills in the context of academic themes serves to link the small and big components of reading and writing. Connected learning experiences related to important and interesting themes deepen students' understanding of academic content while helping them master the oral and written skills that are critical for academic success. In this chapter, we use the theme of Pancakes or Pancakes Around the World to illustrate how to teach early reading and writing skills in context. This theme might sound frivolous at first glance, but it is rich with content connections, among them learning about Africa, African village life, farms and farming, the interdependency of communities, liquid and dry measurement, nutritional foods, and the producer-to-consumer cycle as it applies to food products (grain to pancakes, tortillas, bread; collection and consumption of maple syrup). Through this enjoyable theme, students can also learn about similar foods that are eaten around the world and common cultural practices in their new country (county fairs, pancake breakfasts, and the like). More will be said about these content connections later in this chapter. See the Additional Resources for Teachers section at the end of this chapter for books related to pancakes; we refer to these as we explore teaching strategies that support emergent ELL readers and writers in the sections that follow. You may be familiar with many of the books in our list.

Teaching Initial Literacy to ELLs

Before sharing teaching strategies, we outline a number of instructional guidelines and strategies for promoting initial literacy skills in English for ELLs upon which all teaching strategies should be based. These guidelines and strategies are especially important for students who have the daunting task of learning how to read and write for the first time as they simultaneously acquire functional competence in oral English and learn to fit into a new culture. The guidelines that we present are based on eight key principles.

PRINCIPLES OF EMERGENT LITERACY INSTRUCTION

1. Literacy activities in school should be meaningful, interesting, and interactive to ensure that students are engaged and motivated and they should be highly useful so that students build the literacy skills they need.
2. Literacy instruction should build on and expand ELLs' oral language skills in English and link to their background knowledge and experiences to ensure that we are building upon their existing strengths.
3. Reading and writing skills (e.g., phonological awareness and strategies for reading comprehension) should be taught directly and modeled for students. When small unit skills are taught directly, it is important to do this in meaningful ways so that ELLs understand the importance of them for functional aspects of reading and writing as a whole.

4. The component skills of literacy (e.g., sound-symbol correspondence; letter formation/handwriting) should be taught systematically, but in an integrated and meaningful fashion—small unit skills with big unit skills, and with an eye to ELLs' later literacy development as well as immediate growth. High-frequency words can be taught as sight words.
5. Reading instruction should be connected with writing instruction so that each can build on the other.
6. ELLs must have lots of opportunities to read and write to ensure that they acquire fluent reading and writing skills and that they catch up with their native English-speaking peers as quickly as possible.
7. Literacy instruction must address all aspects of literacy, both reading and writing, and for both social and academic purposes.
8. Literacy at school must connect to and build on literacy experiences in the home and community.

Make Literacy Instruction Meaningful, Interactive, and Useful

Using the Pancakes theme, we show you how good themes can make instruction pleasurable and meaningful to students learning to read and write. Effective literacy instruction is interactive—it facilitates student-teacher interaction around reading and writing. Different varieties of pancakes are eaten all over the world: American-style pancakes in the United States, *banh xeo* in Vietnam, *beghrirs* in Morocco, *blinis* in Russia, *chapatis* in India, *okonomiyaki* in Japan, *kartoflane placki* (potato pancakes) in Poland, spicy chickpea or black-eye-bean pancakes of Africa, or *tortillas* in Mexico. The universality of this type of food and the enjoyment experienced by most people when eating pancakes makes this theme fun and meaningful for most young students. This theme also lends itself to creating language experiences during which students make and eat pancakes and in doing so build their oral language skills. The antics described in some of the books on pancakes add humor and delight to

Research Finding

Genesee and Riches (2006) found that the most effective teaching strategies with ELLs included direct instruction of specific reading-related skills and strategies, as needed by students, using interactive activities that engage students with one another or their teacher. Interactive activities allow students to learn from others and to seek out the input and feedback they need to master literacy skills.

book reading and exploration as students see the pancakes running away in *The Runaway Tortilla* (Kimmel 2000) or *The Runaway Latkes* (Kimmelman 2000), the sticky situation the pig gets into in *If You Give a Pig a Pancake* (Numeroff 1998), or the predicaments of the little old lady who lacks ingredients to make pancakes in *Pancakes for Breakfast* (dePaola 1978). When you select books for your classroom, you should always choose books that interest your students and use them in ways that match their attention spans, sense of humor, and background knowledge so that you can engage them actively in literacy.

You will also want to ensure that your instruction is useful and interesting. Using the Pancake theme to build an instructional unit, you can construct activities that actively engage students in literacy by reading recipes to make pancakes or by having students write reviews of the best pancakes they have ever had (potato, banana, blueberry, wheat, oatmeal, etc.). Students reading the *The Runaway Tortilla* could draw maps of the route that the runaway pancakes take as they escape, thereby teaching students useful skills with respect to directionality, distance, orientation, and even geography. The clear story lines in these books allow students to retell them, thereby teaching them useful language skills related to sequencing information. Presenting information in sequence is an oral language skill that is also useful when children talk to one another about everyday events or in a science unit when they have to follow a specific procedure to get seeds to germinate, for example. Reading a number of books related to the same theme gives students lots of practice with all these important skills in their new language.

Link Literacy Instruction to Oral Language Development

Oral language is the foundation of literacy. We can begin building this foundation before students can read by using wordless picture books. Let's see how this can be done using *Pancakes for Breakfast.* This book provides a wonderful opportunity for students to learn nouns, adjectives, action verbs, prepositions, and conjunctions. With guidance from the teacher, students can invent dialogue, share idioms (e.g., s/he's a bad egg, all your eggs in one basket, don't cry over spilt milk, sell like hotcakes, a piece of cake, flat as a pancake), show how tone of voice and loudness affect meaning, and introduce various verb tenses (present progressive, past, future). You could "frontload" all of this language by doing a language experience activity around making pancakes, or you could begin the book and proceed to develop vocabulary as you explore the story through reading. Frontloading is very important with ELLs; it builds the oral language and background knowledge they need to support storytelling and comprehension before they actually get into the book.

An advantage of wordless picture books is that they can be used to differentiate vocabulary instruction, with one student learning basic words (like *lady, rug, table*) and another learning complex noun phrases (*ordinary elderly woman, braided wool carpet, cozy kitchen table*). They can also be used to teach word-formation skills, for example, how some words, like *pancake*, are compounds that are made up of other words. Words that are introduced orally while "reading" a wordless story book can appear in writing on labels around the room, preferably accompanied by pictures. The task of producing the labels can be given to beginning-level students, thus giving them a chance to practice basic writing skills. The idea is to build the vocabulary that children need to tell the story and then to use that vocabulary in the classroom to enhance comprehension and early writing skills.

In this section, we have illustrated how, in order to help students tell a story in English, it is important to build foundational skills using books and other realia. When you do this, you can introduce useful new vocabulary and sentence patterns and create opportunities for students to use new language skills in literacy-related ways (in this case storytelling) that are engaging and interesting. (For a quick overview of frontloading, storytelling, and retelling with wordless books and other teaching strategies presented in this chapter, see the chart in Appendix B).

Using Wordless Picture Books to Support Emergent Literacy

1. Select books with pictures and themes that encourage language expression.
2. Model storytelling for learners with the same or another wordless book. Demonstrate how to invent a narrative and/or dialogue page by page.

3. Have students view the book with you and then invite them to produce a story.
4. Let several children tell their versions of the story.
5. Create a story and write it down.
6. Use the story for word work and reading comprehension activities.

Wordless picture books are ideal for ELLs for many reasons, largely because they are very flexible. They can be used to support language and literacy development of English at school, and they can provide a useful link between school and home. Students can take the books home and discuss them with their parents because they are not language specific. Parents can tell their children a story using the home language using the same book that is being used at school. The child can record their parent's story and bring it to school for the listening pleasure of other students who speak the same language. Additionally, students can record their own story in English or the home language to accompany the wordless picture book. This can also serve as a "read-aloud" for other students to enjoy. This affords an opportunity to bring in students' home languages even in English-only classrooms. Eventually, bilingual books that students illustrate can be created and placed in the school or classroom library, showing the school's respect for the students' home languages. (For more ideas about use of bilingual books in English-medium classrooms, see Chapter 3.)

Once stories have been introduced, the class can enjoy other literacy projects, such as dramatizing the story, writing a prequel or sequel, creating drawings to accompany the story, and inventing their own parallel wordless picture books with similar plots (Jalongo et al. 2002). There are many wordless picture books; the Additional Resources for Teachers section at the end of the chapter provides a few leads to get you started.

When you select picture books, keep the language-learning needs of emergent ELLs in mind; for example, books like *Pancakes, Pancakes!* (Carle 1970) have a repetitive text structure that is important for building language. Repetition allows students to focus on learning

Research Finding

Text features, like word repetition rates and the rate at which new words are introduced, are very important in supporting early literacy. Another feature that matters is the use of words representing familiar concepts; concrete, high-imagery words are learned and retained better than words that are low in these characteristics. Pacing, repetition, and ratio of new to total words are also features to monitor (Hiebert et al. 2004).

one new word at a time; in this case, pancake ingredients are presented one at a time on each page. Books with repetitive sentence patterns or phrases help ELLs learn grammatical patterns in English, which helps them to read more efficiently.

Even before the book is read, you can do a Total Physical Response (TPR) activity (Asher 1982) or sing a song about pancakes. To do a TPR activity with *Pancakes, Pancakes!*, you can obtain picture cards at www.teach.virginia.edu/go/wil/Pancakes_Pancakes_Activity_Card.pdf. To find a song related to pancakes, go to www.kididdles.com/lyrics/p047.html. The song you will find at this website is wonderful because it shows that in everyday speech, we often leave off word endings (*mixin'* instead of *mixing*, *fryin'* instead of *frying*, etc.). Students will learn how language is used in real life and be able to acquire both social and academic English as they compare the words in the song to the language in their books.

Instead of singing, these phrases could be performed as a *jazz chant* (Graham 1998). Jazz chants are snappy, upbeat poems that are typically divided into two alternating parts, with one group or person saying a line and another group or person saying the next in a rhythmic, fun way. You can encourage children to clap or tap the beat to heighten involvement and enjoyment while saying their parts. After this language play, the story could then be read multiple times and ways.

Following all of this, you can do a picture-sequencing activity with picture cards to see if students really comprehend the story by putting the picture cards in the order of the events in the story. If they have the proficiency to do so, they could also try to tell the story as they point to their cards.

Teach Directly and Model Reading and Writing Skills for Learners

Once you have selected books that match your students' stage of literacy development and you have built their oral language and background knowledge to support working with the book, you can then identify the specific foundational and comprehension skills you want to focus on directly either by direct teaching or by modeling during shared reading and reading aloud to children.

The template in Figure 2.1 on page 51 shows how to integrate objectives when planning instruction based on *Mama Panya's Pancakes: A Village Tale from Kenya* (Chamberlin, Chamberlin, & Cairns 2006). The template highlights four essential areas for development, along with possible objectives for each. You will notice that the template lists many possible objectives for each domain, especially oral language. Clearly, not everything that is listed can be taught. Therefore, once all possible objectives have been identified, it is necessary to select the specific objectives for particular groups of students in your class. Let's take a closer look at each of these essential areas of development now.

- *Oral Language.* It is useful to review the book or books you have chosen to use in a unit and then compile lists of oral language skills that can be taught using these materials, like the list of oral language that is attached to the template. Then, select the specific oral language skills you would like to focus on for different subgroups of learners in your class.
- *Background Knowledge.* By going through the book and identifying the themes and topics embedded in the text, you can determine background knowledge that students need to understand the story. In the case of *Mama Panya's Pancakes,* for example, we might identify knowledge associated with Kenya, village life, and what goes on in outdoor markets as important. If you think that your students do not have this background knowledge, then you would do some preteaching to ensure that they do.
- *Decoding/Encoding Skills.* We spend additional time on this topic because it is so important and often misunderstood. Phonological awareness is a critical component of developing decoding and encoding skills. Some ELLs will already have acquired some phonological awareness, in English or the home language, before they start school; others will not. Therefore, it is important to identify what students already know and then provide direct instruction to students with limited phonological awareness. In our unit on pancakes, we might do this by teaching the phoneme /*p*/ in initial consonant position with words like: *pan, pat, pail, pot, people*; by teaching onset and

rhyme with *p-an* (short vowel); or by teaching rhyming words like *p-an, m-an, f-an, r-an, c-an, th-an,* etc. The phonogram /*-an*/ is a very high-frequency phonogram in English and, thus, easier for students to grasp. Or, you could ask students to count the number of syllables in words (*pan-cake*). The very title of the book *Perfect Pancakes If You Please* (Wise 1997) introduces word play, and children can be invited to invent their own alliterative sequences, like *perfect puffy pancakes* or *potato, poppy, and pumpkin pancakes.*

> **Research Finding**
>
> Genesee and Riches (2006) and August and Shanahan (2006) both concluded, after reviewing research findings on teaching reading to ELLs, that direct and focused instruction of certain literacy skills is effective in promoting acquisition of those skills. It is effective for small-unit skills, such as phonological awareness, and big-unit skills, such as reading comprehension strategies. Direct instruction should be used judiciously on an as-needed basis in conjunction with interactive, functional approaches.

For ELLs in the emergent literacy stage, you should always start with an activity that is meaningful (like reading a story) and work on the small parts of reading (related to words, sounds, symbols) once the students are meaningfully engaged. The amount of time spent on the parts should be a small fraction of the time spent on meaning—word meaning and story meaning. Nevertheless, you need to be systematic in teaching the foundational skills because students who do not master these skills can have difficulty later on when it comes to comprehending text.

Of course, you will need to focus on different decoding/encoding skills for different groups of learners. For example, you will notice that we identified the /*–an*/ phonogram as in *pancake, can, African, sand,* and the initial consonants or consonant blends listed in Figure 2.1 as possible targets to be taught using this book. Next, you would want to decide which of these to make the focus of attention based on your students' needs.

- *Reading Strategies.* After the book is read or during a second reading, we can begin to model or directly teach reading comprehension strategies, like using picture cues to uncover the meaning of unknown words. As with the other areas, the strategies selected would be based on what can easily be taught and practiced using the book and the needs of learners.

Teach Sound-Symbol Correspondence and Sight Words Systematically in Meaningful Ways

English has what is called a deep or opaque orthography. This means that the link between the way words are pronounced and spelled is

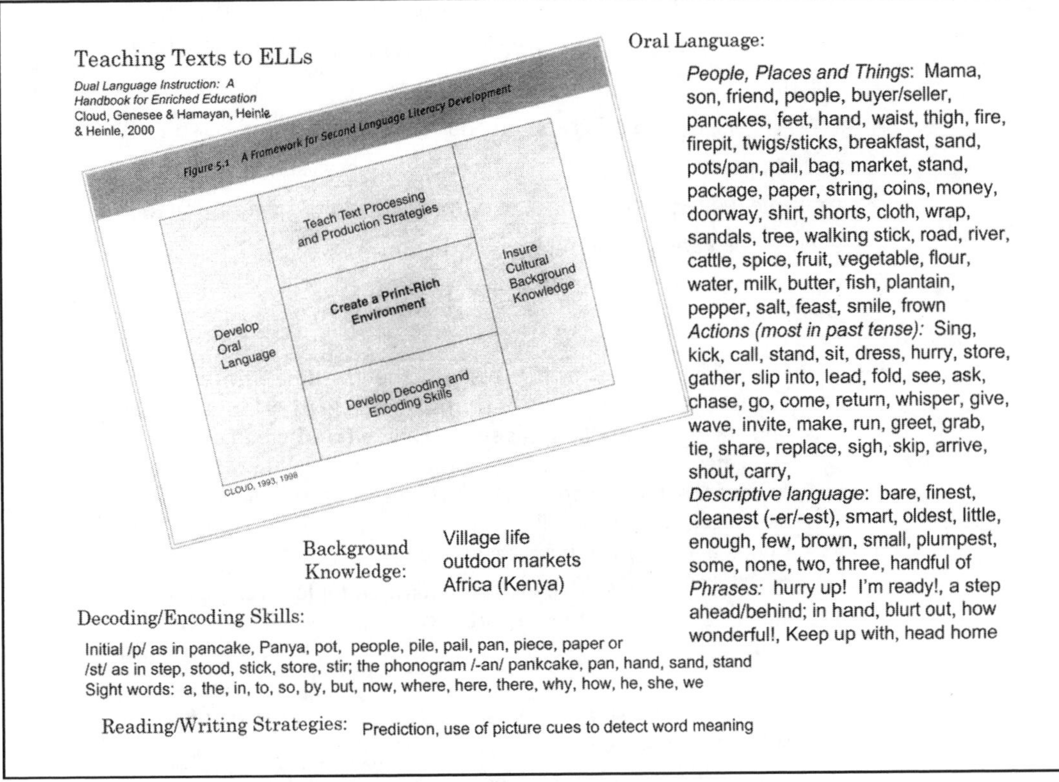

Figure 2.1 Planning Template

complex and not always regular. Some languages, like Spanish, in contrast, have shallow orthographies because the link between word sounds and spelling is consistent and transparent (Bear et al. 2007). As a result, it is difficult, even for native speakers, to learn English spelling patterns. To make the task easier, teach initial and final consonants first, then move on to simple vowel patterns in the context of regular consonant sounds (Hiebert et al. 2004)—for example, initial consonant /*p*/ words (*pot, pan,* etc.) before consonant blend /*st*/ (*stir, store*). In the beginning, expose children to words with regular one-to-one letter-sound correspondences for both vowels and consonants, and then move on to more complex letter-sound relationships—for example, short /*a*/ as in *had, bag, sat,* before the sound variants of vowels such as in "*r*-controlled vowel" words like *market, smart.* Words that contain high-frequency and consistent spelling-sound relationships are easier to learn (i.e., /*-an*/ phonogram—*man, pan, ran*) so this is a good place to start. These kinds of words do not require the same number of repetitions as words with infrequent patterns (Hiebert et al. 2004).

Because English spelling patterns are so complex, you will need to teach sound-symbol correspondences systematically and in multiple contexts, but always in conjunction with meaningful themes, such as the Pancake theme we have been using.

Here are some useful steps to follow:

- ❑ Identify decoding skills to focus on throughout the theme. In our Pancake theme, we could also work on the hard /c/ sound in cake and show students that this sound can be represented by /c/ or /k/. Later we might want to show the long vowel rule of *a-e* (*cake, take, make, bake, plate*, etc.). Whatever the focus, be sure to focus on specific decoding skills and embed that focus throughout the theme and texts you have chosen to use.
- ❑ Reinforce the target decoding skills. For example, when reading stories, ask children to find particular words and explain what they know about how the target letters are read (pronounced) in those words.
- ❑ Do word work using the target words. You might teach prefixes or suffixes, do picture sorts, or find rhyming words.
- ❑ Use the words for handwriting practice. Teach letters in meaningful groups based on their utility for early decoding (e.g., initial consonants before final consonants).

It is also important to remember that ELL students may use native language knowledge about letter names and sounds to name letters in English that also occur in their home language (e.g., the letter *j* exists in both English and Spanish but is named and pronounced differently). Therefore, when they see particular letters, they may be tempted to give it a different name or say a different phoneme than the one English expects.

Research Finding

Shanahan and Beck (2006), in their synthesis of research on the effectiveness of alternative instructional strategies for teaching literacy to ELLs for the National Literacy Panel, report that "teaching specific reading and writing elements can be beneficial to second-language students" (436). They go on to point out, however, that explicit instruction is probably more beneficial if it is part of the larger instructional goal of expanding ELLs' English oral language proficiency. In other words, explicit instruction of the elements of reading and writing probably should not be done in isolation. Genesee and Riches (2006, 140) drew a similar conclusion from their review.

More is said about this in Chapter 3, but it is wise to remember that they bring information from home that may or not be useful to them in their attempts to decode English. Perhaps their task is to learn new letters and new sounds, but it could also be to learn new letter names and sounds for known letters.

With *Pancakes, Pancakes!* (Carle 1970), we could conduct picture or word sorts based on consonant blends, initial consonants, or vowel sounds or have students enter words with target features into word study notebooks. Alternately, focusing on meaning, we might sort target words by categories—such as household items, pancake ingredients, actions, animals, or story characters. (See Bear et al. 2007, concerning picture and word-sort activities.)

When you work on letter formation (handwriting), it is most common to introduce printing before cursive writing and capital letters before lowercase (although there are some professionals who argue that cursive is easier to write than print for young children or new writers with little fine-motor muscle control [Blumenfeld 1994].) Practice letter sequences that are similar with respect to their formation, as suggested in methods like *Handwriting Without Tears* (i.e., the letters *p r n m h b*). Practice writing the letters alone and then in words that appear in the pancake stories (i.e., *pan, ran, man*). (See www.hwtears.com/whyitworks/teachingorder.)

Research Question

Teachers may want to explore this question by teaching one group of students to print first and then introduce cursive, while taking another similar group of students and teaching cursive first. There may be factors that affect the response of learners to each manner of teaching handwriting, such as age of the learner, motivation to write in ways similar to peers, motor control, and so forth. These factors, once identified, could guide teachers in which method to select for a particular group of emergent writers.

After practicing single letters, practice writing high-frequency words that appear in Fry's 1,000-word list, Hiebert's word zones, or other word lists—words like: *she, said, make/made, asked, eat, measure, table*; words that students are likely to need when they write their own stories (Fry & Kress 2006, Hiebert 2005). Even though we suggest you refer to these lists for ideas, we do not intend that you engage in rote practice with these words; rather, use these lists to pick out the high-frequency words that appear in the stories your students are reading. Consult the lists quickly before starting a unit, or consult them as activities unfold, making note of the high-frequency words you can reinforce. Be sure to work on high-frequency words in the same way you would work with any key vocabulary from the stories—in meaningful ways.

High-frequency words can also be taught as sight words. While some sight words are phonetically decodable (words that follow the rules—for example: *big, here, little, make*), others are not (for example:

NOTE FOR UPPER GRADE TEACHERS

When planning emergent literacy instruction for older learners, be sure to select high-interest themes and motivating materials that are age-appropriate but at the emergent literacy level. Once you do, then you can proceed in the same manner as listed here.

the, have, said, come, give, of, again). Sight words that are not phonetically decodable require lots of practice so that learners can decode them automatically or write them easily in their own texts. Therefore, when you select sight words to practice with students when reading specific pancake books, writing a class story about pancakes, or for them to use when writing captions for pictures they are drawing of important story events, pay special attention to those words that are not phonetically decodable and give your students more time to practice them. In *Pancakes, Pancakes!*, for example, you might select one or two of the following words for sight word practice: *the, was, said, have, how, an, a, look, like, will, can.*

Research Finding

Hiebert et al. (2004) found that high-frequency words are particularly difficult for ELLs to read. Many are not phonetically regular (e.g., *the, come*) and they have meanings that are abstract (e.g., *an*) or ambiguous (e.g., *saw*). Sometimes they are homophones like *their, there* or have graphic features that are difficult for new readers to distinguish (i.e., *the, then, them*).

Connect Reading and Writing

An important goal of early literacy development is to connect reading to writing and vice versa, and to connect both to students' emerging oral language skills and prior life experiences. Devise instructional activities in which students can read what they have written and can write about what they are reading and discussing in class. Additional ideas about how to connect reading and writing as well as a discussion about instructional strategies that can be used to reinforce those connections are presented in Chapter 5.

Provide Lots of Opportunities to Read and Write

The emergent literacy classroom should be filled with books and materials that encourage students to read and write. To do this, stock your classroom library with audio books, video books, and text sets, like those suggested for our Pancake unit. A *text set* is a collection of reading materials that is organized around themes—be it literary (African folktales) or informational (nutritional foods). A good text set includes a wide variety of written texts and materials that vary in length, difficulty, and structure, and encompasses texts that are interesting, relevant, and accessible to most students. A good text set gives students options for independent reading and provides students with opportunities to practice new reading strategies and to learn content information (Tovani 2004, 43). Text sets have numerous advantages for ELLs in the emergent literacy stage:

- ❑ They provide ELLs with opportunities to learn the same high-frequency vocabulary appearing across a number of books, words that they can use in their own early writing.
- ❑ They permit ELLs to develop schema associated with a particular theme and to build networks of related concepts to talk and write about.
- ❑ They build ELLs' confidence and fluency in reading because they encounter words and phrases they have seen before.
- ❑ They give ELLs the chance to hear words with the same sounds so they can start to create stable associations between English sounds and symbols.
- ❑ They develop ELLs' comprehension skills so that they can tackle new books.

Bear et al. (2007, 19) suggest that opportunities for reading and writing can be expanded by engaging students in a variety of activities, including: reading to students, reading with students, writing with students, word study, and talking with students about books. Writing is particularly challenging for ELLs, so give them plenty of opportunities to write, as early as possible.

"There is a reciprocal relationship between reading and writing development. Reading informs writing, and writing makes for better readers and spellers."

(Bear et al. 2007, 7)

Some engaging writing activities for emergent writers could involve taking digital pictures of family members and of their neighborhoods and writing labels and short captions for them; or they might make lists of things they miss about their home country and things they enjoy in their new country; or similar activities that involve writing. The digital photo and caption in Figure 2.2 demonstrates how children at the beginning proficiency level still want to share their world with others and communicate powerful thoughts through simple text. It also shows how places that we may see as just another building in the community take on special significance for our learners and allows us to appreciate what matters to them.

Figure 2.2 Storefront. Permission for use of student work granted by the Charles N. Fortes Elementary School (a Museum School), Lori Hughes, Principal, Providence, RI.

To encourage early student interest in writing, collect and display different types of writing paper and writing implements (such as colored pencils, crayons, large pencils with pencil grips, markers, glitter pens, etc.; drawing paper with lines, pretty origami paper, construction paper, oak tag/cardstock paper, postcards, blank books formatted in many interesting formats, etc.). Display different types of student writing to invite your students to engage in similar types of writing. Making books is not the only option. You can also use dialog journals, letters, postcards, posters, and other formats to encourage early writing when students are still in the early stages of learning to write. (See Chapter 5 for more ideas.)

Always be sure to match instructional activities with students' stages of development. Emergent writers are most likely to be at one of the first three stages, or breaking into the fourth stage, as described below:

> "Graves (1979) and Calkins (1983) documented children's extraordinary growth as writers/thinkers/perceivers in classrooms where children not only wrote but were taught by a teacher who constantly challenged and attended to the writer and his or her ideas. . . . (Their) data show that writing occurs and develops through, not merely in, contexts."
>
> (Edelsky & Jilbert 1985, 64–65)

STAGES OF WRITING DEVELOPMENT

- Pre-Writing: scribble writing and drawing, where often the scribbles reflect the orthography of the native language.
- Pretend Writing: strings of letters, with no sound-letter correspondence (pre-syllabic).
- Pre-Phonetic Writing: use of letters to represent whole words or thoughts, some sound-symbol correspondence, some correctly written high-frequency sight words (syllabic).
- Phonetic Writing: Emerging standardized writing, with patterned writing and longer messages; cross-linguistic inventive spelling and some conventional spelling and punctuation.
- Conventional Writing: Use of standard forms.

(Samway 2006)

Use All Types of Literacy

When teaching emergent readers and writers, use all types of texts to promote reading and writing development, including different genres (narrative, expository) and formats (handwritten language, printed material, multimedia, and Internet presentations of text) for both social and academic purposes. Poetry and rhyme are especially effective in supporting early writing because they are predictable, recursive, rhythmic, and fun. The poem on page 58 is based on our Pancake unit and can be used to engage students in pantomime while they or you read the poem. By having students act out the words and phrases of the poem using gestures or pantomime, their memory for what they are reading is enhanced because they are physically engaged with language. This is why TPR is so effective with beginning-level second-language learners (Asher 1982). Anthologies like *A Chorus of Cultures* (Ada et al. 1993) offer lots of variety so that students can recite, chant, and perform poems of diverse kinds.

Mix a Pancake

Mix a pancake,
Stir a pancake,
Pop it in the pan;
Fry the pancake;
Toss the pancake,
Catch it if you can.

Author: Christina G. Rossetti, 1830–1894
www.scrapbook.com/poems/doc/3068/53.html

Texts with simple structure, rhythmic repetitive language patterns, and rhyming words are a good choice for ELLs of any age who are just beginning to read. Books that lend themselves to being performed are especially effective because they enrich students' language experiences. Picture books—both narrative and expository—are also good choices because they provide models that students can use to create their own early texts. Books with clear visual displays that are closely related to the written text are also very effective with ELLs because comprehension is supported by the photos that accompany the text. Letter name and alphabet books can also be effective, especially if they contain culturally appropriate content (for example, *Eating the Alphabet* [Ehlert 1996] introduces fruits and vegetables from around the world).

Folktales and fables, especially if they are traditional tales from the students' own culture, are good ways to engage students in early reading and writing activities. As well, using multimedia and Internet sources is important so that ELLs become familiar with computers, CD players, and the Internet and how to interact with these to access literacy experiences, if they are not familiar with these already. For a list of multicultural book companies that publish folktales and fables, see the Additional Resources for Teachers section at the end of this chapter.

Connect Literacy at School with Literacy at Home and in the Community

There are many opportunities to connect literacy activities at school with those at home and in the wider community. To do this, you need to investigate the literacy levels of parents and other family members and also their availability to engage in literacy activities in the home. Since many ESL parents are highly literate in their native language, encourage them to read to their children in that language, especially if this is their stronger language (Cappellini 2005). Even parents who are not fully literate or are preliterate can contribute to the literacy development of their child and should not be discounted, provided they have the time to get involved. Fieldwork conducted by Alma Flor Ada (1988) has shown that having parents serve as audience while their children read is as valuable as having parents read to their children in promoting early literacy.

Adjusting to life in a new city or country is very demanding. It may not be possible for parents to engage actively in literacy activities because they are busy getting their family settled into their new home or making sure there are sufficient economic resources to support their family. If parents are not readily available, perhaps an older sibling, cousin, or family friend can serve in this role (Cappellini 2005). Every text set should include books that make parent and family involvement possible—for example, a wordless picture book for oral storytelling or book enjoyment or a book in the native language on the theme. For more ideas about working with parents, see Chapter 3.

Linking school literacy to the home and community is easier if you can find out what literacy practices and resources exist in each cultural and linguistic community. Many community libraries host family literacy nights, and some schools have home-school reading programs

Research Question

Research on effective strategies to engage parents in their children's literacy is not extensive. Therefore, teachers may want to explore what works best with the parents of their students by devising different activities to be done at home and monitoring how effective each is. By sending alternative activities to parents with different linguistic and cultural backgrounds, you could even see if each group is more responsive to some activities than others.

"Meaningful interaction with parents and daily conversations about meaningful topics . . . result in more academic gain for children. . . . Knowing that their parents have a high regard for the learning process makes the children more eager to do well in their schoolwork."

(Ada 2003, 136)

where the entire family is encouraged to read together for enjoyment. Both can be very effective because they extend and widen the literacy experiences of new readers and writers (Ada 2003, Cappellini 2005).

Promoting Growth in Literacy for Beginning ELLs

The acquisition of high-level and fluent reading and writing skills is a developmental process that takes time. The focus of instructional attention shifts somewhat as students progress from *beginning* reading and writing, to *beginning intermediate* reading and writing, to *intermediate advanced* reading and writing, and finally to *advanced supported.* In the early stages of learning to read, mastery of word-level skills is important, while at the same time teachers show students how to connect what they are reading and writing to their lives, the curriculum, and the world around them. To move ELL students from their current literacy level to the next stage of literacy development, devise activities that help students acquire the skills and behaviors associated with the next stage of development. Scaffolded activities help students stretch into the next stage. This can be done using guided reading and writing activities, by modeling reading and writing skills that you want students to acquire, and through direct instruction of skills that students need for the next stage.

> **Research Finding**
>
> The National Literacy Panel on Language Minority Children and Youth notes that "literacy development is a process that begins early in childhood, long before children attend school, and involves many different skills and experiences" (see Lesaux et al. 2006, 77).

Promoting Growth from One Stage to the Next

1. Identify the student's stage of development.
2. Use scaffolded activities to help the learner acquire the behaviors associated with the next level.
3. Provide lots of modeling and time to practice.
4. Monitor the student's learning.

Guided Reading Methods

Guided reading is a "gateway" into second language and literacy learning because teachers model efficient and supportive reading behaviors for their learners and show them how the language and other text features function (Avalos et al. 2007). Using the interactive guided reading process described next helps students understand the reading process and how to use the various features of text and other cuing systems that support reading: linguistic, picture, background knowledge, and experience.

STEPS IN GUIDED READING

- ❑ Select four to six students who are the same stage of development.
- ❑ Select a culturally relevant text.
- ❑ Model fluent reading aloud.
- ❑ Provide detailed vocabulary instruction.
- ❑ Teach students about word and sentence structure.
- ❑ Develop cultural knowledge.

Begin by doing an analysis of the text so that you can identify elements in the text that you want to teach directly. For our text set on pancakes, these elements might be any of the elements described in the following box.

TEXT ANALYSIS

1. Oral Language: Locate unknown vocabulary and phrases. Teach about words with multiple meanings (*table = kitchen table, water table, multiplication table*) across different content areas.
2. Word Structure: Teach about homophones (*bear/bare*); synonyms (*sticky, tacky*) and antonyms (*dry/wet ingredients*); compound words (*pancake*; *flapjack*; or in *If You Give a Pig a Pancake—suitcase, mailbox*); or figurative language (pancakes as fluffy as clouds).
3. Decoding: Identify common phonetic patterns and high-frequency sight words.
4. Cultural Background Knowledge: Focus on cultural referents that may be unknown (maple syrup, county fairs, pancake breakfasts for fundraising, etc.).

5. Reading Comprehension: Focus on text structure (e.g., comparison/contrast, sequential) because it has been shown that knowledge of text structure can enhance reading comprehension (Carrell 1984, 1985; Coiro 2001). Focus on comprehension strategies. Teach reading strategies like predicting, using visuals to enhance understanding, word-solving strategies (use of cognates), and the like.

During the shared reading portion of guided reading, follow along as students read and listen for miscues; these can form the basis for "minilessons" during subsequent guided reading sessions. Careful observation of students is critical during the emergent literacy stage so you can see what they are struggling with and where they need direct assistance during future lessons. See Chapter 6 for more information on conducting observations for assessment purposes.

Flores (2008) created a novel approach for guided reading she calls "mini shared reading." She developed this method because she observed that most students were not paying attention during whole-class shared reading or could not see the text the teacher was reading. So instead of everyone reading from one book, each student is given a copy of the book and the teacher meets students in small groups of three to five for at least thirty minutes. She recommends that teachers choose books that are slightly beyond students' independent reading level. Other steps in the process are described next.

MINI SHARED READING PROCEDURE (FLORES 2008)

1. Introduce the book with the cover (each child can look at her own book).
2. Read and talk about the title.
3. Connect the book to prior experiences and knowledge.
4. Engage students in an animated picture walk of the book ("walking" through the book page by page before reading, guessing what the story will be about, or just noticing what is happening on each page). Spend a lot of time talking and using new vocabulary and patterns.
5. Read the entire book aloud as students listen and look at their individual copy.
6. Have students echo-read as the teacher reads the text again (looking at their own books).

7. Read the text a third time as a choral read; notice the difficulties students have as they read along chorally.
8. Revisit the text and guide students to notice certain text features of the various cueing systems that make up written text: semantic (new words), syntactic (recurring parts of speech; phrasing), graphophonic (recurring letter/sound correspondences, sight words), orthographic (family spelling patterns), and mechanics (conventions such as spelling, capitalization, and punctuation) as well as the visual supports available.
9. Create a collaborative text by having students work together to construct their own story following the patterns they have seen in the shared book.
10. Have children read the original and their collaborative texts on their own or with a partner.

Guided Writing Methods

In order to guide students in learning to write, you need to take note of the strategies they use to write words or phrases. You will notice that students often make excellent guesses about how to spell words based on similarities between English and their home language. For example, they might use letter-sound correspondences in Spanish to write English words (*chaket* for *jacket*); or, they might spell English words the way they say them in English (i.e., *escul* for *school*). Inventive spelling of this sort is unique to second-language learners; you should expect to find it in their writing. It is another example of how resourceful ELL learners are (see Chapter 2 in Bear et al. [2007] for a full discussion of how to analyze the spelling errors made by second-language learners of various language backgrounds).

Flores (2008) has devised a procedure she calls "collaborative text writing" that can be useful with students in the emergent writing stage. Using our theme of Pancakes, here are the steps to follow using her guided writing procedure.

COLLABORATIVE TEXT WRITING PROCEDURE (FLORES 2008)

- ❏ Select a pattern, such as "I like pancakes, said ***Jack***," or "Here's the ***milk*** shouted Jack," or "Let's make some ***pancakes***."

- ❑ Together with the students, generate modifications to this text for the words shown in italic and list the new story lines on chart paper or a transparency.
- ❑ Create a new story using the students' suggestions based on their own lives or stemming from story events (e.g., "I like pancakes," said Ludmila; "Here's the flour," said her cousin. "Let's make some pancakes." or "I like pancakes said the farmer." "Here's the flour," said the miller.).
- ❑ Ask the students to choose a newly invented story line they would like to illustrate.
- ❑ Have the students sequence the story lines they have illustrated to fit their new story to create new books.
- ❑ Have the students read their new book.

Putting It All Together: Daily Schedules and Unit Plans

Teachers may wonder how to plan the literacy block when working with emergent ELLs. A sample of how you might allocate time, using a ninety-minute literacy block, follows.

Sample Literacy Block Schedule (90 Minutes) for Emergent Literacy Students

COMPONENT	MAJOR ACTIVITY TYPES	TIME ALLOTTED
ORAL LANGUAGE DEVELOPMENT		
Frontloading of vocabulary; sentence patterns and background knowledge	Language experience activities Wordless picture books TPR Chants Songs Poems Word Walls with pictures/illustrations	15 minutes
READ-ALOUD		
Use key book from text set based on content focus	Teacher/school librarian read-aloud Parent read-aloud Cross-age student read-aloud Recorded book (video/DVD, cassette tape)	20 minutes

COMPONENT	MAJOR ACTIVITY TYPES	TIME ALLOTTED
WORD WORK		
	Word sorts (by sound, category, etc.) Finding story words with the same: initial/final consonant; vowel sounds, etc. Labeling pictures and underlining the target sound-symbol correspondence Teach sight words for reading and writing Spelling words from story when dictated by a peer or the teacher	5 minutes
READING PRACTICE		
	Guided reading (focus on emergent reading strategies) Shared reading Partner reading Independent reading (select stories based on language level, expected background knowledge, and interest level); choose books with good picture support and patterned stories	20 minutes
WRITING PRACTICE; WRITER'S WORKSHOP		
Including work on handwriting, spelling, sentence patterns	Guided writing (focus on emergent writing strategies) Collaborative writing (story retelling, writing prequels/sequels) Partner writes	25 minutes
CONNECTIONS TO HOME AND COMMUNITY		
	Sharing activities done at home with parents/family members Showing resources produced with parents/family member (e.g., recorded books for class library in home language) Lists of information gathered at home and in the community that together form a class book on that topic (stores in our neighborhoods, etc.)	5 minutes

Another useful model we offer is how unit delivery might look over a three-week period of instruction (see the Pancakes Units Plan on pages 66–67).

Pancakes Unit Plan—Three Weeks

With potential links to Africa, African village life, farms and farming, communities, liquid and dry measurement, nutritional foods, and the producer-to-consumer cycle as it applies to food products (e.g., grain to pancakes, tortillas, or bread; collection and consumption of maple syrup); pancakes around the world; U.S. cultural practices with respect to pancake breakfasts, county fairs, etc.

KEY	
OL	Oral Language Development (vocabulary, sentence patterns/structure)
CC	Content Connection
RW	Reading-Writing Connection
HC	Home Language/Community Connections
CA	Classroom-Based Assessment

WEEK 1

ACTIVITY 1	ACTIVITY 2	ACTIVITY 3	ACTIVITY 4	ACTIVITY 5
Language Experience Activity	**Play with Theme Language**	**Read a Theme Book As a Read-Aloud**	**Word Work**	**Story Retelling**
• Make pancakes • Name ingredients as you make them **(OL)** • Have students engage in measuring the ingredients using dry and liquid measures **(CC)** • Model the reading of a recipe • Ask students to find words in the recipe for key ingredients **(RW)**	• Do a TPR activity **(OL)** • Sing a pancake song or perform a pancake chant/poem **(OL)** • Assign parts • Let the children clap or tap to feel the beat of the words and music	• Select a story to read as a read-aloud from the pancake text set • Read the book aloud to children • This could be done as using the Mini Shared Reading procedure (Flores 2008) or you can do a traditional whole-class read-aloud • Monitor students' understanding of the story as you read **(CA)** • Assess and build background knowledge and vocabulary as needed **(CA)**	• Identify words in the story to teach: –beginning/ending sounds –initial blends or digraphs –vowel sounds • Or teach compound words from the story • Or teach about syllabication • Or work on sight words • Or do word sorts using picture cards for objects, actions, people, etc. • Practice finding the target sounds/words in the story	• Using picture cards of key story events on the chalkboard tray or in a pocket chart, have children retell the story with assistance **(OL)** • If you like, children can practice in pairs before telling their story to the class to build their abilities to tell about the story **(OL)** • You might also review key terms during the second reading of the story **(OL)**

WEEK 2			
ACTIVITY 1	**ACTIVITY 2**	**ACTIVITY 3**	**ACTIVITY 4**
Guided Reading	**Independent Reading (DEAR time/SSR Time)**	**Illustrating Story Events and Writing Captions**	**Telling a Story to Parents Using a Pancake Wordless Picture Book**
• Work with students in small groups with one of the theme books that is appropriate for their levels • Teach students a reading strategy you want them to know how to use • Monitor and reinforce their use of the strategy **(CA)** • Note other problems as they read using your observation journal **(CA)**	• Assign students a book that you know they can read or look at • Assign wordless picture books to those who cannot read independently • Assign books with limited text and/or recurrent text structures to the others • Be sure they notice the high-frequency words on your illustrated Word Wall so they can use this as a resource while they read	• Give each student or pair of students a story event from the read-aloud to illustrate • Have them write a caption for their picture using the Word Wall and each other for support **(RW)** • Put the story events together as a class book • Use the students' pictures to retell the story their own way to each other, or to the class. **(OL)**	• Have students take home the wordless picture book from your Pancake theme **(HC)** • Ask them to prepare to tell the story to their parents in their native language **(HC)** • Have them practice telling the story several times prior to telling the story to their parents **(HC)** • Record the students telling the story to their parents **(HC)** • Put the recording in the class for others of the same home language to listen to **(HC)**

WEEK 3			
ACTIVITY 1	**ACTIVITY 2**	**ACTIVITY 3**	**ACTIVITY 4**
Collaborative Text-Writing Procedure	**Guided Writing**	**Read-Aloud and Dramatic Performance of the Story**	**Recording/Copying a Pancake-like Recipe from Home**
• Using a repetitive pattern found in one of the theme stories, have students create a new story in small groups on chart paper **(RW)** • Allow each group to tell or read their story • Allow students to add illustrations to their chart and to sign their names as the authors • Post the charts around the room	• Provide instruction on sound-symbol correspondence that you know the group has difficulty with using words taken from the class read-aloud, or invented stories • Concentrate on initial or final sounds, long or short vowels, digraphs, and blends as appropriate • Dictate story words to write, and monitor their production **(CA)** • You might also practice writing compound words taken from the story, using high-frequency sight words: *pancake; door-way*	• Choose another story to be read aloud, for example *Mama Panya's Pancakes*, one that leads to cross-cultural and content learning **(CC)** • Build background knowledge and vocabulary for the story **(OL)** • Ask students to tell their favorite part **(OL)** • Dramatize all or part of the story	• Have students ask the person who cooks in their home if they have ever made something like a pancake (e.g., *beghrirs* in Morocco, *blinis* in Russia, *chapatis* in India, *okonomiyaki* in Japan, or *tortillas* in Mexico) **(HC)** • Ask them to make a list of main ingredients together with their parent or to copy the ingredients from a cookbook. **(HC)** • Make a class book of lists of pancake ingredients for different types of pancakes.

Learning to Read in a New Cultural Context

ELLs often come from families with social norms, values, and customs that are different from those of the school or those that are depicted in the texts they are reading. When the cultural context of a book is unfamiliar, making sense of a story or a paragraph written in a new language becomes even harder. Two things can be done to lessen the effect of an unfamiliar cultural context.

First, as described in other sections of this chapter, make the context more familiar by doing prereading/prewriting activities that give students a sense of why things are done the way they are in a story. For example, in *Pancakes for Breakfast,* students may not understand why the old woman would go next door to borrow ingredients for her pancakes from a neighbor. In *Mama Panya's Pancakes,* they may not know why Adika would dress in his finest shirt and cleanest shorts just to go to the market, or they might not be familiar with the cultural values that cause him to invite everyone he sees to his house for pancakes, even though this may mean they won't have enough food to go around. Build background knowledge that helps students understand the cultural values that explain these events.

Second, whenever possible, choose books that have cultural context that is familiar to students so you are not obliged to provide extensive explanations for every book, as this can detract from story enjoyment.

Selecting Culturally Familiar Texts and Topics

Using culturally responsive literature gives ELLs an opportunity to talk about experiences they have had in their countries of origin, such as fishing, planting, caring for animals, participating in family or community events, or traveling extensively within their native country. Lots of children's literature like this is available. The list in the Additional Resources for Teacher section at the end of this chapter provides a partial compendium of sources for multicultural books about different cultures and groups of people. Teachers will always want to be sure that they read books from all the cultural groups represented in the school and community, not exclusively about one group or the same few groups. They will also want to match books to the kinds of prior experiences their students have had in urban, suburban, or rural communities.

Using Familiar Themes and Tapping the Life Experiences of ELLs for Writing

You can engage newly arrived students in writing by prompting them to write about experiences that are unique to them as second-language learners or recent arrivals. As well, books like *I Hate English* (Levine 1995), *Amigo Means Friend* (Everett 1999), or *Abuela* (Dorros 1991) let you tap into the experiences of students who have lived the immigrant experience or who have recently arrived in a new country. These experiences can be the basis for student writing; ELL students are often anxious to tell stories about similar experiences they have had.

With older students who are learning to read and write for the first time, themes that tap their bicultural life experiences, longing for the homeland, or being surprised by their new surroundings are all good choices. We want students to be able to write about what is on their minds and in their hearts. Books like *Going Home* (Bunting 1998) or *My Little Island* (Lessac 1987, a Reading Rainbow title) are good choices for opening up older students' feelings about trips back to a home that is very much missed. Excerpts from *I'm New Here* (Howlett 1993) can be read to promote talk about the feelings of being a stranger in a new place. When students see that their experiences are published in books, they get excited about reading. They also realize that what they bring to the classroom is valued and worthwhile.

NOTE FOR TEACHERS WORKING WITH STUDENTS WITH LIMITED FORMAL SCHOOLING

For those of you working with ELLs with limited formal schooling, see *Closing the Achievement Gap: How to Reach Limited Formal Schooling and Long Term English Language Learners* by Freeman, Freeman, and Mercuri (2002) for a discussion of the issues and review of effective practices for this population.

Using Literature for Cross-Cultural Learning

While we want to honor the experiences of our students and use their life experiences to promote early literacy development, we can also use literature to support learning about new cultures and, thus, support student's integration into ethnically diverse English-speaking countries. When students learn about pancakes, they are learning about life in their new country, and they can see that families from different backgrounds can make and enjoy pancakes. They can learn about growing grain, milling, and tapping trees for maple syrup. In *Pancakes for Breakfast* they can learn about farm life and the pets we keep in our homes and snowy days. In *Curious George Makes Pancakes* (Rey 1998), they can learn about pancake breakfasts, fundraising, blueberries, forming lines in order to be served food, and games like dunking tanks at community fairs. With each book they read, students enter a new cultural world and learn a lot more than language.

Using Multicultural Literature to Promote Cross-Cultural Understanding

Helping ELLs navigate their new multicultural world and promoting cross-cultural understanding are important goals of instruction. This is where using a theme like Pancakes can shine. Stories using the same theme are told across cultures, like in the story of *The Great Pancake Escape* (Many 2002), *The Runaway Latke,* and *The Runaway Tortilla.* These stories are quite similar, and yet it would be important to notice how they differ and what is unique to each telling of the tale. Pancakes and making food form the basis of many books, songs, poems, and rhymes, as we have seen in this chapter. Using these variations on a single theme, you can show how surface and deep cultural values differ across cultures by comparing *Mama Panya's Pancakes* to *Mr. Wolf's Pancakes* (Fearnley 2001), to *Sunday* (Saint James 1996) in terms of story events, setting, characters, and plot. By comparing stories, students can see that in *Mr. Wolf's Pancakes,* you take care of yourself, whereas in *Mama Panya's Pancakes,* you care for the community and the community cares for you. They can learn in *Pancakes for Breakfast* "If at first you don't succeed, try, try again," whereas in *Curious George Makes Pancakes,* "Everyone has special talents and abilities that can help the community." It is important to engage ELLs in discussions of deep cultural values and differences. This is much more important than learning that people in different parts of the world wear different clothes or make different types of pancakes depending on the natural resources of a particular country (blueberries or chili peppers).

Orienting Learners to U.S. Values and Cultures Through Literature

The Pancakes theme also provides a context for orienting ELLs to well-known characters, themes, and core values in their new country. They can get to know familiar book characters like Curious George and learn commonly known nursery rhymes in *Mr. Wolf's Pancakes.* They can also learn that being expected to do things by themselves and celebrating unique talents of individuals (individualism) are valued in their new country, as shown in *Mr. Wolf's Pancakes* and *Curious George Makes Pancakes.* The story *Pancakes for Breakfast* shows them that perseverance is valued and that following recipes is a common way of cooking in the United States. All of this helps ELLs come to understand the common practices and predominant values of their new communities. This, in turn, will help them feel at home because they know what is expected of them. Books on a theme offer ELLs rich opportunities for learning about their new culture.

Curriculum Development for ELLs

In this final section, we use all that the chapter has outlined to formulate curriculum design principles for teachers of emergent readers and writers and suggest ways of evaluating school and classroom library collections to ensure that students have books they can read inside and outside of school.

Curriculum Design Principles

Across this chapter we have suggested many ways of working with emergent ELL readers and writers. Following is a summary of the most important points with respect to how teachers can construct curricula for their students so that they are as supportive and effective as possible.

1. Start with what learners know—investigate your ELLs' home language abilities in reading and writing, their oral language and literacy levels in English, and their experiences with print in the home and community.
2. Build themes around students' interests, lives, and learning needs.
3. Organize materials into text sets; make sure the sets start with wordless picture books and extend to multimedia and Internet-based texts that are above their independent reading level but can be read aloud to students.
4. Ensure that what goes on in the classroom is linked to the home and community; invite parents to participate in any way that they can (as audience, as models reading and writing in their native language, as co-learners of English in Family Literacy Programs).
5. Identify students' developmental stages of reading and writing, engage in activities that draw on the skills of that stage, and promote acquisition of skills at the next stage.
6. Tie reading to writing and both to oral language development.
7. Plan for oral language development. Identify goals for oral language, reading, and writing for every lesson.
8. Personalize instruction and provide focused feedback.
9. Teach skills in context.
10. Monitor student progress and alter the curriculum as needed.
11. Discard books and materials that do not engage learners or are not at the right level.

There are many resource books for teachers working with beginning-level students that will advance your understanding of how to teach ELL learners who are at this critical stage of literacy development listed in the Additional Resources for Teachers section at the end of the chapter (see Basic Books on Emergent Literacy with ELLs). These books reflect the principles outlined here.

Evaluating Classroom and School Libraries

Entering the school or public library can be overwhelming for emergent readers and writers because libraries do not organize books by proficiency level but rather by author, genre, or topic. Sometimes books are in collections called "Easy Reading," but this does not guarantee that they will be easy for emergent ELL readers. Work with the school or local public librarian to show them what makes books supportive for early readers who are second-language learners, namely:

- ❑ Predictable and patterned text, with limited amounts of unknown vocabulary, and simple sentence structures.
- ❑ Books with supportive visuals that tell the story and closely match the text.
- ❑ Books with a limited number of pages so that the learner does not fatigue before finishing the book.
- ❑ Books with themes that tap background knowledge and life experience and match age-level interests.
- ❑ Books with interesting plots and/or information that engage students.
- ❑ Text that invites talk and reader response.

Overall, the teacher's job is to identify where ELL students are in the process of developing reading and writing and to provide supportive instruction, focused and well-targeted feedback, and lots and lots of interesting and pleasurable opportunities to engage in reading and writing.

Summing Up

Here are the big ideas about teaching beginning readers and writers to keep in mind as you work with ELL students:

1. The most supportive early literacy environments for ELLs focus on developing vocabulary, building oral language, and sharing literacy experiences.
2. Effective teachers use techniques like read-alouds, shared reading, shared writing, and modeled writing to support emergent literacy.
3. Effective teachers focus on top-down processing (building concepts, background knowledge) before building bottom-up reading and writing skills.
4. Successful teachers use rich themes that promote high levels of engagement and promote language and literacy development across a range of texts.
5. Responsive teachers promote language learning and cross-cultural understanding and tap the rich cultural and experiential reservoirs of our learners.

Additional Resources for Teachers

Books for the theme: Pancakes, Pancake Day, or Pancakes Around the World [Books and book descriptions taken from a lesson by Paul Many, Language Arts K–4, available at www.lessonplanspage.com/LAMDMardiGras-PancakeDayUsingBooksK4.htm]

Curious George Makes Pancakes

From the character created by Margret Rey, H. A. Rey (Illustrator)

Written and illustrated in the style of the Reys by Vipah Interactive
Houghton-Mifflin (Boston, 1998)

Curious George, an inquisitive monkey, causes quite a stir when he tries his hand at making pancakes at a fundraiser for the children's hospital.

The Great Pancake Escape

by Paul Many, Scott Goto (Illustrator)
Walker & Co. (New York, 2002)

When their bumbling magician father accidentally uses the wrong book to make pancakes, his children are led on a merry chase through town trying to catch their wiggly, sneaky breakfast.

If You Give a Pig a Pancake

by Laura Numeroff, Felicia Bond (Illustrator)
Laura Geringer Book (New York, 1998)

One thing leads to another when you give a pig a pancake.

"If you give a pig a pancake, she'll want some syrup to go with it. You'll give her some of your favorite maple syrup. She'll probably get all sticky, so she'll want to take a bath. She'll ask you for some bubbles. When you give her the bubbles . . ."

Mama Panya's Pancakes: A Village Tale from Kenya

by Mary Chamberlin, Richard Chamberlin, & Julia Cairns
Barefoot Books, Ltd. (London, 2006)

Mama Panya is alarmed at the market when her son Adika invites all of their friends to come over for pancakes. However will she feed them all? This clever and heartwarming story about village life teaches children the benefits of sharing as well as introducing simple Swahili phrases.

Miss Mabel's Table

by Deborah Chandra, Max Grover (Illustrator)
Harcourt Brace Jovanovich (San Diego, 1994)

A cumulative counting rhyme presents the ingredients and techniques used by Miss Mabel to cook enough pancakes to serve ten people.

Mr. Wolf's Pancakes
by Jan Fearnley
Tiger Tales M E Media LLC (Wilton, CT, 2001)
Mr. Wolf asks some of his neighbors to help him make pancakes, and even though they all rudely refuse, when the pancakes are done they expect to share the feast.

Pancakes for Breakfast
by Tomie de Paola.
Scholastic (New York, 1978)
A little old lady's attempts to have pancakes for breakfast are hindered by a scarcity of supplies and the participation of her pets.

Pancakes, Pancakes!
Written and illustrated by Eric Carle
Knopf (New York, 1970)
By cutting and grinding the wheat for flour, Jack starts from scratch to help make his breakfast pancake.

Perfect Pancakes, If You Please
by William Wise, Richard Egielski (Illustrator)
Dial Books for Young Readers (New York, 1997)
King Felix loves pancakes so much that he offers to marry his daughter to the man who can make the perfect pancake.

The Runaway Latkes
by Leslie Kimmelman, Paul Yalowitz (Illustrator)
Whitman & Co. (Morton Grove, IL, 2000)
When three potato latkes (pancakes) escape Rachel Bloom's frying pan on the first night of Hanukkah, everyone including the cantor, the rabbi, and the mayor joins in the chase.

The Runaway Tortilla
by Eric A. Kimmel, Randy Cecil (Illustrator)
Winslow Press (Delray Beach, FL, 2000)
In Texas, Tia Lupe and Tio Jose make the best tortillas—so light that the cowboys say they just might jump right out of the griddle. One day, a tortilla does exactly that.

Sunday
by Synthia Saint James
Whitman & Co. (Morton Grove, IL, 1996)
This book portrays an African American family as they spend a typical Sunday eating a pancake breakfast, going to church, and visiting their grandparents.

Other children's books referenced in this chapter

Bunting, E. 1998. *Going Home.* New York: HarperCollins.

Dorros, A. 1991. *Abuela.* New York: Dutton.

Ehlert, L. 1996. *Eating the Alphabet.* New York: Harcourt Children's Books.

Everett, L. 1999. *Amigo Means Friend.* Mahwah, NJ: Troll Communications.

Lessac, F. 1987. *My Little Island.* New York: HarperCollins.

Levine, E. 1995. *I Hate English.* New York: Scholastic.

Howlett, B. 1993. *I'm New Here.* Boston: Houghton Mifflin.

Wordless picture book lists

- http://picturingbooks.imaginarylands.org/resources/wordless.html
  Lists fifty wordless picture books.
- http://nancykeane.com/rl/317.htm
  Lists 135 wordless or almost wordless picture books.
- www.colorincolorado.org/read/forkids/wordless
  Lists twenty books with annotations and suggestions for their use.
- http://people.ucsc.edu/~ktellez/wdlesspicbooks.htm
  Your local school and public librarian may keep other useful lists like these.

Selected multicultural book companies that publish folktales and fables

- Culture for Kids (www.cultureforkids.com)
- Asia for Kids (www.afk.com)
- Bilingual Books for Kids (www.bilingualbooks.com)
- Shen's Books (www.shens.com)

Selected multimedia and internet sources

- *Reading Rainbow* (http://pbskids.org/readingrainbow/books/index.html)
- *Living Books/books on CD Rom* (www.KidsClick.com)
- *We Read* (free online books at www.weread.org/index.asp)
- Sesame Street (www.sesameworkshop.org/sesamestreet)
- National Geographic Kids (http://kids.nationalgeographic.com)
- Yahoo Kids! (http://kids.yahoo.com; exists in Japanese and Korean as well)

Helpful sources of multicultural children's literature

1. Hadaway, N. L., S. M. Vardell, and T. A. Young. 2002. *Literature-Based Instruction with English Language Learners K–12.* Boston: Allyn and Bacon.

2. Ada, A. F. 2003. *A Magical Encounter: Latino Children's Literature in the Classroom. Second Edition.* Boston: Allyn and Bacon.
3. www.multiculturalchildrenslit.com (which lists African American, Chinese American, Japanese American, Korean American, Latino, Middle Eastern, and Vietnamese books).
4. NEA's site *50 Multicultural Books Every Child Should Read* (www.nea.org/readacross/resources/50multibooks.html).
5. A World of Difference *Recommended Multicultural and Anti-bias Books for Children* (www.adl.org/bibliography)

Basic books on emergent literacy with ELLs

❑ Ada, A. F. 2002. *A Magical Encounter: Latino Children's Literature in the Classroom. Second edition.* Boston: Allyn and Bacon.

This helpful teaching resource book is divided in four major parts: (1) theoretical principles, reflections on the role of literature for children and adolescents in the language arts curriculum, the basic tenets of "Transformative Education," the "Creative Reading" methodology; (2) an overview of the evolution of Latino literature for children and adolescents in the United States, with an extensive bibliography of books published by Latino and Latina authors; (3) the role of the various literary genres in the classroom; and (4) helpful teaching suggestions, with examples using specific books. A rich resource for teachers working with Latino children and families.

❑ Bear, D. R., L. Helman, S. Templeton, M. Invernizzi, & F. Hohston. 2007. *Words Their Way with English Learners: Word Study for Phonics, Vocabulary, and Spelling Instruction.* Upper Saddle River, NJ: Pearson/Merrill Prentice Hall.

Helps teachers understand what learners are bringing from their home languages into English in terms of their knowledge of print, based on native language orthographies. Describes the emergent stages of reading and how to promote phonics and word recognition with ELLs at the beginning literacy stages. In writing, focuses on letter recognition and production and how to work with learners at various stages of spelling development.

❑ Boyd-Batstone, P. 2006. *Differentiated Early Literacy for English Language Learners: Practical Strategies.* Boston: Pearson, Allyn and Bacon.

Discusses emergent literacy with ELLs emphasizing oral language and vocabulary development as the base. Offers helpful charts that break out teaching strategies and student activities by proficiency level. See Chapter 5 for how to develop vocabulary and promote reading fluency and Chapter 6 for how to conduct book walks, craft minilessons, develop fluency, conduct shared read-alouds, and select books for ELLs.

Chapter 4 outlines how to teach ELLS to write letters using TPR and other techniques and how to teach spelling rules. Chapter 7 focuses on teaching writing across the various proficiency levels, within a process-writing framework. Offers many useful templates and rubrics to support writing development.

- ❑ Cappellini, M. 2005. *Balancing Reading and Language Learning: A Resource for Teaching English Language Learners, K–5.* Portland, ME: Stenhouse.

  In addition to chapters on setting up the learning environment, welcoming parents as partners, and thematic planning, describes how to do read-alouds, shared reading, guided reading, and independent reading with ELLs of various developmental levels. Throughout discusses how to develop oral language through literacy. Highly practical.

- ❑ Dargan, P. B. 2005. *A How-To Guide for Teaching English Language Learners in the Primary Classroom.* Portsmouth, NH: Heinemann.

  Describes ways to effectively integrate ELLs into the primary classroom, facilitate oral language development through poetry and music, and use shared reading and picture books to help children acquire language and learn to read. Highlights thematic teaching and integration of the arts to promote literacy development.

  This book focuses on emergent literacy in the early grades. Describes ways to promote writing and publishing with English language learners throughout the book and ways to connect with families. Great ideas of how to use art and projects to prompt early writing. See especially Chapters 10 and 12.

- ❑ Freeman, D. E., & Y. S. Freeman. 2000. *Teaching Reading in Multilingual Classrooms.* Portsmouth, NH: Heinemann.

  Introduces core principles of effective reading practice for teachers working in linguistically diverse classrooms. Promotes the use of themes and demonstrates how teachers can plan their instruction, select books for students, and formulate text sets. Gives checklists for teachers to use when they have multilevel classes to ensure they are meeting the needs of all students, especially of beginning students who are English language learners. Shows teachers how to link with the home language, promote vocabulary development, and link oral language to literacy activities. Discusses early literacy practices like picture walks, read-alouds, language experience, and partner reading. Also answers questions teachers have about phonics and phonemic awareness with students who are new to English.

- ❑ Hadaway, N. L., S. M. Vardell, & T. A. Young. 2002. *Literature-Based Instruction with English Language Learners K–12.* Boston: Allyn and Bacon.

Very teacher-friendly book on how to organize for literature-based instruction with ELLs. Great chapters on developing oral language and reading skills through literature: multicultural literature, folklore, poetry, and expository texts. Provides excellent ideas on setting up productive classroom environments and a range of practical strategies for teaching. Discusses beginning language learners in every chapter.

While this book primarily concentrates on literature-based instruction with ELLs for the purpose of oral language and reading development, it also includes helpful strategies on how to build English learners' writing skills around quality children's literature and nonfiction texts. See Chapters 6 and Chapter 11.

- ❏ Peregoy, S. F., & O. F. Boyle. 2008. *Reading, Writing, and Learning in ESL: A Resource Book for K–12 Teachers.* Fifth Edition. Boston: Pearson, Allyn and Bacon.

  While other chapters may be of interest, Chapter 5 addresses emergent literacy in terms of teaching beginning reading and writing. It discusses environments that nurture emergent literacy, strategies that promote early literacy, and specific strategies for teaching sight words, phonics, and spelling.

- ❏ Samway, K. D. 2006. *When English Language Learners Write: Connecting Research to Practice, K–8.* Portsmouth, NH: Heinemann.

  An extremely helpful review of the most important findings from ELL writing research is accompanied by stories of individual ELL writers and what supported their development. The author suggests ways to connect reading to writing instruction and ways to support reflective writing in the classroom. Individual chapters offer teachers ideas about how to connect read-alouds and textbook reading to writing and ways to use learning logs, dialogue journals, questionnaires and interviews, bookmarks, and letters to prompt reflection through student writing. The book ends with very helpful suggestions of how to set up a classroom environment that supports and encourages writing, from emergent stages forward.

HELPING ENGLISH LANGUAGE LEARNERS BECOME BILITERATE

CHAPTER 3

Critical role of the home language *82*

Different levels of biliteracy *88*

Using the home language to support English *93*

Social aspects of biliteracy *104*

Implications for all teachers *110*

Summing up *112*

Additional resources for teachers *113*

MANY ELLs COME TO SCHOOL WITH LITERACY IN THEIR HOME LANGUAGE; OTHERS ARRIVE NOT HAVING DEVELOPED READING AND WRITING SKILLS AT ALL. WE BELIEVE THAT ALL ELLs HAVE THE POTENTIAL TO DEVELOP FULL LITERACY IN ENGLISH AND AT LEAST SOME LITERACY IN THEIR HOME LANGUAGE.

They can become biliterate, regardless of the type of program they are in, be it a mainstream program with ESL push-in or pull-out support, a sheltered ESL classroom, or a full-fledged bilingual program. Mainstream teachers who are not bilingual themselves can help ELLs achieve some level of biliteracy. It is up to you, their teachers, to see that they reach that potential; this is the main message of this chapter.

Some teachers might find it difficult to accept that this is possible, especially since schools in most English-speaking countries, including the United States, focus on oral and written competence in English only. It is easy to forget that the majority of the world is bilingual and biliterate and, in many cases, multiliterate. Many politicians, school board members, and school administrators are still under the misconception that if ELLs spend any time learning their home language, the development of English proficiency, whether oral or written, will suffer. As will become clear in this chapter, the home language actually facilitates, rather than hinders, the development of English, especially when it comes to reading and writing. The most important reason to consider the development of literacy in ELLs' home language is that it offers significant and well-documented advantages in learning to read and write in English; a goal upon which we all agree.

"... most people in the world speak more than one tongue, and in [some] places ... it is common to speak three or four distinct languages and a dialect or two as well."

(Gibbs 2002, 85)

This chapter is designed with your role as an ESL or mainstream classroom teacher in mind and takes into account that, in many cases, you are not proficient in the home languages of your ELLs. This chapter is not written exclusively for bilingual professionals; rather, it is written for all teachers. There are two reasons we focus on biliteracy in this chapter: (a) It is critical that you understand the role of the home language in the development of literacy in English, and (b) even monolingual mainstream teachers can help ELLs become biliterate. Helping ELLs learn to read and write in English and in their home language is not only possible in all schools but also extremely important in order to better prepare students for the linguistically complex globalized world that they will live in once they have finished school.

Critical Role of the Home Language

Although the primary goal of schooling in English-speaking countries like the United States is acquisition of English, teachers should not ignore the critical role that ELLs' home language can play in achieving that goal, especially when it comes to learning to read and write.

Numerous systematic reviews of research on the educational outcomes of ELLs have shown that ELLs are most likely to develop high levels of literacy in English when they are given some instruction in their home-language. Teachers who understand the powerful role that home-language literacy plays in promoting literacy in English are able to harness that power, even in the mainstream classroom, in the service of promoting English literacy. This well-established research finding runs counter to what many people believe. Many believe that the best way to teach reading and writing in English is to teach reading and writing only in English. According to this view, supporting literacy development in the home language takes away time from learning English and creates the possibility of interference between the home language and English. It turns out that the development of literacy skills in a second language is much more complicated than that. In this chapter, we explain what is really going on.

> **Research Finding**
>
> Contrary to what some people may think, research shows that beginning to learn how to read through the primary language is not a "waste of valuable time." Skills developed in the first or primary language support literacy in English in many important ways (Genesee & Geva 2006; Genesee et al. 2006; Reese et al. 2000; Riches & Genesee 2006).

> **Research Finding**
>
> In an extensive review of research on alternative forms of education for ELLs in the United States since 1980, including programs that provide instruction through the home language, Lindholm-Leary and Borsato (2006, 201) conclude "there is strong convergent evidence that the educational success of ELLs is positively related to sustained instruction through the students' first language. . . . Most long-term studies report that the longer the students stayed in the (bilingual) program, the more positive were the outcomes."

Regardless of the type of program ELLs are in (ESL, sheltered English, bilingual, or dual language) and regardless of their grade level, ELLs who know how to read and write in the home language acquire higher levels of competence in academic oral and written English than ELLs without this advantage. In a nutshell, and as many reading experts point out, you only have to learn to read once; if you can read in your home language, then learning to read in another language is halfway there. Moreover, as proficiency in reading and writing English grows, proficiency in reading and writing in the home language also grows and, thus, contributes to students' biliteracy.

> "... students instructed exclusively in their second language may apply the second language writing skills when writing in their first language."
>
> (August 2006, 72)

ADVANTAGES OF DEVELOPING LITERACY IN THE HOME LANGUAGE

- Beginning literacy instruction is more efficient and effective if it takes place in a language students already know since students do not have to learn a new language and literacy at the same time. Oral skills in the home language can serve as a platform for literacy development, as when ELLs start school and are introduced to literacy in their home language. Some districts capitalize on this advantage by offering a bilingual or dual language program for ELLs.
- ELLs who have had initial literacy instruction in the home language come to English literacy understanding what it is and view themselves as literate individuals. As a result, they not only have a conceptual understanding of reading and writing, they also have confidence that they can learn to read in another language. All ELLs in your classroom with literacy skills in their home language have this advantage.
- Students have linguistic identities, just as they have cultural identities, and teaching literacy in the home language strengthens their identities as competent individuals. This, in turn, strengthens and deepens the process of learning to read and write in English. We will share ways to capitalize on this advantage in your classroom.
- There are aspects of home-language literacy that transfer to English literacy and, thereby, facilitate the acquisition of English literacy skills. We describe the transfer process in detail later.
- When students are allowed to develop literacy in their home language, they come to appreciate their own literature and the value of being biliterate; they are also able to participate in two literate worlds. We share ideas of how to promote reading in two languages in and outside of school for students who are literate in their home languages.
- If students learn to read first in their home language, we can be highly systematic when introducing literacy in English. This is critical to classroom ESL teachers working in English.

Spending time promoting ELLs' ability to read and write in the home language, be it at home or in school, does not take away from learning to read and write in English, but rather contributes to it. Understanding this relationship is linked to two key concepts: "cross-linguistic transfer" and "metalinguistic awareness." We discuss both of these concepts in the following sections.

Cross-Linguistic Transfer

Cross-linguistic transfer occurs when specific knowledge and skills in one language are used in another language. Teachers who are teaching only through English need to be aware of this phenomenon in order to make the most of the home language to support ELLs' acquisition of English literacy skills. When it comes to reading and writing, the more similar the home language to English (as is the case for Spanish and English in comparison to Farsi and English, for example), the greater the transfer. As evidence of cross-linguistic transfer, ELLs whose home language is Spanish might read the word *have* as "av-ey" since the *h* is silent in Spanish and all vowels are pronounced; they might write the English word *helper* as "jelper" since the letter *j* in Spanish is pronounced like *h* in English; or they write sentences without explicitly stating the subject, such as "ate his lunch," because Spanish allows this.

When ELLs use knowledge of the home language in these ways, they are actively filling in gaps in their English by drawing on corresponding skills and knowledge from the home language; this is what researchers call bootstrapping (August & Shanahan 2006; Genesee et al. 2006). They are also showing us that they know that there is a correspondence between written letters and sounds in language—a critical foundational skill in learning to read and write in any language. Students who demonstrate this kind of transfer do not need to learn phonological awareness skills because, as you can see by these examples, they are aware of phonemes. All they need is to learn the letter-sound correspondences in English. ELLs who do not make these kinds of transfer may be at a preliteracy stage and, therefore, may require instruction that helps them develop their phonological awareness skills.

Students also transfer general strategies to figure out the meanings of new words or to comprehend text. While these strategies may not be obvious cases of transfer, they often are. You can tell when this is the case because ELLs in your class who do not already have literacy skills will not use these kinds of strategies when they come across a new word or have difficulty comprehending text. When students transfer skills from the home language to English that produce the correct result in English, the influence of the home language is invisible; we simply think that they "got it right."

> **Research Finding**
>
> Langer, Barolome, and Vasquez (1990) found that ELLs successfully made use of competencies in the home language to make sense of reading material in English. For example, they often thought of words and ideas in the home language as a comprehension aid when reading English, especially when the level of reading was difficult.

To better understand how your ELLs are using the home language to bootstrap into English, get to know how the various home languages of your ELL students compare to English in sounds, word formation, grammar, and meaning. These aspects of oral language underlie and support reading and writing because, after all, written language is a graphic representation of oral language. ELLs' existing knowledge of these aspects of their home language creates expectations about how written language in English represents oral language and meaning (see Bear et al. 2007, 3). This is true even when students have not been taught to read or write in the home language. You can see evidence of this in your native English-speaking students when they use inventive spelling—their inventive spellings correspond to how the word sounds to them. In fact, sometimes their renditions of how to spell irregular words are more regular than conventional spelling. ELLs likewise draw on their knowledge of their home language to spell, write, and decode English, as has already been seen in the examples provided.

> **NOTE**
>
> For those of you working with ELLs who come from home languages that have a different alphabet system than English:
>
> Even in highly dissimilar orthographies, students who come to English literate in their home language know that symbols represent sounds and words. This level of awareness of what reading and writing entail is useful when learning a new symbolic system. There is evidence of transfer across languages of reading comprehension even when the languages have different types of alphabets (August 2006).

It is useful to know something about the spelling systems of your ELLs' home languages. For example, is the writing system in the student's home language alphabetic or logographic (like Chinese); and what is the directionality of print—left to right or right to left; is reading left to right in horizontal rows from the top, or from top to bottom in vertical columns? In alphabetic languages (like English), you can compare letters and sounds that the home language and English have in common and those that differ and even conflict, like the letter *i*, which by itself is a long-sounding vowel in Spanish whereas in English it is a short vowel (Hiebert et al. 2004). This difference could cause Spanish-speaking ELLs to say the word *hit* as "heat." In logographic codes (like Chinese), sound and meaning are represented very differently from English. In Chinese, the majority of written characters are semanto-phonetic compounds: They include a semantic element, which represents or hints at their meaning, and a phonetic element that shows or hints at their pronunciation (Bear et al. 2007). Explaining these differences to students can enhance their metalinguistic awareness. See the Additional Resources for Teachers section at the end of this chapter for a list of language resources.

Capitalizing on Cross-Linguistic Transfer to Promote Metalinguistic Awareness

Cross-linguistic transfer is a strategy that students use automatically to figure out how English literacy works. They do this whether we encourage it or not. In fact, we should encourage it because research has shown that ELLs who use these kinds of strategies learn to read and write in English more easily than students who do not. Linking literacy instruction in English to the home language also serves to engage ELLs in the learning process because they can demonstrate what they know long before their competence in English is fully developed. Limiting ELLs to English often highlights what they don't know rather than what they do know. We engage monolingual English-speaking students in learning to read and write by drawing on their knowledge of English when we do rhyming or other types of word games that tap into their oral vocabulary skills, like asking students to name as many animals as they can whose names start with the */b/* sound, and so on. ELLs are unique in that they have a reservoir of bilingual skills and knowledge that you can draw on to engage and teach them. The more you learn about this reservoir, the more you can tap into it and promote learning, for example, during guided reading and writing activities or during individual writing conferences.

> **Research Finding**
>
> Jimenez, Garcia, and Pearson (1996) found that successful ELL readers and writers used the same strategies during literacy tasks in both the home language and English, and they viewed reading in the home language and English as similar but with language-specific differences. In contrast, unsuccessful ELL readers and writers thought the home language was a source of confusion when reading and writing in English.

By explicitly talking with ELLs about their two languages, you also develop their metalinguistic awareness (Bialystok 2007). This in turn promotes the acquisition of reading and writing skills because good readers and writers have explicit insights about how written language works. By encouraging ELLs to learn and think about their two language systems explicitly, you can promote their competence in the following areas (Mora 2007):

- Awareness of and knowledge about the cueing systems used to read and write: sounds (phonology), word formation (morphology), grammar or word order (syntax), and word meaning (semantics)
- Strategies for figuring out the meanings of new words or comprehending complex text
- Students' confidence in their capacity to grow as readers, writers, and language users

As you can see, metalinguistic awareness is linked to many skills that contribute to literacy, but perhaps none more important than vocabulary learning (Graves 2006). In his four-part vocabulary program, Graves (2006) highlights several aspects of word learning that depend on "metalinguistic awareness":

1. Word consciousness—Awareness of and interest in words and their meanings; understanding why some words are used instead of others and the power of words.
2. Using parts of words to unlock their meanings—Using word roots, prefixes, and suffixes to figure out the meaning of new words; for example, words that begin with *in* or *un* often refer to the lack of something, like *incomplete* or *unsure.*
3. Using *cognates* (words that are identical or almost identical in two languages and which have the same or highly similar meaning) to figure out word meanings.

When it comes to learning vocabulary, students with two languages often spontaneously notice similarities and differences in word meanings, word formation rules, and usage in their two languages. Some students are more apt to see similarities and differences than others; all students can benefit from being asked explicitly to engage in cross-linguistic comparisons. This can be a great tool for teachers. There are even published, research-based vocabulary programs for ELLs that are designed to promote "metalinguistic awareness" to advance student learning. (See *The Vocabulary Improvement Program* [Lively et al. 2003]; a grade 4–6 program.) You will certainly want to

Research Finding

Nagy, Garcia, Durgunoglu, and Hancin-Bhatt (1993), in a study of Spanish-speaking ELLs, found large individual differences in students' ability to recognize cognates in English and Spanish and that students who were better able to do so had higher levels of metalingusitic awareness about the role of word-formation rules. This suggests that teaching students about cognates and how certain parts of words are the same in different languages enhances transfer.

develop your ELLs' metalinguistic awareness skills. Sharing ELLs' knowledge of their home languages with your mainstream students in class is also a way of showing your monolingual English-speaking students the richness of language diversity and, in this way, developing their metalinguistic awareness at the same time.

DIFFERENT LEVELS OF BILITERACY

ELLs come to school with different levels of literacy in their home languages; some have well-developed literacy skills and some have no literacy skills whatsoever. This is often a result of how much formal reading and writing instruction students have had in their home languages, or is a reflection of how much experience they have had with books in the home language. Most children begin learning to read and write when they start school at around five years of age. However, some ELLs begin learning to read and write beyond the typical age of school entry because they did not have the opportunity to develop literacy skills in the home language earlier. Some of these ELLs may have just joined your class having had their schooling interrupted in the home country because of war or natural disaster; they may have spent several years in refugee camps or moving from country to country before settling in their new homes; yet others may have gone to school in the United States but did not get instruction in their home language. Clearly, there are large individual differences in how literate ELLs are in the home language when they begin schooling in English, and there is likely to be consid-

> "... ELLs' language proficiency, in both L1 and L2, runs along a continuum. ... Some ELLs have fully developed L1 across the language domains. others may be strong in their L1 oral language but may not have had prior experiences with literacy."
>
> (Gottlieb 2006a, 121)

erable variation in how literate they are in the home language even when they finish school. When we talk about ELLs becoming biliterate, we are well aware that this does not mean equal and full proficiency in both English and the home language for all students, although this is a worthwhile goal for programs to promote.

How you plan literacy instruction for ELLs will depend on the level of literacy they have acquired in the home language when they join your class. We distinguish among three types of ELLs in order to provide guidance for literacy instruction that is differentiated according to students' level of home language literacy development:

1. **No home language literacy (NHL)** includes young ELLs with no literacy skills in any language. This group might also include older students who have not had the opportunity to go to school; they are commonly known as limited formal schooling, or LFS, students. These students' oral skills in the home language must nevertheless be used to help them bootstrap into English literacy.

2. **Some home language literacy (SHL)** includes young ELLs with some literacy skills in the home language. These are students who may have been in a transitional bilingual program, or they may have spent a short period of time being educated in the home language in their home country. They may have also been exposed to literacy in the home and community and, as a result, acquired beginning-level reading and writing skills in those contexts. This group might also include students who have opportunities to practice literacy in the home language outside school, and they have spontaneously transferred skills and strategies they are acquiring at school in English to the home language. Transfer of literacy skills in English to the home language is most likely when the home language and English share the same alphabet and where there is encouragement to transfer what is being learned at school to literacy activities outside school. These students have oral skills and some literacy skills in the home language that can easily be developed further and that can be used to promote literacy in English.

3. **Expected home language literacy (EHL)** includes ELLs who are at grade level in home-language literacy skills when they join your class. These students often have been in late-exit bilingual or dual language programs, or they may have attended community-based literacy programs. They may also

be new arrivals with strong schooling backgrounds and have been systematically taught to read and write in their home language and have used literacy skills for learning in the home country. The home-language literacy skills of these ELLs should definitely be used to promote English literacy, and teachers can easily help them maintain and further develop literacy skills in the home language.

Evaluating Literacy in the Home Language

Regardless of the language of instruction or type of program offered in your school, it is essential to assess how well your ELLs can read and write in their home language. Chapter 6 focuses on this topic. Even teachers who are teaching only through English need to know the literacy level of their ELLs in the home language because students who come with age-appropriate literacy or emergent literacy skills in the home language are quite different learners than those who come without these skills. Students with pre-existing literacy skills (for example, SHL and EHL students) will use their literacy skills in the home language to break into English reading and writing, as we noted earlier; teachers can systematically draw on those skills in lesson planning and delivery to facilitate their acquisition of reading and writing in English. ELLs who have not acquired basic literacy skills in the home language need to start from the beginning, and mainstream teachers need to plan instruction that helps them do that.

It should be clear that knowing the reading and writing skills of your ELLs in their home languages has very important implications for instruction and, therefore, is essential information to collect. When you assess your ELLs' pre-existing competencies in reading and writing in the home language, you should look at literacy with respect to both academic and everyday contexts, for example, by asking students to read popular magazines, CD jackets, comic books, store flyers, event announcements, restaurant menus, or road signs. Students may find it easier to demonstrate their reading abilities if you use everyday texts than if you use academic texts with topics that are unfamiliar to them.

Even teachers who do not know their ELLs' home language can obtain valuable information about their literacy skills easily because most literacy assessments involve paper-and-pencil tasks—for example, students can be prompted to write descriptions or draw pictures of their family, their favorite TV programs, or a sports event. Teachers who do not know a student's home language can still use the types of descriptions they provide to assess their overall level of literacy; students with no literacy skills will be able to draw only pictures. In contrast, students with basic literacy skills will be able to write single words, while ELLs with more developed literacy skills in the home language will be able to write sentence-length or longer descriptions. Students who have produced written descriptions can be asked to read them out loud so you can see how fluently they read. Their different ways of writing and reading provide invaluable information even if you do not know the languages, information that you can use to plan differentiated instruction. At a minimum, all mainstream teachers can and should carry out this kind of informal assessment. If you don't, you risk ignoring valuable information about your students and teaching them as if they are all the same. Assessment strategies that can help you discover ELLs' skills in the home language are described in greater detail in Chapter 6.

More detailed assessments of students' reading and writing skills in the home language may be desirable, and these will require the use of formal assessment procedures and perhaps even the help of someone who knows the student's language. This is easier to do in some languages, like Spanish, than others because of the availability of commercially developed assessment instruments; in Spanish, for example, you could use *Evaluación del Desarrollo de Lectura* (EDL) available at www.pearsonschool.com, the *Brigance Assessment of Basic Skills–Revised, Spanish Edition* available at www.curriculumassociates.com, or *English-Español Reading Inventory for the Classroom* (Flynt/Cooter) available at www.allynbaconmerrill.com, to name a few. Formal assessments are essential in the case of ELLs who might be suspected of having reading difficulties but are also useful for all ELLs if you have the assessment materials and linguistic competence to carry them out. It is inappropriate and invalid to assess students who might be at risk only in English because it is impossible to distinguish ESL learners who are simply slow to learn from students with a reading difficulty if you assess in English only.

An alternative method of assessing students in their home language is to use *benchmark books* in the student's home language. Benchmark books are books that have been classified by reading level. By asking ELLs to read benchmark books and/or to answer questions based on benchmark books in the home language at, above, and below their current grade level, you can judge their general reading level (see *PM Colección* at http://rigby.harcourtachieve.com, and *Spanish Early Intervention Levels* at www.hampton-brown.com).

You can also use benchmark texts to do running records (see Chapter 6) or devise cloze passages[1] to evaluate your students' reading skills. Running records and cloze procedures can be conducted in any language and produce highly similar results in different languages (Gottlieb 2006b). To carry out these kinds of assessments, you need to identify someone who knows the target language sufficiently well to construct, administer, and score the assessment. This may not be as difficult as it might seem since individuals with the necessary linguistic and cultural skills can often be found in the school or community and are often happy to help out. Such people are an invaluable resource worth finding; they can also probably help you with other issues, such as the cultural appropriacy of your materials or instructional activities.

NOTE FOR ADMINISTRATORS

Competence in the languages and cultures of ELLs in your school may be something that school administrators would look for when hiring new teachers or paraprofessionals. Regardless of the type of program offered for ELLs, administrators should always be on the lookout for people who can help work with ELLs in their home languages.

As for writing, you can ask parents for samples of a student's writing or elicit writing samples directly using prompts in the home language. These samples can then be evaluated with the help of someone who is proficient in the home language using rubrics (such as the *6+1 Trait Writing Assessment in Spanish* www.thetraits.org/products/Spanish). Alternatively, you can use subtests of the *Brigance Assessment of Basic Skills–Revised, Spanish Edition* www.curriculumassociates.com, or the *Language Assessment Scales Reading/Writing (LAS R/W)—Spanish* www.ctb.com to look at spelling, handwriting, and writing skills. For Spanish as well as other high-frequency languages, useful tools for evaluating writing are provided in books like *Words Their Way with English Learners* (Bear et al. 2007). In the second chapter of this book, the authors provide spelling inventories in Spanish, Chinese, and Korean and suggest ways of assessing spelling developmentally in these high-frequency languages.

Indirect indicators of students' reading and writing abilities can be had by reviewing their previous report cards or previous

---

[1]Cloze assessment is a form of assessment where you take a passage of known difficulty and delete every fifth or seventh word; students fill in the blanks with appropriate words, drawing on all of their linguistic cueing systems (vocabulary, grammar, etc.) and literacy skills (decoding, reading comprehension). It can be scored for exact or appropriate word replacement, and the percentages of words satisfactorily filled in determines if the text is at the student's independent, instructional, or frustration reading level. (See O'Malley & Valdez Pierce 1996.)

teacher and/or parent reports, or by interviewing students themselves about their abilities or about the way their school functioned at home. In some countries, as in the United States, students are not promoted to the next grade if they do not master all the skills of their current grade. In these cases, grade-level placement can shed light on a student's level of functioning in his/her home language. In other countries, students are promoted to the next grade, but they must "carry" with them specific content areas that they did not pass; these are listed in their school records. Students are expected to keep working on the content areas they did not pass until they meet the criteria set for their grade level. *Understanding Your Refugee and Immigrant Students: An Educational, Cultural, and Linguistic Guide* (Flaitz 2006) is a useful book that can help you understand the educational systems of other countries. It provides charts called *Education at a Glance* for countries in Central and South America, the Caribbean, Eastern Europe, the Near East, Asia, and Sub-Saharan Africa. Each chart reveals if there is preschool education, the language(s) of instruction, if instruction is compulsory, if there are exams, how the grading system works, what the curriculum consists of for primary and secondary grades, and the enrollment rate as a percentage of the school-age population. This is invaluable information for teachers who seek to understand the skills and abilities of their ELLs.

Using the Home Language to Support English

ELLs in some school districts will have had some instruction in their home language in a bilingual education program. Spanish is the most commonly used language in bilingual and dual language programs in the United States (see www.cal.org). In addition to completing part of the mainstream curriculum in the home language, ELLs in bilingual programs receive language arts instruction in the home language. The discussion in Chapter 2 on emergent literacy and many other strategies described in this book are pertinent and useful for ELLs who are learning reading and writing in the home language at school. For ELLs who are not enrolled in bilingual or dual language programs, the home

NOTE FOR TEACHERS WORKING WITH LFS STUDENTS

Beginning to learn how to read and write through the home language is especially crucial for students with limited formal schooling. It is easiest for these students to break the code and to develop the habit of literacy through a language that they can speak. To teach someone to become literate through a language that is not proficient is stacking the cards against the learner.

language nonetheless can play an important role in two ways: (1) using the home language to teach initial literacy to those students who are not literate in any language, and (2) using the home language to further develop literacy in English. See the Additional Resources for Teachers section at the end of this chapter for some resources for teaching ELLs to read in Spanish. If you collaborate with teachers who teach literacy in ELLs' home language, they may also want to know about these specialized books for teaching literacy in that home language.

For NHL Students: Promoting Initial Literacy in the Home Language

It is extremely beneficial for ELLs who are just beginning to learn to read and write to begin learning literacy in the home language because they already know it. For teachers in schools where bilingual programs are available, insist that NHL students are enrolled in the program so that they are introduced to literacy through their home language. If no such program is available, you can still do the following in mainstream classrooms where teaching is done in English:

Helping NHL Students Take Advantage of Their Home Language

- Find out if there is a community-based literacy program for children and encourage the family to have their child attend.
- In families whose members are literate in the home language, encourage family members to engage in functional literacy activities with the child in the home language whenever possible. For example,
  - Write notes and messages with the child.
  - Make shopping lists or to-do lists.
- Encourage family members to read with the child for pleasure:
  - Read books at bedtime.
  - Write texts in the home language based on wordless books.

- Make books based on family stories; the child can make the actual book in arts class or as a special project at school.
- Make books based on folktales.

- Guide family members to do language experience activities (described in Chapter 2) in the home language; be explicit and detailed in the guidance you give since families may not know what you want them to do.
- Encourage family members to use poems, rhymes, and finger plays from the home language to engage in early literacy experiences; many such books are available, especially in Spanish: *Mamá Goose: A Latino Nursery Treasure* (Ada & Campoy 2005); related to our theme *Tortillitas para Mamá and Other Nursery Rhymes* (Griego et al. 1988); with older students, you can teach family members how to do read-alouds using books in Spanish related to classroom themes, like *The First Tortilla* (Anaya 2007) or *La Tortillería* (Paulsen 1998).
- Encourage students to think about similarities and differences between English and their home-language; this can also serve the purpose of building your knowledge base of the various languages in your classroom.
- Be sure to talk with parents at parent-teacher nights about the value you place on home-language literacy and how important you think it is to their child's acquisition of English. Sometimes parents think that the school does not want them to promote reading and writing in the home language. Make sure they know how valuable home language literacy is.

See the Additional Resources for Teachers section at the end of this chapter for websites that educate parents in Spanish and English about the importance of engaging in literacy activities through the home language.

Using the Home Language to Bootstrap into English

All students, regardless of their level of proficiency in the home language, use and benefit from drawing on the resources they have in their home language. Even NHL students who have not acquired literacy skills in any language can draw on their oral skills in the home language to facilitate learning to read and write in English. SHL and EHL students likewise bring oral language skills linked to the home language and, as well, their knowledge of reading and writing in the home language. These students use knowledge about literacy that they have acquired in the home language to bootstrap into English. As they acquire skills for reading text in English for meaning and skills for expressing themselves in writing in English, they can apply these skills to reading and writing in their home language. It is only natural that they do this because reading and writing in both languages are interconnected, as we saw previously.

Next we provide some examples of activities that any teacher, including those who are teaching only through English, can do that encourage this type of bootstrapping (for a quick overview of strategies, see the chart in Appendix B).

Activities for bootstrapping from home-language literacy to English and vice versa (for SHL and EHL students)

1. Learn about your students' languages, with an eye to similarities and differences with English.
   a. Ask people who have been educated in those languages about points of similarity and difference; we suggest that you talk to people with formal education because the rules of language are often invisible to people who have had no formal education.
   b. Consult references that describe the differences between various languages and English (see Language Resources in the Addtional Resources for Teachers).
2. Draw students' attention to language in text they are reading: If you are familiar with the home language, point out similarities and differences in the orthographic systems of English and the home language(s); if you are not familiar with the home language, have students work in groups to identify similarities and differences. Teach students to actively apply what they

know in reading and writing in their home language to learning to read and write in English.

3. When students make a "mistake" that is the result of transfer, it is important to view it as an indication of students' resourcefulness. When you do this, you are telling students that you understand and respect their efforts.
4. Ask students why they did what they did; they can often tell you that it is linked to their home language.
5. Observe students from the same language background so you can notice common patterns of transfer.
6. Make a note of common patterns and, whenever the opportunity arises, focus your feedback explicitly on them.
7. Plan minilessons that focus explicitly on differences you have noted and teach these minilessons in the context of what students are currently reading or writing about. For example,
   a. Point out parallels between the two languages: For example, we might teach students how to identify when someone is talking (initial and ending quotation marks indicate dialogue) as this is the same across many languages. In *Mama Panya's Pancakes,* the text reads *"Adkia, hurry up," she called cheerfully. "Today we go to market."* We can teach how to read with expression when we see these marks because they indicate what people actually said, and this, in turn, calls for authentic expression.
   b. Point out contrasts: In our Pancake theme, a mini reading lesson could focus on how vowels sound in English versus some romance languages like Portuguese, Italian, or Spanish. For example, *cake* is an English word that is one syllable and has the rule CVCV = long-sounding first vowel, silent second vowel. In Spanish, words with CVCV patterns are pronounced as two syllables because each CV is sounded: *cabe*—"cah/bey," or *bate*—"bah/tey." Many words like this appear in *Mama Panya's Pancakes* that Spanish speakers might be tempted to sound as two syllables—*bare, five, spice, make, pace, save.* You could also show students that when writing English, possession is usually expressed using an *'s* at the end of the word, as in *Mama Panya's Pancakes,* whereas in Spanish possession is expressed using *de* + the name of the possessor, as in *las tortillas de mamá.*
   c. Eventually, have students investigate similarities and differences in their two languages themselves. This can be done

even if you do not know the home language well. What is important about these cross-linguistic metalingusitic activities is getting students to think explicitly about how language works.

8. Teach reading and writing strategies that would be particularly helpful with common "mistakes" that are sure to arise, like "Always pronounce the *h* in the beginning of words in English (since */h/* is silent in Spanish)."
9. When students read in their home language, ask them to think about the strategies they use to figure out the meaning of new words or text, such as predicting what will happen, finding the main idea, or comparing what they think is happening in the text to their real-world knowledge, and does the text make sense. Then ask them to read a similar text in English and use the same strategies. When it comes to writing, ask students how they set the stage for readers and how they choose the right word to express their intended meaning when they write in their home language. Then, have them use the same strategies as they prepare to write in English.

Using Bilingual Books

Making texts available in students' home language is advantageous, not only for ELLs who are acquiring literacy skills in the home language but also for ELLs in all-English classrooms. Even in all-English classrooms, think about ways to make the literacy environment bilingual; in most cases, in fact, it is important to include books in several languages because ELLs speak different home languages. If you are a monolingual English-speaking teacher, there is no need to feel threatened or at a loss with books in other languages. In fact, working with other languages that you do not know will help you understand the language-learning experiences of your ELLs. As well, when students see you engaging with books in different languages, they see you as a role model who values their languages. As you will see, there is a great variety of activities you can do with books in other languages that will motivate your students.

Most educators advise against translating or using both languages simultaneously in the classroom. They argue that students will simply stop paying attention when their weaker language is used, and, thus, the weaker language will not develop. However, there is a lot to be said for allowing students to use books in English along with books in the home language or even bilingual books. It is important to be strategic when using bilingual books or books in different languages at the same time; avoid having students rely on their more proficient language, although this is to be expected in the beginning. Rather, help students use both languages to read and write in each. This can happen in all classrooms, including those with English-only instruction. The following are three types of bilingual books that you can have in your classroom and in your school library.

Books in the students' home languages and books written in two languages

Provide ELLs with plenty of books to read in their home language. Even if you have NHL students, you can send books home for the family to read together. As much as possible, obtain books that are written originally in the home language. For example, related to our Pancake theme, you might send home Gary Paulsen's *La Torillería* (1998). If you have trouble finding original books in the home language, you could get books that have been translated or are bilingual in English and the other language. For suggestions of books revolving around the Pancake theme, see the Additional Resources for Teachers section at the end of this chapter.

You can also use books that include traditional rhymes like *¡Pío Peep!: Rimas Tradicionales en Español/Traditional Spanish Nursery Rhymes* (Ada, Campoy, & Schertle 2003) or *Mamá Goose: A Latino Nursery Treasury* (Ada & Campoy 2005). These books are very helpful for early literacy instruction with young students because they draw from a rich history of Spanish and Latin American cultural experiences and traditions. (For a description of different types of bilingual books, see "Bilingual Books: Promoting Literacy and Biliteracy in the Second-Language and Mainstream Classroom" [Ernst-Slavit & Mulhern 2003], *Bilingual Children's Books in English and Spanish: An Annotated Bibliography, 1942–2001* [Cruger Dale 2002], and *A Magical Encounter: Latino Children's Literature in the Classroom* Second Edition [Ada 2003] in the References section at the end of the book.)

See the Additional Resources for Teachers section at the end of this chapter for websites with additional possibilities.

Although bilingual books and books in languages other than English have become quite accessible, be careful which you choose because some can be flawed. Take care in selecting books for children and families no matter the language. For books in languages that you do not read, consult with someone who can. The checklist provided in Appendix A identifies some of the problems that you might encounter when looking for books in various languages. The cautions it includes are not meant to discourage you but rather to underscore concerns regarding the quality of the materials we put in hands of young learners. Appendix A will help you make sure that materials in the home language receive the same scrutiny you would give materials produced in English. Be sure to have both the language and cultural content of books examined by someone familiar with both.

Books that are written by students in English and their home language

Having students write their own books in the home language and English is most useful for EHL students. However, it can also benefit SHL students working in small groups. Having students write their own books using both languages permits them to be maximally engaged because they are drawing on all of their language skills. That is not to say that you would allow them to mix the two languages extensively in the same sentence or paragraph, unless the context calls for it, for example, when there is a direct quote or the student is writing a piece in English where one of the characters says something in the home language. Producing their own bilingual books or books in the home language gives students a much needed sense of empowerment (Cummins et al. 2005).

The Multiliteracy Project in Canada (see www.multiliteracies.ca) is an example of how bilingual books, produced by students, can be a central part of the everyday functioning of a classroom. In this project, students work in small groups of the same home language to write texts in English and their home language. These texts often tell the stories of these students' arrival into Canada, the journey that brought them there, and their feelings about being immigrants. For that reason, the texts are called "identity texts." The end product is a bilingual book that is beautifully illustrated. These books can end up as part of the school library collection, available for all to read. The project has been implemented in elementary classrooms across Canada and is equally effective in settings with ELLs where only English is used for instruction and in classrooms where ELLs speak several different home languages. The project does not have to be in a bilingual program to be effective and is ideal for readers/writers workshops.

Students can also create a home-language version of a book in English. This strategy is especially valuable if you are using English texts with simple language for older ELLs; in this case, students can produce home-language text that is more sophisticated than the texts they are given in English. Using student-produced books also elevates the status of books that ELLs are given to read and reduces the possibility that older students are embarrassed at having books with childish-looking text in English. Student-produced books are also interesting for other students to read in the home language for pleasure, for example.

When ELLs write their own version of an English book in their home language or write their own bilingual book, they can fully express themselves and their ideas in print. While students may struggle to say some things in English, the ideas may flow eloquently in their home language. This is evident from how much students write in their home language as compared to English.

NOTE

For those of you working with ELLs who come from home languages that have a different alphabet system than English:

For students whose home language is not written from left to right and bottom to top, you may have to do a little "cutting and pasting" to make the book go the right way for the particular language. Do not, as some publishers do, keep the book in the English orientation and plug in the other language. Not only does that make it confusing for the reader, but it also sends a not-so-subtle message about the status of the two languages.

Books that invite storytelling in any language

Wordless picture books are useful for connecting oral language with literacy because they stimulate students to tell and create stories. The language used in oral stories is like written language in many respects, for example, both involve sequencing, description of characters and settings, dialogue, causal relationships, and so on. Using oral storytelling as a basis for literacy development is especially effective with NHL students who have no prior literacy skills. Wordless picture books are useful in classrooms with ELLs who speak multiple languages because they can be used to create books with text in any language. You may wish to refer back to Chapter 2, where we described wordless picture books in detail, to get ideas about how to use wordless books with ELLs and their parents so that you can extend literacy to the home and community, whether or not students are receiving bilingual instruction. All cultures have traditional stories and, thus, having parents and their children "read" wordless picture books is a great way to engage parents in helping their children develop their literacy skills through oral language activities.

Activities with Bilingual Books

Bilingual texts lend themselves to many useful activities in the mainstream classroom (see also Ernst-Slavit & Mulhern 2003):

- Teachers can use bilingual books to promote metalinguistic awareness, discussed earlier in this chapter.
- They can also be used to prepare students for new content to be taught during social studies or science time—as a preview for what's to come in a lesson.
- Bilingual books can come in handy for self-assessment and to monitor comprehension.
- As you will see in a later section of this chapter, bilingual books are also very useful to demonstrate the value of other languages, to make connections with the community and family, to strengthen the cultural identity of ELLs, and to honor their families.

We are not suggesting that, as a classroom or ESL teacher, you use bilingual books every day. Rather, by regularly including some bilingual books (say one per unit), you demonstrate your support for your students' home languages and you draw upon their reservoir of bilingual skills and knowledge and, thereby, promote their full potential as readers and writers. We describe each of these functions of bilingual books briefly now.

Promoting metalinguistic awareness (for SHL and EHL students)

1. Have your students compare the texts in both versions of a bilingual book; their comparison could include any of the following, depending on their level of literacy:
    a. Have students do a word count of a couple of paragraphs and compare the count in the two languages. Is there a significant difference? Why?
    b. Have students decide whether the tone of the text is the same in both languages.
    c. Ask students to find words that represent slightly different meanings that were used in the two texts and try to figure out why those particular words were chosen.
    d. Have students evaluate the two versions and suggest changes in language that would improve either text.

2. For older learners: Have students discuss subtle differences in the two texts that might lead to perceptions of higher status for one language over the other.

Preparing students to learn (for SHL and EHL students)

1. Introducing a topic to be taught later:
   a. Have students read a story or expository text in the home language on a topic that you will be teaching later; you will need to consult with a bilingual teacher or librarian to help you find appropriate books.
   b. Students can then jot down in one- or two-word phrases what they learned about the topic using their home language.
   c. Students then find the equivalent of those phrases in English, either in a dictionary or in the English version of the text.
   d. This will prepare ELLs to grasp new concepts around that topic.
2. Use the home-language version for preview: While English-speaking students read the text in English to preview a lesson, ELLs can read the text in the home language for the same purpose.
3. Use the home-language version for review: To review what has been taught, ELLs can read a book related to the topic in the home language.

Self-assessment (for SHL and EHL students)

1. ELLs can read a home-language version of a book, then read it in English and see how much they understand by counting the number of words they understood, by answering questions, or completing a post-reading activity.
2. Students can first read the English version, then confirm what they understood by examining the home-language version.

Connecting school with the home and community (for all ELLs)

1. Invite family or community members to come and tell stories that can later be turned into books by the students. Storytelling is highly valued in many countries as is reciting poetry or dramatic readings of text. Find out who in the community has special skills and talents as storytellers or poets and invite

them to the class. A student who is proficient in English can summarize the story in English for those students who do not understand the language that is being used. This can be an exciting way for English-speaking mainstream students to learn new stories and something about the cultures of their ELL peers.

2. Have ELLs bring reading material in the home language to school, such as newspapers, magazines, or food containers with written language. In groups, have them produce English versions. Some families may pick up books in their home language when they visit their countries of origin and these books can be shared in the classroom.
3. Send wordless books home for the family to use to encourage storytelling, to make written texts in the home language, and/or to record oral renditions of the stories that can be shared later as audiobooks with other children of the same language to listen to and enjoy.
4. Create newsletters in multiple languages to inform families about what is going on at school; include descriptions of your current units of study, what students are reading and writing about, or the authors you are featuring. Given this information, parents can coordinate their home literacy efforts with what is going on at school. Newsletters of this sort are also useful ways for you to make concrete suggestions about how they can continue literacy activities in the home.

Social Aspects of Biliteracy

Developing literacy in more than one language has social implications both at the individual and community level. We begin this section by looking at implications at the individual level—namely, how literacy is linked to identity—and then we discuss implications at the community level.

Biliteracy and Identity

We tend to think about reading and writing as if they are strictly cognitive in nature. However, reading and writing and learning to read and write are not simply cognitive skills, disconnected from the social realities in which your ELLs live and learn. Students' sense of identity and the social context in which they acquire that identity can have a significant impact on their acquisition of literacy skills and how they make sense of written text (Cummins et al. 2005, Gallimore & Goldenberg 1993, Moll 2000, Vygotsky 1978). This is true even when there is just one language involved (see Shirley Brice-Heath's classic book *Ways with Words* [1983] for an example of this in English-speaking communities in the United States). The strong link between literacy and identity can be seen in the way we depict ourselves through writing (in two languages, in the case of biliterate individuals) and in the way we relate, or fail to do so, to what we are reading. The identities of bilingual students are complex because there is an additional layer of cultural norms and values that are attached to the home language, and there are complex interactions between home-language norms and values and those of the larger mainstream community. When teaching ELLs, it is important to make sure that their identities are reflected and honored in the classroom in meaningful and significant ways; otherwise, they will always feel like outsiders, trying to get in.

> "Literacy in the minority language not only provides a greater chance of survival at an individual and group level for that language. It may also encourage feelings of rootedness, self-esteem, the vision and world-view of one's heritage culture, self-identity and intellectual empathy."
>
> (Baker 2006, 328)

In the Multiliteracy Project mentioned earlier in this chapter, ELLs produce bilingual books that describe their experiences as second-language learners and as immigrants and refugees who are learning to live in a new society. These texts, sometimes called "identity texts," affirm students' cultural and linguistic identities. When these bilingual books are produced by the students in ways that accord them high status (for example, by being produced in high-quality long-lasting material), they show that the languages of the students' families have a significant place in the classroom and throughout the school (Cummins et al. 2005). When these student-produced multilingual books are placed in the school or classroom library for all to see and share, the value of ELLs' home languages and cultures is confirmed to everyone in the school. By creating a truly multicultural reading and writing environment in the classroom and throughout the school, you validate and honor the languages and cultures of your minority language students. When you do this, they feel like they belong and this sense of belonging enhances their motivation and stimulates them to invest and take risks in learning.

Multicultural literature

One way of affirming students' identities is to make sure that books in the classroom and school libraries reflect their cultures. In an earlier section of this chapter, we examined different types of books from the perspective of the language(s) they are written in. You should also consider the cultures that books represent. As discussed in Chapter 2, there is a wealth of multicultural literature at your disposal (see the resources listed in Additional Resources for Teachers at the end of the chapter). You can use the Types of Linguistically and Culturally Diverse Books chart to ensure that you have a full range of books in different languages and about different cultures in your classroom and school libraries. Use this chart to count how many books in each category you can find in your classroom and school libraries. If a specific type of book is in short supply, you may want to focus your next purchases on that type of book. Some books will be bilingual and some may be in only one of the home languages represented in the classroom or school—that is all right as long as a full range of languages and text genres is represented to ensure that your ELLs have access to a range of text types in their language. Some books may be linked to topics

Types of Linguistically and Culturally Diverse Books

CULTURAL CONTEXT LANGUAGE	REPRESENTS AN ELL CULTURE	REPRESENTS MAINSTREAM CULTURE
English		
A Home Language		
In English and a Home Language		

that are closely linked to one of the cultures of the ELLs in the school, whereas others may be more general and relate to topics that are also linked to mainstream culture.

One way of using multicultural literature is to conduct author studies using authors who write in ELLs' home languages. An excellent resource for Spanish-speaking authors you might consult is *Latina and Latino Voices in Literature for Children and Teenagers: Lives and Works (Updated and Expanded)* (Day 2003). An excellent way of involving mainstream students as well is to choose a book written in a language other than English that has been translated into English. Have all students read the same book, in whichever language they find easiest, and discuss cultural as well as linguistic similarities and differences.

The following suggestions can help you build and display book collections in the school, classroom, or parent lending library.

Tips for Classroom and School Libraries

- Choose books of high quality, with strong covers and binding and full color; make sure there are no status differences between the quality and attractiveness of books in one language over another.
- Choose a prominent section of the library to display the books. Do not hide books in other languages in a basket or on a cart as this shows they are not a part of the regular collection.
- Be sure to have books at a range of levels. Wordless books can be distributed across the English and home-language collections, based on theme or cultural source.
- Include books with audiotapes or DVDs, multimedia books, as well as print resources.
- Always show "new arrivals" so that students and parents are aware that the collection is growing and changing.
- Avoid translated books in the home-language collection, or at least make sure that they are kept to a minimum. Having only Dr. Seuss or Corduroy books in other languages is not a good reflection of authentic literature in the home language and gives a message about the importance of English. It does not celebrate and reflect the authentic children's literature in the languages of your learners.

Biliteracy and the Community

By bringing multicultural literature into your school and by making the home language part of the everyday life of the classroom, you are linking the school with the students' families and communities at the same time as you promote literacy experiences that are authentic and relevant to them. In other words, by including multilingual books in your library, you are integrating students' home and school lives with school life. This is important because the community can ensure and reinforce the development of their literacy skills in the home language. For ELLs who do not have the opportunity to get much support for literacy in the home, the community becomes important in developing and maintaining high levels of literacy in the home language. When children see others reading in the home language for pleasure or for getting news and information, then the importance of being able to read and write is enhanced, and ELLs are motivated to invest in learning to read and write inside and outside school. Some cultural groups do not see that it is their role to get involved in the work of the school; educating children is the work of schools. It is important for students and their families to see that the community has a role to play in promoting literacy and that this is not interfering but helpful.

In families that read and write in the home language for everyday purposes, ELLs will probably be expected and perhaps even taught to do so by a parent, an uncle, or a grandmother. It is particularly important that ELLs learn to read and write in the home language in some families so that they can communicate with family members who are not within affordable calling distance, through letters, emails, or text messages. ELLs who are literate in the home language as well as English can also serve as brokers with outside agencies to decode written forms and instructions that may be problematic for their parents. In communities where the home language is vital, resources are more accessible and the role that written language plays is more visible. The community may even have a well-established Saturday school or a community center where literacy in the home language is reinforced. However, books, newspapers, and magazines in the home language are not always available. In these cases, schools have an important role to play in obtaining print material in students' home languages to fill these gaps.

For all of these reasons, it is important that you become familiar with the "literacy landscape" of your ELLs outside of school. It is especially important to know if they move back and forth between language communities—do they return to the home country frequently and do they attend school while there? ELLs who revisit the home country have strong needs to develop biliteracy so they can continue to learn in the home country. Some suggestions to help you find out more about literacy in the students' communities follow.

As you can see by the tips for investigating the literacy landscape, not only is it important to find out about the literacy landscape of your ELLs' communities, you also need to support activities that strengthen and lend vitality to the home language in the community. By supporting the development of literacy in the home language outside school, you enhance ELLs' literacy development in school. By helping ELLs develop literacy skills in the home and community, you can help them become biliterate and enjoy all of the benefits of biliteracy.

Tips for Investigating the Literacy Landscape

- Ask your students or their parents if they write to friends and family members in the home language.
- Ask your students or their parents if there are newspapers or radio and TV stations in languages other than English that they use.
- Investigate the public library and ask if there are materials (print and nonprint) for pleasure reading and/or services (computer classes, tax preparation services) in community languages.
- Investigate students' neighborhoods to check out stores, billboards, and signs for evidence of print in other languages.
- Investigate if there are bookstores that sell books in other languages in your community. If not, do your families bring books and other reading material from their home country?
- Investigate to see if there are events in the community in languages other than English—events that involve literacy, such as meetings, plays, and exhibits.

- Investigate if the post office provides services in other languages. Is letter writing an important form of communication?
- Are other languages used for voting in the community or in other civic functions—such as rallies and public hearings?
- Are there after-school or weekend schools that teach or promote literacy in the home language? Are there dual language schools or programs available (charter or magnet schools)?
- Are there other institutions in the community that use languages other than English to transact business, such as hospitals or banks?
- Is there an office of the consulate or embassy of the countries of origin and, if so, do they support educational initiatives locally?

Implications for All Teachers

One of the best predictors of literacy in English is whether students have had instruction in reading and writing in the home language in school. However, not many schools provide instruction in the home language in an extended way and definitely not in all of the languages that ELLs speak. Regardless of what kind of program you have in your school and regardless of your proficiency in the home languages of your ELLs, you can help ELLs become biliterate. Following are suggestions for developing literacy in the home language, even in schools where formal instruction in the home language is not possible and only ESL programs are offered. We start with the absolute minimum and move on to the ideal. To tackle the "To-Do" list below on your own can be daunting. We suggest that you collaborate with teacher colleagues and administrators; together, you can accomplish a lot.

Absolute Musts for All Teachers

- ❑ Raise the status of ELLs' home languages in the school.
- ❑ Encourage ELLs and their families to engage in literacy in the home language outside of school.

- ❑ Set up informal programs for English-speaking students and teachers to learn about the home languages of ELLs in the school.
- ❑ Encourage and help the community to keep their home language vital.
- ❑ Make the home languages as visible and useful as possible around the school.
- ❑ Set up a formal home-language buddy or small-group system so students can complete projects together; these systems can also be used so students can help each other in content area classes.
- ❑ Collect literature and content area texts in the home languages and display them prominently in your classroom.
- ❑ Do an inventory of books in the classroom and school libraries and fill any gaps in home-language and home culture materials.
- ❑ Accept homework in the home language when students are not yet proficient enough to do work in English; find someone who can help you interpret and assess it.
- ❑ Set up group writing projects that can be done in the home language.
- ❑ Prominently display student work and other material in all the home languages prominently in the classroom and throughout the school.
- ❑ Whenever possible, have students do research projects in their communities.
- ❑ Include family members in key roles in your classroom, especially in activities that involve reading and writing in the home language.

Closer to the Ideal

- ❑ Hire paraprofessionals who read and write the home languages of your ELLs to work with classroom and content area teachers.
- ❑ Set up after-school clubs that use the home language—for example, book clubs or pen-pal projects with schools from other countries.
- ❑ Whenever there is an opening, hire bilingual teachers, even if they would be teaching in English.

- ❑ If students come from a bilingual program in the school or district, ensure that they get continued support in the home language after they have left the program.
- ❑ Make sure that mainstream teachers and administrators continue to encourage the use of the home language at home.
- ❑ Support families with print materials and multimedia resources that promote and maintain literacy in the home language.
- ❑ Investigate whether a dual language program might be appropriate for the student population in your community.

Summing Up

Three things are important to remember about fostering the ability to read and write in two (or more) languages:

1. Literacy in the home language facilitates the development of literacy in English.
2. All ELLs have the potential to become biliterate to the extent that, together with the family, you create the conditions for this to happen.
3. All teachers can contribute to literacy in ELLs' home languages. You do not have to be bilingual to honor and foster the languages of all members of the school community.

Additional Resources for Teachers

Language resources

- Bear et al. 2007: Has spelling inventories that show where transfer is most likely to happen. Chapter 2 and its appendices show inventories and spelling development in Spanish, Chinese, and Korean (pages 36–41); they also have assessments of orthographic knowledge in many languages. Chapter 2 shows how to assess spelling developmentally, and it lists errors often made by ELLs.
- Coelho 1991: Linguistic information regarding students from the Caribbean.
- Haghighat 2003: Linguistic comparisons for sixty-seven languages.
- Nathenson-Mejia 1989: Shows examples of cross-linguistic spelling and the regular substitutions that would be made by Spanish speakers when they attempt to spell English words.
- Swan and Smith 2001: Examples of interference from various languages when learning English.
- Two other useful sources for learning about particular languages and their writing systems are Comrie, Matthew, and Polinsky (1996) and Nakanishi (1990).

Professional books for bilingual teachers who teach reading in Spanish

- August and Vockley. 2002. *From Spanish to English: Reading and Writing for English Language Learners, Kindergarten Through Third Grade.* Pittsburgh: National Center on Education and the Economy and the University of Pittsburgh New Standards Project.

  Discusses phonemic awareness, phonics, decoding accuracy, fluency, self-monitoring and self-correcting, and reading comprehension. Provides useful charts of what transfers from Spanish to English for children who have been taught first to read in their home language. Comes with CDs of actual case studies of children to support the principles of instruction introduced in the text. Also describes writing development in the early grades.

- Beeman and Urow. (in press). *Teaching Spanish Literacy in the United States: A Practitioner's Handbook.* Philadelphia: Caslon.

  Based on the premise that teaching literacy in Spanish in the United States is different from all other literacy endeavors in that country. It places the discussion of lesson planning and instruction in the context of standards and assessment and describes strategies for teaching comprehension, word knowledge, fluency, and writing. It offers suggestions for scheduling, unit planning, and lesson planning.

- ❑ Carrasquillo and Segan. 1998. *The Teaching of Reading in Spanish to the Bilingual Student.* Mahwah, NJ: Lawrence Erlbaum.

  Describes theories and methods for teaching reading in Spanish to Spanish-English bilingual or Spanish-dominant students. The text is written in English and Spanish. It reviews basic reading methodologies, reading in the content areas, and uses of technology in instruction. It also has some treatment of teaching reading in Spanish to special-needs learners.

- ❑ Freeman and Freeman. 2006. *Teaching Reading and Writing in Spanish in the Bilingual Classroom.* Second Edition. Portsmouth, NH: Heinemann.

  This second edition of the Freemans' classic text updates their ideas and strategies in response to new research and changing contexts for teaching reading and writing in both English and Spanish. The book gives teachers research-based instructional advice about the most effective methods for teaching reading and writing to students in two languages. The new edition includes: approaches to teaching reading and writing in bilingual and dual language classrooms, scenarios of effective teaching, and bibliographies of literature and content books in Spanish and English that support theme-based instruction. Highlights instructional strategies that match students' developmental levels.

Websites that educate parents in Spanish and English about the importance of engaging in literacy activities in the home language

- ❑ ***Learning in Two Languages: Questions Parents Ask (in Spanish/English)***

  A PBS Parents Website: Because educating multilingual children offers unique opportunities and challenges, parents may have questions as to what to do at home in each language. This article provides answers to many of these questions and useful advice, which parents could use to support language development and reading at home. Supports use of the native language to promote language and literacy development in bilingual children. Organized into three sections: (1) Talking with Children, (2) Reading to Children, (3) Other Questions Parents Ask.

  www.pbs.org/parents/readinglanguage/spanish/articles/multifamilies/main.html

- ❑ ***Colorin Colorado for Families: What You Can Do at Home***

  Talks about the gift of two languages and gives parents lots of practical ideas as to how they can sing, talk, read, and encourage their child every day. Encourages parents to do so in their most proficient language. A WETA website (Public Broadcasting Station in the nation's capital), Colorín Colorado receives major funding from the American Federation of Teachers. Additional funding is provided by the National Institute for Literacy and the U.S. Department of Education, Office of Special Education Programs.

www.colorincolorado.org/familias/hogar

www.colorincolorado.org/families/home

Bilingual pancake books

Books written in two languages:

The Day It Snowed Tortillas, El día que nevaron tortillas
(Hayes, El Paso, TX: Cinco Puntos Press, 2003)

The First Tortilla: A Bilingual Story
(Anaya, Albuquerque, NM: University of New Mexico Press, 2007)

La Tortilleria
(Paulsen, San Diego, CA: Harcourt Children's Books, 1998)

Magda's Tortillas/Las tortillas de Magda
(Chavarría-Cháirez, Houston, TX: Arte Publico Press, 2000)

Tortillas and Lullabies/Tortillas y cancioncitas
(Reiser, New York: Greenwillow Books/Harper Collins, 1998)

Books with some Spanish words:

The Runaway Tortilla (Kimmell, New York: Winslow Press, 2000)

T Is for Tortilla: A Southwestern Alphabet Book (Alpers, Santa Fe, NM: Azro Press, 2006)

Books that include traditional rhymes

Mamá Goose: A Latino Nursery Treasury: Un Tesoro De Rimas Infantiles (Ada & Campoy, San Diego: Del Sol Books, 2005)

¡Pío Peep! Rimas Tradicionales en Español/Traditional Spanish Nursery Rhymes (Ada, Campoy, & Schertle, San Diego: Del Sol Books, 2003)

Tortillitas para Mamá and Other Nursery Rhymes (Griego, Bucks, Gilbert, & Kimball, New York: Henry Holt, 1988)

Sources for bilingual materials

www.bilingualbooks.com
www.mantralingua.com
www.cultureforkids.com
www.panap.com
www.letterboxlibrary.com
www.opalaffinitybooks.com.au
www.tulikabooks.com/revivearticle.htm
www.bopobooks.com
http://benito.arte.uh.edu
www.chinasprout.com
www.cincopuntos.com
www.delsolbooks.com
www.greenebarkpress.com
www.lectorum.com
www.leeandlow.com
www.yellowbridge.com
www.EnchantedLearning.com
www.en.childrenslibrary.org
www.childrensbookpress.org

Reading and Writing to Learn

Academic Language and Literacy for ELLs

CHAPTER 4

In this chapter, we describe why ELLs need second language and literacy learning opportunities in every lesson and during every moment of their school day, rather than only during English-as-a-second language (ESL) instruction. We also describe why they need to be learning academic language and content during their ESL or reading support class.

Promoting language and literacy across the school day *118*

Joining forces for language and literacy development *121*

Promoting academic literacy in K–8 classrooms *124*

Strategies for teaching literacy and academic content together *133*

Extending academic learning *147*

Summing up: Learning English while learning content *149*

Additional resources for teachers *154*

Certainly, the primary goal of ESL, and later language arts instruction, is to promote language and literacy skills so ELLs learn to view, listen, speak, read, and write effectively in English. During content instruction, you have a great opportunity to help ELLs apply and further develop their language and literacy skills while they acquire the knowledge and skills of the major subject areas taught in school. Teaching science, social studies, mathematics, health, and other subjects provides plenty of opportunities for mainstream teachers, ESL teachers, and reading specialists to work together to promote language and literacy development while they promote content learning. Conversely, the time spent in ESL instruction and reading support provides complementary opportunities to reinforce the language and literacy skills that ELLs need to learn new academic skills and knowledge. In this chapter, we talk about how the mainstream classroom teacher, ESL teacher, and reading specialist can work together to take maximum advantage of these opportunities to further ELLs' academic language and literacy development.

To understand the unique linguistic demands of each discipline, we describe how language and literacy vary across the major academic content areas of science, social studies, and mathematics. This includes a comparison of how academic language differs from social language, as well as a presentation of the specific academic vocabulary, grammar, and discourse (talk and text) features of each major content area taught in K–8 schools. We also consider how the cultural and experiential background knowledge of ELLs affects both their reading comprehension and their written expression about grade-level subject matter they are learning. We show how teachers can use students' existing cultural and experiential background knowledge to promote content learning, while at the same time building new knowledge bases that are required to read and write well during content area instruction. We emphasize using learner diversity as a resource during content instruction, rather than viewing it as a barrier to be overcome.

We share frameworks for planning instruction that integrate the teaching of language and literacy with content area instruction for mainstream content and ESL teacher use. Next, we present a range of effective research-based strategies for teaching language, literacy, and academic content together. We also provide recommendations for keeping track of language and literacy objectives when assessing the overall success of a content area lesson or unit (see also Chapter 6). For reading specialists who provide support to ELLs, we focus on how to work in tandem with classroom teachers and ESL specialists to promote academic literacy in a new language by aiding ELLs in comprehending and producing expository text. Finally, we suggest ways of tapping the funds of knowledge in each cultural community to support academic learning and ways to reach into the local community through projects and explorations to advance ELLs' academic literacy skills.

Promoting Language and Literacy Across the School Day

Because most ELLs spend much of their school day in mainstream classrooms with their English-speaking peers studying the grade-level curriculum, you need to take advantage of the rich opportunities that this affords second-language acquisition and, in particular, the promotion of academic language and literacy development in English. We know that language and literacy are best acquired when they are embedded in activities that are meaningful and interesting (Chamot & O'Malley 1994; Lightbown & Spada 2006). By collaborating and planning together to take advantage of these opportunities, mainstream classroom teachers, ESL teachers, and reading specialists can maximize their ELLs' language and literacy development (Ontario Ministry of Education 2005).

Mainstream Classroom Teachers as Second-Language Teachers

When you became an elementary or middle school teacher, you became responsible for many aspects of child and preadolescent development, both social and academic. In becoming a K–8 teacher, you are prepared to teach reading and writing as well as mathematics, science, and social studies and to integrate other special subjects (art, music) into your curriculum. You may not have imagined having students in your class who would not know English. However, because many of you now work in multicultural and multilingual settings, you have also assumed the role of second-language teacher and cross-cultural broker. Helping children navigate their passage into English mainstream culture can be a satisfying process. Your students depend on you to help them make this transition successfully. Whether or not you have had a lot of preparation to work with ELLs, this chapter will give you many ideas of how to promote language and literacy in English more systematically and effectively during content instruction to support your ELLs.

When you see yourself as a second-language teacher, you start to notice opportunities to promote language learning in your classroom. Here are seven ways you can help:

Promoting Language Learning in the Classroom

1. See yourself as a language model. Speak clearly and calmly, in an unhurried way. Keep your language constant and augment your spoken language with gestures and actions that aid in capturing the meaning. Repeat important points. If children are literate in their home languages, write important points or words down on the board, an overhead transparency, or electronic whiteboard.
2. Don't let ELLs sit silently, just watching and observing, unless they are new arrivals at the very beginning stages of language acquisition. Give students plenty of chances to speak, read, and write in English. Encourage them to participate in stage-appropriate ways.
3. Study your instructional materials to determine the language and literacy demands. Decide how to modify the materials you plan to use with ELLs, depending on their stage of proficiency. Identify problematic passages that may need to be skipped or rewritten. Avoid examples that do little to connect with your students' lives and prior experience because they will further confuse ELLs.
4. Be a language detective. What kind of language must be mastered? What are the high-mileage words and phrases to teach so that your students can comprehend? What should you ignore (low-frequency, low-utility language)?

5. Stay in the target language and make meaning come through. Use the home language as an occasional support (particularly with abstract language and concepts), but avoid constant translation through adults or children who speak the child's home language. (See Chapter 3 for more on this topic.)
6. Plan for language practice in every lesson. Remember that ELLs are still learning English and will need plenty of chances to try out the words and grammatical patterns needed to communicate.
7. Encourage peer support. Someone just a step above your student's proficiency level is the best partner for him/her because they have empathy for the language learning process, yet know a little more English than your target student. A native speaker may overwhelm the new learner, so be sure to instruct him/her on how to be a good conversation, reading, or writing partner, if they are the only partner you can provide.

ELLs need as many opportunities as possible in school to build their language skills in English so that they can become critical thinkers when listening and reading and strong communicators when speaking and writing. As a classroom teacher, you are in the best position to provide this practice as you teach key subject matter in class. It just takes planning on your part to build these opportunities into every lesson by designing activities that are appropriate for ELLs' current stage of development in English.

ESL and Reading Specialists as Academic Language and Literacy Teachers

If you are an ESL or reading specialist, your primary role in your school is to promote language and literacy development. As reflected in the national Pre-K–12 English Language Proficiency Standards (Teachers of English to Speakers of Other Languages 2006) and in many state English Language Proficiency (ELP) standards, your work with ELLs must include an emphasis on the development of academic literacy to ensure school success. When you do so:

- ELLs will find language and literacy instruction more relevant and meaningful because they will acquire critical language and literacy skills while learning valued grade-level content.
- You will be able to integrate all state and national standards into your units of instruction, thus ensuring that your students are working on both content and language standards in an integrated manner to perform successfully on state assessments.
- ELLs will learn the language and literacy skills needed to support them across the curriculum. This is the ideal way to teach a second language to ELLs because the forms, functions, and uses of language are best acquired and learned in context, in the service of other learning, with students offered input they can comprehend and see as important (Chamot & O'Malley 1994; Crandall 1987; Echevarria, Vogt, & Short 2008; Mohan 1986; Short 1993; Snow & Brinton 1997).
- Instruction by different teachers will become more interconnected as students move from one instructional context to the next. This counteracts the fragmentation of services that can sometimes occur when a student receives services from multiple providers (classroom teacher, ESL teacher, reading specialist, etc.).

Joining Forces for Language and Literacy Development

When ESL, reading, and mainstream classroom teachers work together, many benefits result for students and teachers alike. We know that provision of cohesive, well-integrated instruction that occurs when teachers collaborate with one another leads to:

- Increased academic achievement of students, including gains in language and literacy
- Improvements in student behavior and attitude
- Reduction in feelings of isolation among teachers when they work separately
- The possibility of more creative lessons because two or more teachers are planning together
- Decreased teacher burnout and increased teacher enthusiasm for teaching

- ❑ Improved teacher satisfaction through positive professional relationships
- ❑ Career rewards for teachers, such as professional recognition and sharing of expertise

(Friend & Cook 2000, Haynes 2007, Inger 1993)

Research Question

To answer the question, "Does collaborative instructional planning result in better plans than plans devised by only one teacher," try doing the following simple action-research. Compare a unit or lesson plan you have devised on your own with the same plan after you have consulted with an ESL specialist and/or the reading specialist in your school. Identify ways in which the plan is different and then go on to identify improvements that have resulted from collaboration.

This "win-win" situation is a primary reason that teacher collaboration is so desirable. Luckily, current school-based initiatives, such as common planning time, are making it easier for teachers with different roles in the school to collaborate effectively. It is critical that you take advantage of these opportunities to maximize the learning opportunities for your ELLs.

Effective Collaboration

First and foremost, you must create opportunities to plan together on a regular basis if you are to deliver instruction in a well-coordinated manner. Here are suggestions from research on teacher collaboration on ways to get the time needed to work together and on how to make effective use of your time together (Showers & Hansen 2006; Templet, Squires, & Stickler 1999):

1. Consider instructional collaboration as a professional development activity. Use half-day and full-day professional development sessions for large-scale co-planning. Classroom teachers can systematically show ESL and reading specialists the content of their science, math, and social studies curriculum and when during the year certain units of instruction are commonly taught. Collaborating teachers can come to common understandings as to which content areas (science, social studies, or mathematics) or units of instruction (marine mammals, regions of the United States, polygons) will be used in common to jointly promote language and literacy development. This type of curriculum mapping and instructional integration is highly recommended to promote curriculum coherence (Jacobs 1997, Drake 2007). For their part, ESL and reading specialists can demonstrate specialized teaching strategies to classroom teachers for promoting language and literacy in their ELL students. This promotes bidirectional sharing of expertise.

2. Use technology to collaborate. Use phone, email, online chat rooms, and message boards once collaborative efforts are underway. Create online groups at free sites to share templates and teaching ideas. Classroom teachers might use a chat room to give reading and ESL specialists advanced notice of when particular units will start so they can be thinking about and planning for their instructional time with students, or share observations about student performance and particular skills students need help with.
3. Work to ensure that each teacher who contributes to ELL students' language and literacy development has common planning time with the classroom teacher on a regular basis—at least bimonthly, preferably weekly. Ways to get this time include: (a) shortening the school day by five minutes at both ends of the day, thereby providing fifty minutes of paid, contractual, after-school time per week; (b) adding calendar days to the school year; (c) use of early dismissal or late start times; (d) use of substitutes to cover classes in a rotating fashion so that different teams can receive collaboration time by hiring a single substitute; (e) use of staff meeting time; (f) late afternoon paid teacher meeting times with light refreshments; (g) joint extended lunch times; (h) paid half-day Saturday sessions; or a combination of these.
4. Enlist the assistance of the principal to guarantee that time is provided in the ESL teacher's and reading specialist's schedules for active collaboration. If all of their time is used for direct provision of services to students, then coordination can occur only before and after school, making it far less likely that it will occur on a regular basis. If ESL and reading specialists are given one period per day in their schedule for active coordination, the inclusion of this time in their schedule should be done in such a way as to ensure that they can find a common planning time with each teacher with whom they work.

Here are some important co-planning activities that will facilitate your work as language and literacy development collaborators:

Important Things to Co-Plan

- Identify the current stage of proficiency of individual ELLs in oral language, reading, and writing. Agree on the types of strategies that are most beneficial for each ELL at this stage—those that can be implemented in the classroom, and that need to be implemented in a specialized language-learning setting.

NOTE FOR ADMINISTRATORS

Since it is ideal for the reading and ESL specialists to meet with the classroom teacher at the same time, schedule the ELLs at each grade level into one classroom, thus minimizing how many mainstream classroom teachers the specialists must meet with. Teachers at the same grade level could take turns accepting the ELLs students into their classes so that, over time, all grade-level teachers would gain expertise in collaboration and in ESL service delivery. You can also create incentives for teacher collaboration. Options can include payment, offering of professional development credits, provision of lunch/dinner, or even flex time. By all means, create accountability for teacher collaboration time so that everyone feels that this time is a well-planned and supported professional activity, without creating burdensome reporting systems. Administrators may check in regularly with teams or may look for evidence of joint planning when supervising and evaluating teachers during the year.

- Agree on the language and/or literacy skills you will target. In oral language, this goes beyond identifying target vocabulary to identifying grammatical structures and word forms (i.e., prefixes, suffixes), and the communicative functions ELLs need in English (defining, describing, labeling, justifying, etc.).
- Share resources and strategies with one another when you meet on a weekly basis, including how you will evaluate the effectiveness of your instruction.
- Plan for the ways you will encourage language use. What types of grouping structures, tasks, and roles you will set up in your respective teaching contexts. Consider the following questions: Will you the teacher be the conversational partner or will other students serve this role? How will you monitor and support student performance during the activities you provide to promote language use?
- Plan the roles and responsibilities of each instructor. If you work together in the same classroom, what will the role of each teacher be and how will you ensure that the skills of both teachers are maximized? What will be the role of the paraprofessional, student teacher, or practicum student assigned to the mainstream classroom? How can volunteers and paid staff contribute to your goals for the student?
- Use weekly common planning time to identify the language and literacy skills you will work on together. Determine which materials will be used in the support setting and which will be used in the classroom. You may be able to use some materials in both settings, but the important thing is that you talk it all through and agree on a coherent way to work together.

Promoting Academic Literacy in K–8 Classrooms

In order to work together effectively, all teachers must have a common understanding of two types of language that ELLs are learning: social and academic. Social or conversational language is relatively easy to acquire, provided ELLs have access and exposure to native English speakers. This type of everyday language involves talking, reading, and writing about familiar content using high-frequency vocabulary and simple sentence structures, generally in the active voice. Social language takes place in face-to-face interactions that support understanding, whether inside or outside of classrooms.

However, unlike social language, academic literacy is a special kind of language that takes time to learn (Schleppegrell 2001). It is the ability to talk, read, and write about academic content that is less familiar and more abstract, using more sophisticated, low-frequency technical vocabulary like *producer/consumer, quotient,* or *cell membrane,* and complex grammatical patterns, like "if–then" constructions. Here ELLs must comprehend and use highly explicit language and complex sentence structures, frequently in the passive voice (Ontario Ministry of Education 2005, 50). Not only is academic literacy complex and cognitively demanding, it also varies from subject to subject (Short & Fitzsimmons 2007). As teachers, you are quite aware that the language of mathematics is different from the language of science and social studies. Each involves specific vocabulary, and text is organized in particular ways as required by the discipline. Each subject area tends to use particular *text structures* or organizational principles to present the concepts, facts, and skills of the discipline. In social studies, for example, the text presents many facts and definitions; chronological or sequential organization of text is common; and the past tense dominates. In contrast, in science the present and future tense are more common and comparison/contrast passages are more frequent. Ragan (2005) argues that three areas of language cause students particular difficulties in handling content texts: vocabulary (words with subject-specific meanings, multiword phrases, technical terms), grammatical structures (particular tenses, sentences with

Research Finding

L2 oral proficiency is most important when learning to read when comprehension of text is important; it is relatively less important during the word-decoding stage of acquisition. Overall, aspects of oral proficiency that are important for learning to read are quite specific and are those aspects of oral language that have fairly direct links to reading and writing—breadth and depth of vocabulary, knowledge of complex grammatical skills, use of pronouns for reference, and listening comprehension of complex oral language. In other words, it is not enough for ELLs to simply have high levels of general proficiency in their home language or English for them to improve their reading acquisition skills. They must acquire academic language skills (Genesee & Riches 2006, August & Shanahan 2006).

Research Question

An important question when devising classroom instruction is whether ELLs make better progress in mastering academic objectives if they can draw on all of their linguistic resources, including those related to the home language. To answer this question, do the following classroom experiment. Teach two lessons in science during separate weeks. Divide the ELLs who speak Spanish into small working groups of about four so that some of them speak English and Spanish quite well while others speak mainly Spanish. During one of the lessons, encourage the students to use Spanish along with English to figure out word equivalencies in the two languages; during the other lesson, stick to English. Observe whether the students who speak mainly Spanish are more or less engaged when their home language is used and whether they grasp the material better if Spanish is used along with English or if only English is used. Several days later, examine the students to see how well they have retained what you taught and whether they acquired new English vocabulary associated with the lessons. Also, observe how your native English speakers respond—do they show interest in the other language and/or does it interfere with their learning?

multiple embedded clauses), and cohesive devices (linking clauses; conjunctions).

The Language and Literacy Demands of Academic Content Areas

We begin by outlining some of the language and literacy demands of each content area, so that teachers can be aware of the uniqueness of each. This will also help you identify the language scaffolding that students may need as well as language that can be taught when teaching each content area. This includes specific vocabulary, language structures (e.g., grammatical patterns), and communicative functions (the communicative tasks students are trying to accomplish in English). In effect, for students to succeed in the content areas, they need to learn the style of discourse or "register" appropriate for each academic subject. Once you understand the demands of academic discourse (oral and written) associated with a particular content area, you can identify and teach reading and writing skills and strategies that will help them learn academic registers effectively. For each major content area taught in grades K–8, we outline the features of text and talk that characterize that particular content

"A register is the constellation of lexical and grammatical features that characterizes particular uses of language (Halliday & Hassan 1989, Martin 1992). Registers vary because what we do with language varies from context to context. . . . For any particular text type, these features can be described in terms of the lexical and grammatical features and the organizational structure found in that text type."

(Schleppelgrell 2001, 431–32)

domain and offer suggestions about how you might use this information to guide your teaching.

The academic language demands of science

Science discourse (talk and text) is marked by particular features as you can see in Chart 4.1 (Biber et al. 1999, Kessler & Quinn 1987, Quaglio & Lauth 2006) on page 129.

The academic language demands of social studies

Coelho (1982), Short (1993), and Quaglio and Lauth (2006) have documented the academic language demands of social studies for ELLs (see Chart 4.2 on page 130).

The academic language demands of mathematics

Mathematics has unique vocabulary, sentence structure, and text features as shown in Chart 4.3 (Dale & Cuevas 1987) on page 131.

As you review these charts, think of things you can do to support students when they listen or read and also what you can do to help them acquire this language so they can speak and write effectively in each content area class. See Building Academic Language and the Ability to Communicate About Content for a few suggestions of what you might do with the information provided in the charts.

Building Academic Language and the Ability to Communicate About Content

- Preteach essential concepts and vocabulary (the big ideas) using multisensory methods (visual, kinesthetic) that do not rely exclusively on language for understanding.
- Help students recognize cognates—words that are identical or almost the same in both languages (their native language and English) to aid their comprehension.
- When identifying linguistic goals, try to teach grammatical features and vocabulary you know students need to communicate effectively. Directly teach the grammatical features students will encounter, such as the predominant verb tenses (present, past, conditional) or sentences with complex grammatical patterns, such as clauses that begin with *if* or *when*.

- When identifying communicative goals, favor the high-frequency communicative functions that are appropriate to the students' stage of proficiency: naming and labeling for beginners, explaining and justifying for more advanced students. Scaffold instruction so students of all proficiency levels can perform the functions that predominate in the discipline—such as recounting events or explaining phenomena, using visual supports and objects, as needed.
- Focus on reading/writing strategies and skills you know students will need.
- Work to simplify text and talk features. Break longer sentences into shorter sentences. Keep language consistent so terms can be learned. Change passive voice to active voice so students can understand better what is going on.
- Help students process text by reiterating major points. Underline or highlight key terms and phrases. Write notes in the margin, if possible, to help students.
- Identify major text structures and use graphic organizers that reflect these (for example, for comparison/contrast text structure, use Venn diagrams; for enumeration text structure, use word webs).
- Teach students to identify the common transition words that occur with the particular text structures in use, and what these terms indicate.
- Give students models and use guided writing to show how to organize their written output; provide word boxes and other aids (writing frames/templates) to help them speak or write about important content concepts they have been learning about.

Constructing Needed Background Knowledge and Building on Existing Background Knowledge to Promote Content Learning

Many ELLs come to school with background experiences that are quite different from those that are assumed in content area textbooks. When classroom texts and discussion topics match students' background

Academic Language of Science

TEXT/TALK FEATURES

- complex sentence structures made up of multiple embedded clauses
- highly specific vocabulary that conveys scientific concepts and understandings
- if/then sentences
- use of the conditional tense (what could/might happen)
- active explanations and descriptions of phenomena
- use of metaphors–"a comet is like a . . ."; "think of a comet as a . . ."
- high level of visual support–diagrams, photographs, illustrations

MAJOR TEXT STRUCTURES/FEATURES OF TALK

definition; description/enumeration; cause/effect; chronological/sequential; comparison/contrast; problem/solution

SUBJECT MATTER MATTER-SPECIFIC VOCABULARY

e.g., *omnivore, vertebrae, lava, mineral, stamen, thorax, molecule, electron, carbohydrate, amphibian*

WORDS USED IN NEW WAYS

e.g., *cell, space, cycle, crust, matter, front (weather), property*

COGNATES (SPANISH/ENGLISH)

e.g., *adaptación/adaptation; anfibio/amphibian; bacterias/bacteria; camuflaje/camouflage; dióxido de carbono/carbon dioxide*

PHRASES/LEXICAL BUNDLES BUNDLES (WORDS THAT OFTEN CO-OCCUR; COMMON SEQUENCES OF WORDS)

e.g., *food chain, water cycle, cloud formation; the nature of ___; in the form of ___; the way in which ___; as a result of ___; the size/shape of the ___; as shown in Figure ____*

COMMON TRANSITION WORDS; LOGICAL CONNECTORS

unless; although; finally; because; also; consequently, therefore

COMMON COMMUNICATIVE FUNCTIONS

name; classify/categorize; ask and answer questions; report; describe; explain; predict; hypothesize; defend

HELPFUL READING/WRITING SKILLS AND STRATEGIES

visualize what is read; find information; use of text features (bold, italics); distinguish between main idea and supporting details; draw inferences; use root words and affixes to discover word meaning (hydro, proto, -ose); write summaries; record observations; use graphic organizers to record information; use diagrams to process text

Chart 4.1 Academic Language of Science

Academic Language of Social Studies

TEXT/TALK FEATURES
• complex sentences with independent and dependent clauses; descriptions of related events; causes and effects • verb plus infinitive (refused to obey, offered to write) • time references; temporal phrases • third-person pronouns that refer to actors previously named in the passage (he, she, they) • causative words
MAJOR TEXT STRUCTURES/FEATURES OF TALK
compare and contrast; generalization-example; enumerative; cause and effect; sequential/chronological; problem-solution
SUBJECT MATTER–SPECIFIC VOCABULARY
e.g., *continent, landform, goods, services, raw material, consumption, patriotism, rebel, boycott, taxes, delegates*
WORDS USED IN NEW WAYS
e.g., *party; capital; assembly; press (as noun); lobby*
COGNATES (SPANISH/ENGLISH)
e.g., *historia/history; extinto/extinct; patriotismo/patriotism; partido/party; estado/state; dinastía/dynasty; nación/nation;* same word, both languages: *colonial; capital; local; global*
PHRASES/LEXICAL BUNDLES
e.g., *at the same time; had the right to; became known as; one of the most; had the right to; as a result of; the fact that the*
COMMON TRANSITION WORDS; LOGICAL CONNECTORS
from that time forward; after the war had begun; furthermore, he thought that; by the nineteenth century; as a result; finally; so; never before
COMMON COMMUNICATIVE FUNCTIONS
explain; describe; define; justify; give examples; sequence; compare; answer questions; clarify/restate
HELPFUL READING/WRITING SKILLS AND STRATEGIES
use the resources in textbooks (index, table of contents, glossary, etc.); find the main idea and supporting details; present an oral report; write a cause-and-effect essay; use note-taking strategies; use graphic organizers to record information; conduct research; prepare reports; summarize; paraphrase; use timelines, graphs, maps, and charts

Chart 4.2 Academic Language of Social Studies

Academic Language of Mathematics

TEXT/TALK FEATURES

- conceptually packed
- high density of unique words with specific meanings
- great deal of technical language with precise meanings
- requires multiple readings
- requires a reading rate adjustment because text must be read more slowly than natural language texts
- uses numerous symbols
- many charts and graphs

MAJOR TEXT STRUCTURES AND FEATURES OF TALK

cause and effect; comparisons; logical or chronological sequence

SUBJECT MATTER–SPECIFIC VOCABULARY

e.g., *divisor, denominator, integer, quotient, coefficient, equation, protractor, place value, proper/improper fraction*

WORDS USED IN NEW WAYS

e.g., *table, column, variable, carry, irrational/rational, mean, factor, term, expression, odd, set*

MULTIPLE WAYS OF SAYING THE SAME THING (SYNONYMS)

e.g., *add, plus, combine, and, sum, increased by, total; subtract from, decreased by, less, minus, differ, less than, have left*

COGNATES (SPANISH/ENGLISH)

e.g., *base/base; centímetro/centimeter; columna/column; concepto/concept; número/number; ordinal/ordinal; grupo/group; identificar/identify; secuencia/sequence; ángulo/angle; círculo/circle; diferencia/difference; dividir/divide; línea/line; multiplicar/multiply*

PHRASES WITH SPECIFIC MEANINGS; LEXICAL BUNDLES

e.g., *least common multiple, standard deviation, square root, a quarter of, divided by vs. divided into, as much as, common factor, the size of the, greater than or equal to, not more than*

TRANSITION WORDS; LOGICAL CONNECTORS

if . . . then, if and only if, because, that is, for example, such that, but, consequently, either

COMMON COMMUNICATIVE FUNCTIONS

following directions in a sequence, show, tell, ask and answer factual questions, predict, explain, justify, hypothesize, conjecture

HELPFUL READING/WRITING SKILLS AND STRATEGIES

adjust reading rate, reread difficult text, confirmation checks/summarize as you go, take notes while reading, use graphs, number lines, and charts to complement the understanding of text

Chart 4.3 Academic Language of Mathematics

knowledge and experiences, ELLs are enabled by what they naturally bring to the act of reading or writing. However, when texts and topics are "foreign" or outside of ELLs' experience, reading and writing are much more complex. When students decode but still don't know what is being talked about or when asked to write say "I don't know what to write," they may be telling you that the demands you have placed on them are unreasonable, because of the mismatch with their prior life and educational experiences.

It is for this reason that "frontloading" takes on special importance for ELLs. We must either select texts and topics that match ELLs' background knowledge and experience, or we must build background knowledge and experience before expecting texts to make sense or for writing to be realistic for ELLs. Because this is of particular importance in reading and writing content area texts, we add this special caution so that you consider what students know about the topics you are teaching, especially if the topics are country or region specific (e.g., U.S. government, states/regions of the United States or provinces of Canada, English measurement system, animals and plants that live in the northern woodlands, weather conditions they have never experienced).

When you learn about the special knowledge and skills that ELLs bring to school and the values they hold, you can use that knowledge to promote learning. You want to tap the "funds of knowledge" (Moll et al. 1992) in your ELLs' communities—that of your students, their parents, and other community members. For example, in a unit on measurement, you might find out what knowledge your students bring—such as their existing knowledge of the metric system or temperature measurement using the Celsius scale, as well as special skills and abilities that exist in their families, skills and knowledge gained from professions in construction, designing or making clothing/sewing, cooking/culinary arts, furniture making, boatbuilding, or architecture. Engaging students in discussions of values could explore what size of home or food portion is considered "enough" and what length of distance is considered "far" or "near" in particular cultures. This is just one example, but when you are planning lessons, you will certainly want to think of how you can bring in the rich resources your ELLs and their families bring to each content lesson.

Research Question

Try a simple experiment in class during storytime to answer the following question: "Are ELLs more engaged and do they use more language during storytime when they select the pictures used to tell the story and when they can draw on their home language in comparison to storytelling that is based on a teacher-selected picture without the benefit of using their home language to fill in gaps in their English?" On one day, give students a picture that you have chosen from a magazine and ask them to describe and talk about it—perhaps to tell a story about it. On another day, ask students to bring a picture that they like from a magazine and ask them to do the same thing. Allow the ELLs to use their home language if they want or need to, with other bilingual students providing translation when they do. Observe how much your students, and especially your ELLs, are engaged when they describe a picture they have selected and when the other language is used. Does use of the other language interfere with the activity? Check to see if the ELLs are learning new English vocabulary from other students who are translating for them. See if the mainstream students are interested in the other language when it is used. Do they learn some words in the new language?

Strategies for Teaching Literacy and Academic Content Together

To illustrate how to teach literacy and academic content together, we move beyond the children's literature unit on the theme of Pancakes presented in Chapter 2 to more intensive academic content learning. In the sample unit on pages 150–53 we model how to use a content-oriented text set that focuses on the economic cycle from producer to consumer, as taught in the upper elementary grades in social studies (grades four to six, depending on your state or local curriculum). In this social studies unit, the following would be the key concepts:

> "There may be a gap between what the schools expect and what students bring, but that does not mean that these students do not bring anything. They each have a language, a culture, and background experiences. Effective teachers draw on these resources and build new concepts on this strong experiential base."
>
> (Freeman, Freeman & Mercuri 2002, 16)

1. Raw materials are gathered, transported, and processed to produce finished goods.
2. People use natural resources to support their basic needs.
3. People from around the world hold different values with respect to sharing and protection of natural resources.

While some teachers may want to expand the unit to other content areas by focusing on nutrition, dry and liquid measurement, or the planting and growth cycle of plants, we focus on the social studies/economics unit "From Producer to Consumer."

See the text set we have gathered in the Additional Resources for Teachers section at the end of this chapter. It includes recorded books for nonreaders/early readers and texts for independent or group reading at reading levels of grade 2.5 and above. All texts include many visuals that support the text and they also are selected to represent various geographic settings, cultural groups, and life experiences. We provide a transition book from our literature theme to model how to transition from a literature-based thematic unit to a social studies thematic unit.

In collecting text sets for ELLs, you will want to keep in mind the following, as we did in selecting texts for our text set:

- ❑ Students' proficiency levels
- ❑ Students' literacy levels (in L1 and L2)
- ❑ Students' life experiences and background knowledge
- ❑ The kind and level of text support needed by students in terms of photographs, pictures/drawings, diagrams, charts, or pull-out boxes
- ❑ The amount of print per page that students can handle and their need for text features such as bolding, italic, and so forth to identify key concepts; their need for L1 support
- ❑ Aspects of the texts that students would find motivating and attractive
- ❑ The emotional and affective response produced by the text; the sensory qualities of the text (the phrasing, cadence, and rhythm of the text; the images evoked by the text)
- ❑ The inclusion of features such as a table of contents, glossary, or index that will allow you to teach your students how to locate specific facts in informational texts

Preparing to Teach an Informational Text: Frameworks for Planning

In Chapter 2, we provided one framework for planning lessons for ELLs (see Figure 2.1 on page 51). Chart 4.4 is another framework that you might find useful.

When using either of these planning tools, it is important to account for the background knowledge needed by ELLs and also to make explicit the language and literacy objectives that will be targeted while teaching particular subject matter to students. In the planner shown as Chart 4.4, we also account for language proficiency and content standards being addressed in the unit.

Identifying language, literacy, and content area objectives

You can find your content objectives by consulting your district curriculum guide, teacher's guide, or state content frameworks. Once the content objectives have been identified, select appropriate strategies for teaching them. Be sure to determine how you will assess whether your students have met all of the objectives—content as well as the language and literacy objectives.

TOPIC: CONTENT STANDARDS: TEXT(S):		ELA/ELP STANDARDS:	
Teaching Activities (Built upon ELL Research-Based Reading/Writing Strategies)	Background Knowledge Needed	Target Vocabulary and Language Forms	Reading/Writing Skills to Practice

Chart 4.4 Template for Planning Instruction

A Sampling of Research-Based Strategies

In the sections that follow, we highlight some strategies that conform to the principles of instruction presented in Chapter 2; they are also based on research evidence of their effectiveness in promoting literacy in ELLs.

Frontloading vocabulary and concepts: Preparing students for reading and writing

Vocabulary is an essential component of reading and writing in the content areas. You may wonder how to select the words you need to teach. Here is what several vocabulary experts suggest (Carlisle & Katz 2005, Graves 2006):

Selecting Words to Teach

- Select words that are important for understanding the selection.
- Do not exceed the number of words that a student can remember (say around six to ten per lesson, depending on the learners' age or stage of proficiency).
- Select words that can advance student's word learning skills (words with particular prefixes or suffixes, for example).
- Teach words that are frequent, useful, and likely to be encountered in the content area. They should be highly transferrable to other units or content areas.
- Do not directly teach words if students can use context or structural analysis skills to discover the word's meaning.
- Be sure that you select an appropriately leveled passage to begin with, one for which you will only need to teach a small number of words prior to reading.

For our unit on "From Producer to Consumer," we might select concept words like: *needs, raw material* (or *natural resources*), *foods, goods, grow* (*grower*), *produce* (*producer*), *consume* (*consumer*), *sell* (*seller*), *buy* (*buyer*), *process* (as noun and verb). We would select this set of related words because they are needed to understand the passage, and, also, they are highly useful in social studies instruction as well as in daily life. By teaching how to take verbs and turn them into nouns by adding /-*er*/, we also further vocabulary development because ELLs learn that the ending /-*er*/ often indicates the person who does the action. We would also want to use strategies that show the relationships that exist among the words, using semantic webs and diagrams, for example.

According to Graves (2006), we should use the following research findings when teaching individual words to learners:

Research Finding

ELLs benefit from accommodations when learning to read because they have more limited proficiency in English compared to native speakers; as well, they have different world knowledge, familiarity with written language, and cultural backgrounds. An important accommodation is use of the home language. Other accommodations that are beneficial are (see Goldenberg [2008] for more discussion):

(a) clarification and explanation
(b) additional time to complete tasks
(c) preview-review
(d) focusing on similarities and differences between the home language and English
(e) teaching reading strategies in the home language and then having them practice them in English
(f) sheltered instruction using various scaffolds: graphic organizers, redundancy, extra practice time, identifying and clarifying difficult words, use of familiar content, and use of the home language to clarify
(g) use of materials that are meaningful and connect with their backgrounds and experiences (familiarity does not necessarily mean "cultural familiarity")

- ❑ Instruction that involves both definitional information and contextual information is markedly stronger than instruction that involves only one of these.
- ❑ Instruction that involves activating prior knowledge and comparing and contrasting meanings is stronger still.
- ❑ Instruction that involves students in actively manipulating meanings, making inferences, searching for applications, prior knowledge, and frequent encounters is still stronger (Beck, McKeown, & Kucan 2002).

Here are some useful methods for frontloading:

1. Cognate Word Walls or Notebooks. For our unit, cognate words would include: *material* (same word both in Spanish and

Research Finding

Students may need to encounter a word about twelve times or more before they will know it well enough to help them comprehend what they read (McKeown et al. 1985).

English), *natural resources/recursos naturales, produce/ producir,* and *consumer/consumidor.* These could appear on a cognate Word Wall in the classroom or as a chart in student's notebooks. Make sure students interact with their notebook or the Word Wall, perhaps by doing the next activity—student-developed definitions.

2. Student-Developed Definitions (with/without pictures and drawings). Here students write, in their own words, the meaning of the terms. They can add drawings or cut out pictures to help illustrate the term. Students remember words better when they define them in their own words and provide meaningful examples (Gorrell, Tricou, & Graham 1991). A good way to do this is to have students keep dictionaries by content area and theme. Work on definitions systematically and review terms frequently until they are acquired.
3. Semantic Webbing/Word Webs. The use of semantic/word webs is very helpful to ELLs because they reduce language demands while presenting information in a highly conceptual way. For example taking the production/consumption economic cycle, we could create a word web as seen in Figure 4.1.

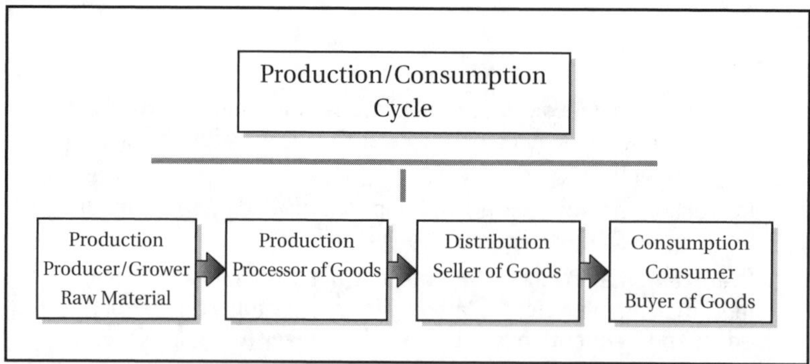

Figure 4.1 Word Web for Production/Consumption Cycle

Semantic feature analysis or attribute charts are also very useful when teaching concept words. With a semantic feature analysis chart or grid, you can examine related concepts and make distinctions between them according to particular criteria across which the concepts can be compared. To create the chart, a set of concepts is listed down the left side and criteria or features are listed across the top. If the concept is associated with the feature or characteristic, the student records a Y or a + (plus sign) in the grid where that column and row intersect; if the feature is not associated with the concept, an *N* or – (minus sign) is placed in the corresponding square on the grid, as shown in the Figure 4.2.

	GROWS OR COLLECTS RAW MATERIALS	TURNS RAW MATERIAL INTO FINISHED GOODS	IS AFFECTED BY SUPPLY AND DEMAND	SELLER	BUYER
Producer	+	–	+	+	–
Processor	–	+	+	+	+
Consumer	–	–	+	–	+

Figure 4.2 Semantic Feature Analysis Chart

4. The Frayer Method: A strategy for teaching challenging or abstract concepts (see Figure 4.3).

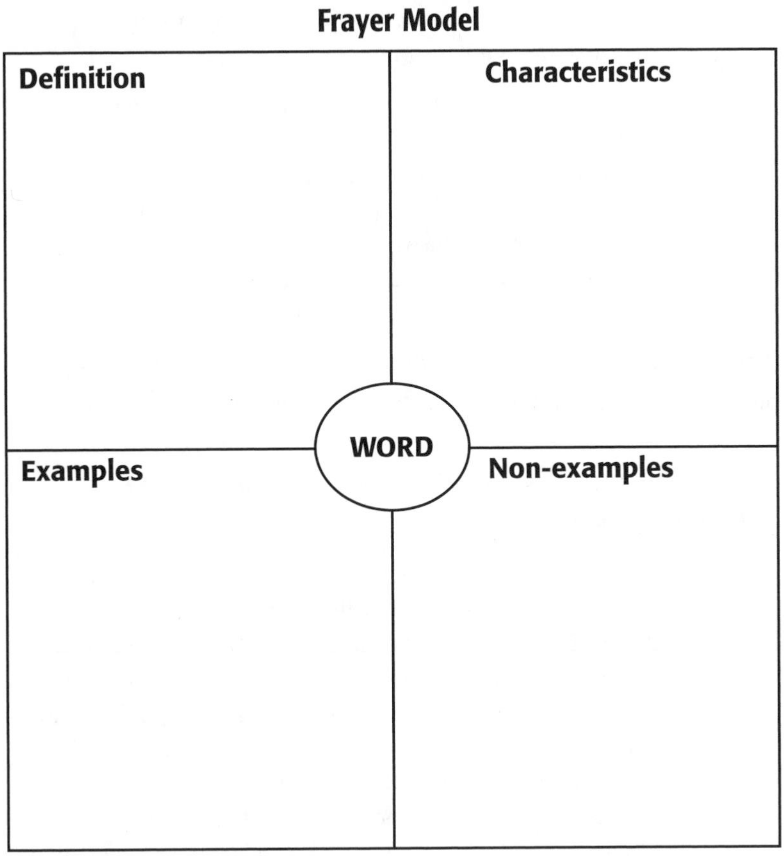

Frayer Model

Definition	Characteristics
Examples	Non-examples

WORD

Figure 4.3 Frayer Method

Research Question

We have argued that ELLs are more engaged and can advance more quickly in their English development and mastery of new concepts and knowledge if they are encouraged to make connections between their home language and English. To see if this is true, try using the Frayer method with and without the option of ELLs using their home languages and see which condition results in more elaborated and sophisticated definitions and descriptions of new concepts.

Use the Frayer chart to:

a. Provide a clear definition and a listing of essential characteristics of complex concepts.

b. Distinguish between the new concept and similar concepts it might be confused with. First, present examples and non-examples, and ask students to distinguish between them. Then have students present examples and non-examples, explaining why they are one or the other, and provide feedback (Frayer, Frederick, & Klausmeier 1969).

This might be done with a term like *raw material* or *natural resources* from our unit. It can be done on word webs, such as the one shown earlier, or word cards—4 × 6 cards divided into four parts that ask the student to list the word, give an illustration or diagram, provide their own definition, and use it in a sentence. The main goal of the Frayer method is to have students elaborate extensively about new concepts to be sure they acquire its full meaning.

5. Word Study (roots, affixes). Word study involves the learning and using of word parts. This is helpful to ELLs because they can learn how words are formed in English and also start to become word detectives, noticing specific parts of words that can cue them as to the word's meanings. As suggested earlier, teaching students about the */-er/* ending would be one such strategy (*consumer, producer, buyer, seller*).

(For a quick overview of frontloading and other teaching strategies presented in this chapter, see the chart in Appendix B).

Using scaffolds to support reading comprehension and written production

1. Graphic Organizer as Mediator. Understanding text structure is critical for comprehending text written in a second language (Coiro 2001; Dickson et al. 1995, Iwai 2007). Second-language learners can have considerable difficulty with text structure in English (Sharp 2004). Graphic organizers are helpful tools for making text structures visible and getting ELLs to reflect on how text is organized. Understanding the structure of text enhances comprehension and helps ELLs to identify important ideas they need to communicate about in either written or oral reports.

Text Structure

STRUCTURE	BEST GRAPHIC ORGANIZERS TO REFLECT THE TEXT STRUCTURE OR PURPOSE OF COMMUNICATION
Enumeration (Main idea/supporting details)	Semantic maps, concept maps, herringbone technique
Chronological/time order/temporal sequence (how to do or make something)	Sequence chart, staircase, cycle graph
Temporal sequence	Time line, staircase, sequence chart, ladder graph
Definition/example	Word map, Frayer
Lists	Bulleted list, enumerated lists
Cause and effect	Fishbone/herringbone map, cause/effect chart, T chart, arrow graph
Compare and contrast	Venn diagram, T chart, compare/contrast charts
Problem and solution	T chart, problem/solution charts
Question and answer	T chart
SIGNAL WORDS (WORDS THAT SIGNAL PARTICULAR TEXT STRUCTURES; RELATIONSHIPS AMONG IDEAS)	
Enumeration/description	*first, second, third (first of all); to begin with; next; then; finally; last; another; also; most importantly; in summary; in brief*
Time order/sequence	*first, second, third; now; before; after; on (date); at (time); when; earlier; always; later; next; finally; eventually*
Compare/contrast	*however; but; and yet; either . . . or; as well as; like; likewise; similarly; not only . . . but also; although; yet; as opposed to; on the other hand; in contrast*
Cause/effect	*because; consequently; therefore; as a result; if . . . then; since; thus; due to; so that*
Problem/solution	*a way this can be solved; the problem is; one solution to this; a solution might be; an explanation for this; the challenge is; the key is; the answer is; a resolution for*

Chart 4.5 Text Structure

Graphic organizers are useful because they limit the amount of language ELLs need to understand a text and yet they are conceptually organized. This helps ELLs better understand the content of written text. Using graphic organizers with ELLs separates large amounts of content into manageable chunks of essential information. However, graphic organizers must be selected to mirror the structure of the text so that students can capture information in the text and later share this information with others in oral or written summaries. Thus, for ELLs, well-selected graphic organizers act as mediators for taking in information and conveying information to others (getting language in and getting language out).

Bouchard (2005, 81–83) provides instructions on how to use graphic organizers and signal words in the text (see Chart 4.5) to teach text organization/structure to ELLs. She suggests that teachers divide the class into groups and give each group an article or selection that demonstrates the text structure being discussed. Each group can be asked to find the signal words in the paragraph as they practice using the graphic organizer to summarize the important information they are learning. They can compare what they have listed in the organizer with other students and determine which points they all agree are the most important to record. Chart 4.5 identifies the types of graphic organizers that can be useful when ELLs are reading or producing particular types of texts. (See Bouchard 2005, 85–91. There is also a list of important signal words.) For downloadable graphic organizers, visit everythingesl.net (www.everythingesl.net/inservices/graphic_organizers.php)

2. Guided Reading/Writing. During guided reading of content area texts, teachers explicitly show students strategies that they can use to support their reading and writing. These can

Research Finding

Focused, explicit, and deliberate instruction in some reading-related skills improves performance, especially when students are having difficulty acquiring these skills, for example, knowledge of the alphabet, knowledge of letter-sound relationships, academic vocabulary, reading comprehension strategies, and use of cognate vocabulary (Genesee & Riches 2006).

include prereading and prewriting strategies, like setting a purpose for reading or brainstorming what you know about a topic before writing. Or they might include "during reading/writing strategies," such as the use of illustrations or text features (bolding, highlighting, marginal glossing) to support comprehension, rereading when reading or writing, or using an editing checklist to guide revision efforts.

Here are some strategies you can teach during guided reading/writing to ensure that your ELLs become efficient in their use of each:

- ❏ Set a Purpose for Reading or Writing. Have students decide before reading/writing what they are trying to accomplish by reading/writing the text.
- ❏ Activating Background Knowledge. Have students think about what they already know about a topic; make associations between what they already know and are about to read.
- ❏ Selective Attention. Have students notice only what is important; focus on key concepts, vocabulary, phrases, and ideas.
- ❏ Self-Monitoring. Have students check to see that they are understanding as they read; check to be sure their writing communicates their ideas effectively.
- ❏ Taking Notes. Have students decide what is important in terms of key concepts and ideas; write accurate notes as they read; organize notes as they write. Notes can be written as simple lists, by filling in partially completed notes, or by writing short statements that summarize important information.
- ❏ Summarizing. Have students write short summaries to show their understandings. These might take the form of learning logs, reader response notebooks, or other types of journaling. GIST (Herrell & Jordan 2008, 272) is a technique whereby at given intervals (specific pages and paragraphs) marked by the teacher, students work together in small groups to discuss and then summarize in one sentence what they have learned in that section. They can then use these statements to form a short summary of the entire selection.
- ❏ Questioning Self and Others to Ensure Comprehension. Have students explore areas of uncertainty by questioning others, asking for explanations or examples. This can be done informally or formally through the use of written interview protocols or questionnaires. Questions for ELLs must be leveled to suit their proficiency in order to ensure that they have the proficiency to do what you are asking them to do. For example, beginners do not have enough proficiency to explain, but they do have enough proficiency to give examples or attributes of a concept using single words.

- ❑ Using Resources. Have students look up additional information, check spelling, look for other words to express their meaning, or use bilingual reference tools.
- ❑ Encouraging Oneself to Sustain Task Engagement. Encourage students to tell themselves that they will "get it" and can do the task, especially when the task is difficult; have them talk themselves through the process.

When you introduce particular learning strategies, present the strategy, provide practice, and then help students determine how and when it aids them (Chamot et al. 1999).

3. Writing Scripts/Frames/Templates. Providing models and supports is very helpful to second-language writers. Use of word boxes, sentence starters, or scripts ("one thing I learned about natural resources is that . . .") are very helpful to ELLs because they help them express their ideas—to find words and phrases they need to communicate their meanings. Writing frames and templates are also very helpful because it shows students what to do first, second, and so on. In the case of our unit of instruction, a simple writing frame might include:

I found the unit "From Producer to Consumer" interesting for several reasons.

I discovered that . . .

I also learned . . .

It was interesting that . . .

Finally, . . .

As you can see, . . .

We have already discussed how graphic organizers can serve as tools for organizing writing. Another way of supporting writing is to work from notes taken on a graphic organizer to write a summary or essay.

4. Cooperative Learning. Using cooperative learning methodologies can be very effective in promoting language and literacy development in ELLs (Kagan 1995) for the following reasons:

1. Greater Comprehensible Input. Students receive more comprehensible input because they are working together with a partner.
2. Natural Context. Language is used in real-life, functional interactions where students are attempting to gain meaning from print or express meaning in writing.
3. Negotiation of Meaning. Students have the opportunity to adjust their understandings of text or their written production by working with each other.
4. Lowered Affective Filter. Students are not as intimidated when they work with one other person as when they work alone or perform in front of the class. Hence they may take more risks or receive input more effectively because they are not as anxious.
5. Peer Support. Students encourage and support each other as they talk, read, or write.
6. Enhanced Motivation. Because students need to understand each other, there is high motivation to listen and read and to speak and write for understanding.
7. Greater Language Use. Using a pair structures such as Pair Share, Partner Reads, or Partner Writes, every student receives active language-learning opportunities.

In Partner Reads students are given guiding questions to frame their reading of text. They read a story or passage silently, then read it orally with their partner. During oral reading, students take turns reading the story aloud, alternating readers at appropriate breaks based on the proficiency of each partner. While their partner is reading, the listener can simply follow along or takes notes. They return to the guiding questions and provide joint responses, rereading as needed to respond.

In Partner Writes, students can write simultaneously and then combine their texts, or you may have students share ideas and then jointly construct a single text with one student acting as the scribe. As they work, each partner takes turns prompting or producing the joint writing piece. They review and revise their draft and then share what they have written.

"Providing collaborative opportunities to construct knowledge (collaborative learning) allows kids to bounce ideas off each other, voice their own opinions, and negotiate solutions . . . thus increasing social and communication skills."

(Railsback 2002, 9)

Jigsaw Reading is another beneficial cooperative learning technique to use with ELLs. Here are the steps for conducting a Jigsaw Reading:

Conducting a Jigsaw Reading

1. The teacher identifies reading materials related to a content area topic. These should be of varying text difficulty and sophistication. It could be one reading, split into sections or parts, or separate short readings.
2. Divide students into several home teams and assign readings so that one member of each team is reading the same material; make sure that each student's assignment is appropriate to her level of proficiency in English.
3. Give students time to read their assigned selections independently. They can take notes or fill in a graphic organizer or note-taking outline provided to list important concepts from their passage. In this way, each student becomes an expert on his assigned reading.
4. Next, all students who have read the same reading join an "expert group" made up only of students who have read the same reading. Together they discuss the concepts they feel are most important. Each expert group also produces a summary of key points, a concept map, a graphic outline, or highlighted notes to be shared when they return to their home team.
5. When the expert groups have finished discussing their own reading, each member returns to her original home team. This is where the jigsaw starts to come together. Each home team member teaches members of the team the important information from their assigned reading. Collectively, they put all the pieces from the readings together.

5. Keeping Learning Logs and Journals. Finally, students can keep learning logs or journals about their content area learning experiences. These can be done as simple lists, bulleted phrases, or in paragraph form, depending upon the students' level of proficiency in English. Logs can be written individually or with partners. The important point is that they be written on a regular basis so that students get regular practice writing in their new language about content area topics.

Extending Academic Learning

Beyond the strategies named thus far, there are two more obvious choices for ELLs: project-based learning and field trips/explorations into the wider community.

Project-Based Learning as a Teaching Strategy

Project-based learning, whether done as a cooperative learning activity or individually, has many benefits for ELLs. Because it is tiring to learn content through a second language, projects provide a welcome relief to ELLs because they can be engaged in hands-on activities. Well-designed projects generate student interest and motivate them to take risks in their second language. Through projects, students make observations, read to investigate a topic of interest, use language to collaborate and communicate with others, and reflect orally and in writing about their learning.

When setting up projects for ELLs, be sure to ensure that:

- ❑ The projects you assign are appropriate for the stage of proficiency and literacy level of the student.
- ❑ Roles are assigned that ELLs can easily fulfill so that they feel successful and can contribute in meaningful ways to their team.
- ❑ Project completion requires students to bounce ideas off one another, voice their opinions, and negotiate solutions with one another. This ensures that students get chances to practice their English in meaningful situations where communication matters.
- ❑ You show models of successfully completed projects so that ELLs understand what they are to do.
- ❑ ELLs are required to explain or demonstrate through performance what they have learned, thus providing accountability.

Of course, it is also advantageous if these projects are co-planned with the teachers you work with—ESL and reading specialists and/or classroom teachers, as the case may be.

Field Trips/Explorations

For similar reasons to those mentioned already, getting out of school and into the wider community is very beneficial to ELLs' language and content learning. When students visit local parks, zoos, arboretums, museums, and historical sites, learning comes alive for them. They are naturally inspired to listen attentively, ask questions, make comments, and take notes in English. Be sure to include sites that have special significance for ELLs and that they may know more about than mainstream students so that they can play the role of expert. Often, by getting ELLs out into the community, you can build on their home languages for learning because local guides may be proficient in the languages of ELL students. By communicating through the home language, local guides can ensure depth of understanding. If the goal is to focus on English language and literacy development, field trips provide the context for deepening the meaning of new terms and phrases for ELLs. Thus, for all these reasons, project-based learning along with field trips and community explorations make good sense for ELLs (Melber 2007, Zehler 1994). Here are a few ways to make field trips successful for ELLs:

Planning Field Trips for ELLs

1. Determine your content and language objectives. Focus on these during the trip.
2. Create opportunities for language and literacy use prior to, during, and following the field trip. Make sure that these are meaningful and motivating, not rote exercises.
3. Create templates and worksheets that allow ELLs to record important information while they are on the field trip.
4. Give ELLs a partner to work with and/or talk to during the field trip about the concepts they have been learning at school. Make sure the partner will cause them to use the language you want them to use during the field trip.
5. Make sure that local guides know ELLs will be on the field trip and give them tips for sharing information with students new to English.

6. Encourage students to formulate questions they have that they would like answered during the field trip.
7. Monitor student language use. Encourage and invite their participation.

Putting It All Together

Now that we have seen what can be useful for teaching language, literacy, and content to ELLs, let's look at how our "Producer to Consumer" unit (see pages 150–53) might unfold over the period of three weeks.

Summing Up: Learning English While Learning Content

In this chapter, we have explored the unique opportunities that exist for teachers of English language learners when teaching math, science, and social studies. We have seen that when teaching particular grade-level topics, not only must you focus on district- and state-mandated content objectives, you must also target specific academic language and literacy objectives. You have learned how to analyze content area texts and teacher discourse to identify the challenging language used to present academic content. Only by identifying specific language and literacy objectives can you advance ELLs' academic reading and writing skills. This is what is unique about teaching content to ELLs. What is normally taken for granted—knowledge of instructional language and relevant cultural and background experiences—must become visible to you when you teach ELLs. In this way, you can systematically develop the background knowledge, language, and literacy skills ELLs need to be successful. You have also seen that by working together and using research-based teaching strategies you can make great strides in advancing the academic language and literacy of ELLs.

Sample Content Area Unit Development—Grades 4–8 (3 weeks)

Social Studies Unit: Producer to Consumer

(with language and literacy activities embedded)

National Council for the Social Studies (NCSS) Curriculm Standards: Production, Distribution, and Consumption; People, Places, and Environment; Global Connections

OBJECTIVES:

- **Content:** Economic cycle of production of raw goods, to finished product to consumption: raw material, goods, production, distribution
- **Communicative:** Naming people and ingredients, retelling a story, explaining a process
- **Linguistic:** Knowledge of target vocabulary, knowledge of commands (Think of . . .) and clauses with "who"
- **Reading/Writing Skills & Strategies:** Using text features to support comprehension; making connections; using visuals to support comprehension; sequencing events; using models and writing frames/templates as scaffolds for writing; using a reference (book) to check accuracy
- **Cross-cultural:** The value of different occupations in different cultures; uses of crops in different cultures; values concerning use of natural resources

KEY

A	Assessment
CC	Content Connection
RW	Reading-Writing Connection
EB	Emergent/Beginning Readers and Writers
HC	Home Language/Connection to Home and Community

KEY CONCEPTS: From Producer to Consumer/Economic Cycle

- Raw materials are gathered, transported, and processed to produce finished goods.
- People use natural resources to support their basic needs.
- People from around the world hold different values with respect to sharing natural resources.

WEEK 1				
ACTIVITY 1	**ACTIVITY 2**	**ACTIVITY 3**	**ACTIVITY 4**	**ACTIVITY 5**
Read-Aloud: *Bread Is for Eating*, D. Gershator and P. Gershator, (New York: Henry Holt and Company, 1995) Book is written in English but uses a recurring song in Spanish throughout; also characters are called by native language terms (*mamita*) (**HC**)	Sing song in book	Introduce content-specific vocabulary with pictures: *earth, seeds, plant, corn, flour, factory, machinery, dough*, etc. Model actions with *dough*: mix, push, squeeze, flatten, bake; with *corn*: harvest, grind, store	Make bread or tortillas	Write story of making bread or tortillas ("How We Made Tortillas")

WEEK 1 (continued)				
ACTIVITY 1	**ACTIVITY 2**	**ACTIVITY 3**	**ACTIVITY 4**	**ACTIVITY 5**
• Read book aloud to students • After the first reading, go back through the book and note on a graphic organizer the steps in terms of how bread gets to the table (**RW**) • Introduce the terms *producer*, *consumer*, *grower*, (in this case *baker*), *seller*, *buyer* (**CC**) • List cognates: *consumidor/consumer* *productor/producer* *cultivar/cultivate* (**HC**)	• With sentence strips, review the story events with students (**RW**) • Check to see if they can correctly sequence the events (**A**) • Then introduce the song (you might play the recording from the Reading Rainbow ® version of the story) • Sing along with the tape several times using the English version of the song • If you have a lot of Spanish speakers you may want to sing the Spanish version, then the English version (**HC**) • Go back to key terms introduced yesterday and ask children to write their own definitions (in pairs) for the terms (**CC**)	• Using word cards with pictures or just cut out pictures for nouns and actions for verbs; conduct a TPR activity (**EB**) • Check to see what words are known by students and what words are new and need to be practiced (**A**) • Continue to conduct the full TPR activity: (1) you do an action; children do the same action on your command; (2) then you command one or several children to do an action while the others watch; (3) then individual children who are ready give commands to the class (**EB**) • Make semantic webs of key terms (nouns, actions) associated with *grower*, *harvester*, *baker*, *consumer* (**CC**) • Point out the suffix */-er/*	• Place children into groups • Allow each to play a part in the making of bread or tortillas, or give each a small amount of dough so they can each go through the process of making bread or tortillas • Finish by collecting information from the students as to what they did first, second, and third on chart paper	• Have students return to the chart paper they produced with you in the previous activity • Check to see if they can copy the correct sequence in which things were done into a writing template (first, then, next, finally) (**A**) • Finish by asking each child to tell the story of making bread or tortillas in a letter to a relative or friend (**HC**) • Mail the letters (**HC**)
Strategies Used	**Strategies Used**	**Strategies Used**	**Strategies Used**	**Strategies Used**
• Use of L1 to support L2 (text has some bilingual words and phrases); use of cognates • Use of graphic organizers to support comprehension • Frontloading of vocabulary	• Frontloading of vocabulary (explain meaning of the phrases "staff of life," "love of my life") • Student-developed definitions • Cooperative learning	• Frontloading of vocabulary and concepts • Preparing students for reading and writing with word webs and conceptual organizers; word study strategies	• Language experience • Guided writing	• Guided writing with writing template • Connection to home/community

(*continues*)

WEEK 2			
ACTIVITY 1	**ACTIVITY 2**	**ACTIVITY 3**	**ACTIVITY 4**
Partner Read with *The Tortilla Factory*, Gary Paulsen (New York: Voyager Books, 1995)	Art project: Illustrated phrases from the story	Group investigations	Writing frames to guide reports

• Put students into appropriately formed pairs (where the one partner is no more than one level above the other)
• Have students follow along to a recording of the story, turning the pages as they listen
• Watch them to see if they turn at appropriate times (**A**)
• Depending on their proficiency, ask the children to read (*intermediate advanced*) or tell the story to one another (*beginning intermediate*); beginners can just name what they see in the pictures (**EB**)
• If they tell the story to one another, check to see what descriptive words they use as they tell the story, if any (**A**)
• Have the students copy words or phrases from the story into their vocabulary notebook that they would like to remember (**RW**)
	• To reinforce descriptive phrases, make a class list of some of the descriptions that students noticed and wrote in their vocabulary notebooks (*hot sun*, *golden corn*, *green plants*) (**RW**)
	• Ask students to choose one and make a drawing using no more than three colors (crayons, colored pencils, paints or Cray-Pas™)
	• They can use the book as a model for their drawing if they like
	• Then post their illustrated descriptive phrases in the hallway or on a wall in the classroom (**RW**)
	• If there is time, do a word sort—all the phrases that go together
		• Put students into groups based on reading level; assign books that are appropriate for their level from the National Geographic Theme Set: *Providing Goods* (Social Studies four-book set), 2004
		  • *From Cotton to Blue Jeans* (Fry 3.2)
		  • *From Trees to Paper* (Fry 3.8)
		  • *From Wheat to Bread* (Fry 5.5)
		  • *From Cows to Ice Cream* (Fry 6.6)
		All of the books are well illustrated and they share certain pages in common so the teacher can work with the entire class to reinforce key learning
		Provide a recorded version of *From Cotton to Blue Jeans* if students are beginners (**EB**)
		• Choose one section to read as a Partner Read (e.g., *Key Concept One: Raw materials are gathered, transported and processed to produce finished goods*) (**CC**); beginners will just listen to the recording and follow along (**EB**)
			• Have students return to their groups and review the part they read so they remember all the steps they learned about in turning raw materials into finished goods
			• Have the pairs write steps that occur under each phase of the particular process they studied using a three-part graphic organizer (gather, transport, process) (**RW**)
			• If more than one group uses the same book, have them check their charts with one another; if not, the teacher can check their charts (**A**)
			• Finish by groups reporting their process—one partner reports while the other shows the corresponding pictures/illustrations to the class (**CC**)

Strategies Used	**Strategies Used**	**Strategies Used**	**Strategies Used**
• Word notebooks • Cooperative learning • Word study (descriptive words for beginning intermediate up [*black earth*, *brown hands*, *green plants*, *golden corn*, *hot sun*] and nouns for beginners [*earth*, *grower*, *seeds*, *plants*])	• Frontloading of vocabulary • Word study (word sorts)	• Cooperative learning (partner reads) • Visual supports as an aid to comprehension; discussion as an aid to comprehension • Frontloading of key concepts	• Guided writing (partner writes) • Graphic organizer as mediator • Writing as a means to check on comprehension of key concepts

(*continues*)

WEEK 3			
ACTIVITY 1	**ACTIVITY 2**	**ACTIVITY 3**	**ACTIVITY 4**
Review of key concepts with graphic organizer and learning log	Venn diagram comparing processes	Make additional content connections	Connect to family and community
• Go back to the original story read to the class: *Bread Is for Eating* • Ask children to complete a graphic organizer that represents the steps in the producer to consumer chain with bread (**RW**) • Ask them to use the graphic organizer to write about what they learned about how bread gets from the producer to the consumer in their learning log (**A**)	• Have pairs of students who read different books get together to compare what is the same and what is different about the processes they studied of how raw materials become finished goods (**CC**) • Check their work to see if they are understanding the key concepts (**A**) • Ensure that they use the academic vocabulary you want them to use by placing words in a word box for their use on the activity sheet	• Show where corn is grown around the world; or compare dry measurement of grains using the English and metric systems; or compare the nutritional value of different grains (**CC**)	• Have students take a book of their choice home from among those you used in the unit to read or talk about with their parents (**HC**) • Have them do one of the activities that correspond to each book: Using *Bread Is for Eating*, have them sing the song with a parent, sibling, or neighbor in Spanish or English (**HC**), then have them make a list of all the types of bread they have eaten OR Using the "how-to" book section in a National Geographic text set book, have them do one of the suggested activities with a parent, older sibling, or other adult; the activities are well illustrated with photographs so that the steps can be easily followed; have them bring their product to class, if feasible
Strategies Used	**Strategies Used**	**Strategies Used**	**Strategies Used**
• Graphic organizer • Learning log	• Academic vocabulary use supported by word boxes • Graphic organizers • Comprehension checks	• Making connections to other content areas and student background knowledge	• Extension to home and community • Use of L1 • Enjoyment of books

ASSESSMENT

(Of Content, Communicative, Linguistic, Reading-Writing Skills/Strategies Taught; Cross-Cultural Understanding)

Use teacher observation during activities or student conferences to assess:

- Affective: Enjoyment of print; self-concept as a reader/writer
- Content: Economic cycle of production of raw goods to finished product to consumption; understanding of concepts: raw material, goods, production, distribution, consumption
- Linguistic: Knowledge of target vocabulary, use of descriptive terms
- Communicative: Naming people, raw materials, retelling a story, explaining a process
- Reading/writing skills: Using text features to support comprehension; making connections (text to self); using visuals to support comprehension; sequencing events; using models and writing frames/templates as scaffolds for writing; using a reference (the book) to check on accuracy of story actions told in sequence
- Cross-cultural: The value of different occupations in different cultures; uses of crops in different cultures; values concerning use of natural resources

Additional Resources for Teachers

Producer-to-consumer text set (raw materials to consumable goods)

- ❏ Transition Book from Literature Unit Presented in Chapter 2: Carle, E. 1970. *Pancakes, Pancakes!* New York: Knopf. Reading level: Grade 3.6; Lexile level: 670.

  Describes the source of all the ingredients used to make pancakes for breakfast as well as the process for turning raw materials into useful food products (butter, flour). Jack collects each of the ingredients in turn so his mother can make his pancake breakfast according to the steps in the recipe presented in the story. The story ends with Jack happily eating his pancakes.

- ❏ Gershator, D., and P. Gershator. 1995. *Bread Is for Eating.* New York: Henry Holt and Company. (A Reading Rainbow® Title in video format so it can be listened to by prereaders through emergent readers.) Some bilingual text. Reading level: Grade 2.8; Lexile level: 450.

  Explains the process for making bread from planting and growing the grain to baking it. There is a built-in song sung in English and Spanish as a recurring chorus across the book.

- ❏ Paulsen, G. 1995. *The Tortilla Factory.* San Diego, CA: Voyager Books/A Harcourt Brace & Company. Reading level: Grade 2.7; Lexile level: 510.

  Describes the planting, growing, and harvesting of corn, grinding corn into cornmeal, and producing tortillas in a factory that are later consumed in households.

- ❏ Thomas, S. 2004. *Providing Goods.* (National Geographic Social Studies Theme Set) Washington, DC: National Geographic Society.

  From Cotton to Blue Jeans (Level A, 3.2)

  From Trees to Paper (Level B, 3.8)

  From Wheat to Bread (Level C, 5.5)

  From Cows to Ice Cream (Level D, 6.8)

  Explains three key economic concepts: (1) Raw materials are gathered, transported, and processed to produce finished goods; (2) the production and distribution of various goods involve different processes; and (3) supply and demand determine which goods are made. Introduces the genre of the "how-to" text, which is compatible with the step-by-step processes introduced across the books included in the text set.

CHAPTER

5

Connecting Reading and Writing

In this chapter, we show how to take advantage of the connections and the overlap that exist naturally among the four skills of language: listening, speaking, reading, and writing. We focus specifically on making the connection between reading and writing, and we show how you can use one skill to advance the other.

Making the connection between reading and writing a routine in the classroom *156*

Strategies for ELLs in the beginning stage of literacy *158*

Strategies for beginning and beginning intermediate stages *161*

Strategies for intermediate advanced and advanced supported stages *176*

Summing up *181*

Additional resources for teachers *182*

We describe teaching strategies where reading is used to promote writing and where student writing is used as individual or class text. The strategies described in the chapter benefit ELLs who are in the beginning levels of English literacy (*beginning*-level students, according to our framework) all the way to those who can read and write in English quite proficiently (*advanced supported*).

Making the connection between reading and writing not only helps advance both skills but also creates more opportunities for writing, a skill that often gets shortchanged in the curriculum. Writing is a complex skill, and it takes a long time for ELLs to acquire the multiple skills that are required to write effectively—vocabulary, phrasing, finding the voice that is appropriate for the context, and fluency or ease of expression. Students need to master these aspects of writing for both social and academic purposes. Thus, ELLs need every opportunity to use their expressive skills. Even in the most interactive classrooms, students get very little chance to speak, so, at the very least, we must create occasions for them to express themselves in writing.

The importance for ELLs spending as much time as possible developing their writing skills is even more apparent when we look at test results that typically show writing to be the least developed English language skill among ELLs. Thus, it is imperative that we give ELLs as many chances as possible to write.

Research Finding

Research shows that writing is a complex and recursive process (Edelsky 2006) and that it is especially taxing for ELLs. Results from the National Assessment of Educational Progress (NAEP) show that ELLs score lowest on the writing segment of the test (U.S. Department of Education 2007).

Making the Connection Between Reading and Writing a Routine in the Classroom

The most effective way to make the connection between reading and writing is to do it whenever the opportunity arises and to train yourself to be on the lookout for occasions when students can read what they have written and write about something they have read. Whenever students are reading something in class, we need to ask ourselves: *What writing activities can stem from the text that students are reading?* And, whenever students are writing something, we need to ask ourselves: *How can I extend this piece of writing so that students will read it for meaning?* In fact, when language is being used for authentic purposes, the two skills are connected to one another, so naturally it is hard to do one without the other.

"Many schools have reading time separate from writing time, but that's an artificial separation. We read what we or someone else wrote; so we can't teach reading separately from writing, and vice versa."

(Beeman & Urow in press)

As you make connections between reading and writing and as you devise tasks and activities that give students opportunities to write, you must remember a few key criteria.

KEY CRITERIA FOR ACTIVITIES THAT CONNECT READING AND WRITING

1. Activities have to be meaningful and functional. Make sure that students can make sense of the activity you are asking them to do and that they understand the purpose that it serves. If you cannot answer the question "*Why am I doing this* (filling in blanks, copying a sentence from the board, etc.)?" in a way that makes sense to the student, then it's probably better to abandon that activity.
2. Activities have to be relevant and interesting to students. Students must be able to make a link between what they are reading and writing about and their daily (or future) lives. If they are asked to write a letter to someone, they must be able to see that indeed they will soon need to write someone like that person a letter similar to the one they are writing at the moment.
3. Activities have to build on oral language. We must use students' oral language as a basis for creating reading and writing activities. Remember, it is much harder to read, let alone write, something that is not part of your oral language ability.
4. Activities must also expand students' language. We must be able to stretch students' language so that it becomes more complex over time.
5. Activities have to connect to the curriculum. Whatever literacy activities students engage in must in some way or other relate to the curriculum. What students write or read about must somehow be linked to the academic subject areas that are being studied.

Strategies for ELLs in the Beginning Stage of Literacy

Many strategies to connect reading and writing are appropriate for ELLs who are in the beginning stages of literacy development in English (for a quick overview of strategies, see Appendix B). However, one strategy is effective for only the earliest stage of reading and writing in English, namely, Mimic Writing. Mimic Writing cannot be used for very long, but if used properly, it can be a very effective first step in learning to read and write among students who are just venturing into the world of text.

Mimic Writing

Mimic Writing is copying but with a very specific purpose: What is being copied must serve a clear function and must somehow be useful to the student. Many of us associate copying with meaningless drill work and consequently shy away from it. But if Mimic Writing is used to write text that serves a real function in the classroom or in the student's life, it can be an effective strategy for ELLs who are just beginning their journey into English literacy. Very simply, Mimic Writing involves students copying words or short sentences, either from the board or from pieces of paper prepared by the teacher. For example, in the beginning of the year, to make the classroom a place that is rich with *environmental print*, you would explain to students that everything in the classroom is going to be labeled. Students can then copy words from a list on the board or from models prepared by the teacher onto pieces of construction paper. These labels would then be fixed to the objects around the classroom. The board would have a label that says "Board"; all the desks would have labels that say "Desk"; the windows would have labels that say "Window"; even the teacher can have a label that says "Teacher"!

These labels will become textual references for the students. Since students learn these commonly used words orally early on, they will read the words to remind themselves of how *chair* is written. They will begin to recognize the words they have written themselves. Labels also serve as spelling guides. Students in "labeled classrooms" are often seen going up to a label during a writing activity and identifying a letter or a combination of letters that they need for a word that they are in the process of writing (Hamayan 1994).

Another effective application of Mimic Writing is to ask students to copy short messages to parents from the board. Instead of sending home a note that you print and copy yourself, you write the note on the board and students copy it to take home. You need to make sure that the students understand what the message says, and you need to make sure that parents are told to let their children "read" messages to them in English (as best as they can) and to have the children translate the message for the parents into the home language. Having students "read" the message to their parents in the home language is an important step in making meaning out of written text.

The messages must be authentic, and they must be about something you really need to tell the parents. As soon as you allow students to copy something they do not need to read, you have stepped into the realm of copying as meaningless and useless drill work. The messages need to be short enough for the student to copy quickly and be able to remember the entire content of the message even if they cannot decode or understand the words. Yes, you are taking a risk because the message may not get to the parent accurately, or at all. But, once students get into the habit of being messengers for things they need from home or things they need their parents to know, they will get more efficient. An example of a good note for copying would be "Your child needs to bring a family photograph to school on Wednesday."

The most efficient way of making this kind of copying a routine in the classroom is for each student to have a notebook that is dedicated only to communication between school and home. In fact, parents can also use it to convey a request or question to the teacher. In many Latin American schools, this system, called *El cuaderno de comunicación,* is used quite effectively for two-way communication between home and school.

Using this technique for written communication with the family can be a tremendous advantage for many parents. Even parents who are not literate in English may welcome the opportunity to say something to the teacher in the emotional distance that writing allows them. Parents who are not literate in English can be encouraged to write in their native language and either the student (if you trust them not to invent!) or another home-language resource can be asked to read the message to the teacher. In order for this to work, parents must feel perfectly comfortable writing in their home language. They must get the message loud and clear from the teacher that not only it is acceptable for them to write in their home language but, in fact, it is encouraged.

In addition to its instructional and family involvement value, the communications notebook provides parents, students, and teachers with a record of the dialogue that has taken place between the parents and the teacher over the school year.

Other appropriate topics for Mimic Writing tasks are homework assignments, field trip permission forms, lunch menus for the following day, a list of snacks that are allowed in the classroom, or, basically, any short text that you normally copy for students to use in class or to take home. When you determine that copying no longer serves a useful learning purpose for a student, you simply stop using it with that student and revert to the note copied on the copying machine. However, if parents are making use of the notebook to communicate with the school, you might want to continue using the notebook by pasting into it the notes that are photocopied and sent home by the school.

What Not to Do with Mimic Writing

- Do not copy new words five times each.
- Do not let students copy whole sentences (as in messages to be sent home) with more than one or two words they do not know.
- Do not give students copying exercises like copying words into blanks or fill in blanks in sentences that are not connected to one another.
- Do not let students copy anything that is not already meaningful to them.
- Do not let students copy anything that does not have a real function in the classroom or in the student's daily life.

The most significant advantage of Mimic Writing is that students begin to view themselves as readers and writers. We set them up for success in a controlled situation. It allows them to feel that they are writing—even though all they are doing is reproducing shapes (words) from the board—because they are producing real written language that carries a meaningful and important message. They are able to "read" because they are reproducing from memory what the message says; and, they are interpreting written text as a meaningful message that someone actually needs to hear. Another important benefit of this technique is that students are introduced early on to the main function of literacy, which is to communicate an idea or a message. In addition to these more general benefits, Mimic Writing gives students a chance to practice fine motor skills associated with writing, to handle writing tools (pencils, pens, or keyboard), to rehearse the direction of print, and to practice forming letters and words. It also gives students exposure to high-frequency and sight words because those are the words that are most likely to be found in Mimic Writing activities.

NOTE FOR TEACHERS WORKING WITH LFS STUDENTS

Mimic Writing is especially useful for students with limited formal schooling as it gives them practice with authentic writing in a structured context and in a way that ensures success.

Strategies for Beginning and Beginning Intermediate Stages

Several strategies are effective for connecting reading and writing with students in the *beginning* and *beginning intermediate* stages of literacy development in English as a second language. These strategies can be varied to suit the oral and written proficiency levels of individual students or small groups of students.

Language Experience Approach

Language experience activities (LEAs) have been described briefly in Chapter 2. They are useful for connecting reading and writing because students (or their teachers) write what has just been said and then read what has been written. Even beginning-level students can read the text because it is based on what they or one of their peers just said, which in turn, is based on an experience that they just shared. The following techniques ensure that the connection between reading and writing is not lost on the student.

Techniques That Reinforce the Connection Between Reading and Writing in Language Experience Activities

For beginning-level students:

- When students dictate the description of the activity for you to write down, sound out the words as you are writing them.
- Take advantage of reading aloud by pointing out "strange" spellings of words, that is, words with low symbol-sound correspondence.
- Start small, with two to four of the most enthusiastic students.
- Point to key words as you read the text aloud.
- If students write their own version of the text into their individual notebooks, encourage them to sound out words as write.

For more advanced students:

- Encourage students to read the text from the perspective of someone who did not participate in the shared activity: How does it sound? Is it comprehensible? Are any details missing? This same text can also be used for assessing the quality of the piece, using a tool such as the 6+1 Trait model of writing, described in a later section of this chapter.

Language experience texts need not be limited to an activity that is completed in the classroom, such as building a bird's nest from twigs; they can also stem from a shared experience that students bring from their community or neighborhood, such as a festival that the neighborhood just celebrated. Thus, language experience texts can directly represent ELLs' rich cultural backgrounds and the traditions that they bring with them to school.

Language experience texts are also effective because they complete the cycle that starts with oral language, goes to writing, and then moves on to reading. When students return later to a piece in order to edit and correct some of the errors that were made when the text was first produced, they are rewriting the text based on their oral language capabilities (see Figure 5.1). They can go through this cycle as

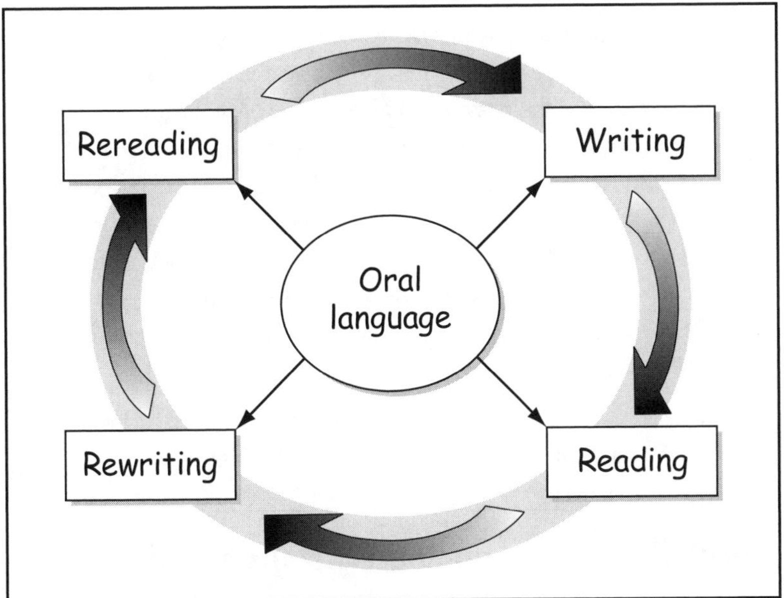

Figure 5.1 The Complete Cycle of Reading/Writing Based on Oral Language in a Language Experience Text

many times as they need to or as time allows, eventually ending up with a final version that they are satisfied with.

Community and Family-Oriented Approaches

Choosing reading and writing activities that are related to ELLs' life at home or in the neighborhood makes it more likely that students can make sense of the text they are working with. It also raises the level of investment and interest that students have in an activity when they are engaged with text. The following are examples of activities that make a connection to the home and the community.

Activities That Connect to the Home and Community

- Show students how to find the numbers and names of buses they and their family members take frequently, for shopping or recreation, for example. Let them write those bus numbers on index cards that can be carried in a wallet or purse.
- Dedicate time during the school day for students to write letters or postcards to family members who live far away.

- Students can bring favorite sayings, *dichos*, from home and can make posters out of these sayings that can be put around the classroom. Whenever the opportunity arises, you can refer to these sayings or proverbs. Thus, when you read Eric Carle's *Pancakes, Pancakes!* you can point to the poster with a saying that one of the students wrote—for example, *Donde hay gana, hay maña* (Where there's a will, there's a way) or *Una abeja no hace una colmena* (One bee doesn't make a hive)—and discuss the relevance of these proverbs to the book.
- Students can also take messages when people call their home and read the messages to their parents or older siblings.

Storytelling Based on Photographs and Videos

We know from our experience as teachers that students enjoy writing about something that comes from them much more than about pictures or topics that teachers impose on them. However, we do not know how the two kinds of texts differ from one another, and to what extent text elicited from a personal illustration or topic is better than text from an outside source. A comparison of the two kinds of texts would be valuable.

For this strategy, students create text based on a photograph (or a set of photographs) or a video that they have taken. Note that this strategy is far less effective if you use photographs from a book or ones that the teacher brings in. There is nothing as dull and uninspiring as trying to describe a picture that has no relevance to your life! When students themselves produce the visuals, they are bringing their personality and their life outside of school into the classroom. By eliciting written text from visuals that belong to the students, you are affirming the value of their home and their community. Also, personal photographs that are either labeled or accompanied by text have a strong allure for others to read, hence, the strong connection between writing (as the first step) and reading (the next step).

Working with a digital camera is very efficient because it allows students to take and to delete pictures freely. Students can also bring photographs from home and base their stories on personal topics; they can write about their life at home, or they can create an autobiography. After thinking about what to say or telling the story orally, students can go about writing text that goes with the visuals. For beginning-level students, this may amount to no more than labels for the photographs. More advanced students can write a whole narrative that describes the photographs or the video. Regardless of the students' level of proficiency, these pictorial texts make wonderful displays, not just for the classroom but for the entire school to see. They can be completed as posters (see Figure 5.2) or as books. Making books could be a language experience activity itself, and it can be a preliminary step in preparing these displays.

Returning to our Pancake theme, if we wanted to use this strategy to expand on one of the pancake books, we might have students take pictures of themselves or a family member making their own version of pancakes. They would then write their own book, perhaps modeled on the original.

This strategy bestows on students the role of authors. Engaging students in such activities acknowledges that they have a story to tell, gives them the time and resources to write their stories, gives them support to revise their writing, and gives them opportunities to share their writing with others by publishing their work. We discuss the topic of students as authors of their own books in more detail in the following section.

NOTE FOR BILINGUAL TEACHERS

Bilingual teachers can take advantage of displays such as those that come out of student storytelling based on photographs to make home-language versions of these stories. Thus, displays around the school will feature both English and various home languages.

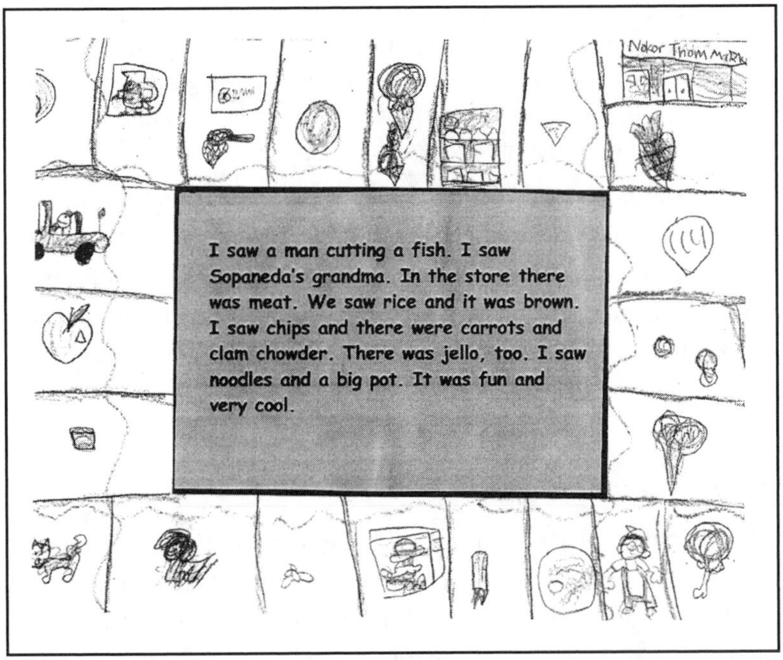

Figure 5.2 A Story, Accompanied by Photographs, Written After Taking a Trip to a Local Market. Permission for use of student work granted by the Charles N. Fortes Elementary School (a Museum School), Lori Hughes, Principal, Providence, RI.

> "We . . . have to be readers to write well. To write using rich, compelling language, we need to hear and read rich, compelling literature. Only a love of reading will promote an understanding and awareness of imagery, tone, voice, and other nuances of good writing. There is no shortcut."
>
> (Routman 2000, 221)

Students as Authors

It is essential that ELLs begin to see themselves as writers, not just people who know how to write but people who write things that others may want to read or as authors who read their work to others.

It is important that ELLs see themselves as authors and feel comfortable in that role; it is equally important that they are acknowledged by others as authors. To accomplish this, you must make sure that:

1. You give students plenty of opportunities to write text that is taken to the point of being produced as a book; that is, you need to give students all the time that it takes to develop their ideas, write them down, get feedback, edit, produce a final draft, and produce the book. If there is a digital library in the school or classroom, the book could be produced digitally. If not, or in addition, a paper version of the book can be produced.
2. Books developed by students adhere to high standards and are treated with the respect that we afford regularly published books. Student books must be made with high-quality materials, they must be clearly written, and they must follow accepted rules of language use.

Once a book is deemed finished, it can be placed in the classroom or even the school library along with other, more traditionally published books. Having students as authors applies to all ELLs, not just the ones who are at a more advanced level of literacy. Students who are at a beginning level of literacy and oral proficiency in English can write books that have more illustrations than written text, as we describe in the next section.

Drawing as early writing

With beginning writers, you can teach them to use cueing systems that support text comprehension and production, such as drawings/pictures and text features such as bolding and underlining. Thus, with our early writing projects, you would want to not only feature drawing as a form of communication but also teach students to use text features like bold print and underlining for emphasis. This method of using drawing to support early writing has been termed "Drawing Out" (Bassano & Christison 1995, Christison & Bassano 1982) and "Draw a Story: Stepping from Pictures into Writing" (NCTE, www.readwritethink.org/lessons/lesson_view.asp?id=45).

By using writing paper that has space for drawing as well as writing, you can show emergent ELL writers how to communicate through graphic means by combining drawing and print (see Figure 5.3). When beginning-level ELLs do not have easy access to written language, their drawings can communicate their thoughts at a more sophisticated level than their writing.

Any format of a book that encourages students to draw and then write text to complement their drawings is highly encouraged for emergent ELL writers. These might include: blank big books, accordion books, step books, tag books, pop-up books, and so on—see www.vickiblackwell.com/makingbooks/index.htm or www.makingbooks.com/freeprojects.shtml for ideas on how to do this creatively.

Begin with drawing and pretend writing, then move on to single-word writing with drawings (labeling, naming, listing), then on

Figure 5.3 Sample Sheet Format for Early Writers

to phrases (captions, simple statements), and finally sentences using models and patterns. For example, in our Pancake unit, you might start by having students draw a picture that captures their favorite scene from *The Runaway Tortilla* (Kimmel 2000) and label items included in their picture or write a caption for their picture, drawing on words on the Word Wall or in a word box. Finally, as children's writing progresses, they might each contribute a page to a book the class is writing together, where each illustrates a scene from the story and a sentence that tells what occurred. You will want to build oral language before, during, and after a book is read, and then take the reading experience and use it for early writing activities. Wordless picture books, such as *Pancakes for Breakfast* in our pancake unit, are ideal for this purpose because the writing is added by the children and is not already provided.

The connections between reading and writing along with connections between written and oral language make this strategy very effective for pushing language proficiency forward. Equally important is the satisfaction of writing something and being able to read it to others or to oneself.

Author's Chair

Some teachers also designate a special chair as Author's Chair and use it when a student author is featured in the classroom. (Naturally, the same chair is used when a published author comes to talk to students.) Thus, students take turns sharing their books with the rest of the class. The Author's Chair also serves the purpose of getting feedback and help while students are still in the process of writing a book (see Graves & Hansen 1983). The featured author gets a chance to ask his or her peers and the teacher to give advice about a plot line or sentence structure or wording. The constant flow between reading and writing when students are engaged in this activity strengthens students' language proficiency in ways that no drill or grammar or vocabulary exercise produced by an outsider can.

Modeling using published books

You can also have students expand their reading into writing by giving them "scripts" and patterned language to support their writing. Because the structure of *The Runaway Tortilla* (Kimmel 2000) is cumulative, ELLs at a beginning level of proficiency in English might each write a page using a phrase like "The (*name of character/animal*) joined the chase." Or children might write sequel pages identifying other characters the tortilla might have run into. With the book *Pancakes, Pancakes!* (Carle 1970), students could each draw a page for one ingredient needed to make the pancake and then use the sentence starter "Here's a (*ingredient*)," said Jack. "Let's make pancakes." These illustrations could adorn the classroom walls or form a class book. After we help children comprehend language (through oral language development and reading), we want to help them communicate messages at a word, phrase, and sentence level so that initial decoding and encoding are related in mutually supportive ways.

Students at more advanced levels can write their own version of a pancake book, for example, turning the pancakes into *chapattis, latkes,* or *atayef.* Alternately, they can write a book they have just read from the perspective of one of the characters in the story or they can extend the plot of the story and write about what happened on the following day. Depending on a student's level of comfort, they can choose to move away from the model provided by the published book or decide to follow the "script" more closely. Students can also start writing a cookbook based on the pancake books, or better, make this a yearlong project and write recipes for all the books with food items that are read that year. Of course, you would bring in some cookbooks for students to look at (see http://childrensbooks.about.com/od/themesubjectbooksby/tp/cookbooks.htm for a list of children's cookbooks). At the end of the year, the cookbook would get published and perhaps given to parents or sold to raise money for a special project.

Writing personal stories based on life experiences

It is also important to give students many opportunities to write about their own lives and interests. Having ELLs use personal life experiences that they bring with them to school as a source for writing is a powerful tool for bridging their two cultural worlds and for integrating their home cultures with that of the classroom. Many educators have done this successfully, mostly with young adolescents or older students. In Chapter 3, we described "identity texts" where students write about their experiences in their new culture (Cummins et al.

NOTE FOR SCHOOL PSYCHOLOGISTS

These personal stories can provide extremely valuable information to a psychologist or social worker who happens to be working with any of your ELLs.

NOTE FOR ALL TEACHERS

If you have students who have come from traumatic backgrounds, such as war or other forms of oppression, be sensitive to the fact that they may be reluctant to divulge much about these incidents.

2005). Weinstein's (1999) *Learners' Lives as Curriculum* is based on stories and memoirs written by students about highly personal issues that provide the material for instruction. Having ELLs write their own stories is a very effective strategy because other students will be highly motivated to read their classmates' stories as well as reading their own stories to their classmates, hence, the connection between reading and writing.

Many ELLs are likely to have some interesting stories to tell that could be novel to their mainstream peers; this will add readability power to their writing, raising not only the popularity of their work with others but also the value of their experiences and their culture in the eyes of others. Unique stories that ELLs can tell include:

- My two languages
- My two countries
- The people I left behind
- The things I miss most about . . . (e.g., my home country)
- A time I didn't understand what was being said
- My first days in the United States
- What it means to be Polish American
- When my parents were children
- How I got my name(s)
- First day at a school in this country
- What people do with my name in this country
- People I miss from back home
- Things I find strange about this country

Intergenerational connections

Research Finding

Research by Jimenez (2000) and Galindo (1993) indicates that ELLs benefit from literacy development experiences that are related to their bilingual abilities and their bilingual status.

Give students the chance to make connections not only between their home and their classroom but across generations. This not only brings in the values, customs, and funds of knowledge of these students' families but also gives everyone in the classroom a sense of history that each student brings with him or her. It allows ELLs to connect the past with the present, making the present less alien (Weinstein 2004). This is especially important for ELLs who came to their new country themselves and had connections between the past and present disrupted. The following activities are effective for making these connections:

Activities That Connect to the Home and Community

1. Students interview family members about their immigrant experiences.
2. Families' immigrant experiences can be compared with student's own immigrant experiences.
3. Students interview family members for stories about life in the home country: What did they play with and what games did they play as children? What chores did they do around the house? What work did they do?
4. Compare these experiences with those of children in the new country.
5. Have students write to their grandparents and older family members.

After students have written their essays or stories, they can read them to their family members. If family members do not speak English, students can interpret (orally) what they wrote in the home language. This can be useful in developing narrative skills in both languages.

Dialogue Journals and Other Types of Interactive Writing

Dialogue journals are written conversations that typically take place between the teacher and individual students on a regular basis. The original purpose of dialogue journals was not language-oriented at all; it was designed as a tool to get to know the students. More specifically, dialogue journals were devised as written conversations to promote learner engagement and help build strong relationships between

Research Question

While many studies have shown a benefit from explicit error correction (Ammar & Spada 2006; Ellis, Loewen, & Erlam 2006; Leeman 2003; Lyster 2004; Mackey 2006; McDonough & Mackey 2006), most of this research had focused on older students and on oral language. Teachers may want to explore how effective explicit correction is in comparison to recasts, a form of implicit correction, in student writing and for different students at different ages.

teachers and students. This, in turn, can lead to greater motivation and investment on the part of the student. Another benefit was soon discovered: ELLs' writing—and more generally, their language proficiency—was advancing rapidly, and they were adopting correct usage even when the teacher did not point out errors explicitly (Hamayan 1994). Thus, dialogue journals became a valuable second-language-development technique (Peyton & Staton 1993). One potential drawback is that it can be time-consuming. Teachers often report that writing well-thought-out responses to students' journal entries can take a lot of time. Many teachers can't fit responding to journals into class time, and they report that in the beginning they tended to be a little resentful of having yet another task to do after work. However, over time, many teachers find that reading students' journals becomes one of the activities that they most look forward to. They say that they can't wait to look at the students' journals, and that it is extremely satisfying to see the amazing advances that their students make. If journals become too cumbersome for you, you can put students on a rotation—four to five students per day. Thus, you would read and respond to only a few journals each day. In this way, you can give each student ample individual attention.

In a dialogue journal, the teacher elicits a response from individual students by writing a message to each of them, usually asking about something that is of interest to the particular student. The student responds and the conversation continues. Unless the student specifically asks for it, you do not correct errors; rather, you simply respond to what the student has written (see Chapter 6 for using dialogue journals for assessment purposes). However, it is always recommended that you recast the student's errors; that is, you need to pay attention to the errors that the student is making and incorporate the correct model into your responses.

Since the goal of dialogue journals is to motivate a student to write authentic messages and to read your responses, you need to engage the student as much as possible: be funny, be outrageous, ask about things that the student brings up in his or her own messages—things you can assume are of great interest to the student. Figure 5.4 shows an example from a fourth grader's dialogue journal with an analysis of what the simple exchange represents.

A few key elements help ensure that dialogue journals serve to advance ELLs' language proficiency and, more specifically, take advantage of the connections between reading and writing.

ELEMENTS OF A SUCCESSFUL DIALOGUE JOURNAL EXCHANGE

- ❑ For your first prompt: Ask the student about something that you know he or she is passionate about—a hobby or a topic that elicits enthusiasm.
- ❑ Modulate your language so that it is at or just beyond the student's proficiency level. There is no formula to follow for this; just go by what feels right and make the best judgment you can.
- ❑ Avoid generalizations such as "Very interesting"; rather, individualize your response to what the student has written.
- ❑ Make your responses personal—tell a story from when you were a child or adolescent that relates to the conversation you are having.
- ❑ Be funny if you wish (but make sure that the student understands the humor).
- ❑ If you feel the student needs prompting, ask a question, but avoid asking too many questions. It is more important for the students to ask you questions because then they will want to read your response.
- ❑ Have fun "talking" to your students; this is a great opportunity to get to know them.

As with Communications Notebooks, the most efficient way of doing dialogue journals is to dedicate a notebook for each student who is participating. That way, you can keep all the conversations that take place with one student in one spot. This allows you, as well as the students, to see progress they have made since they started writing. With the growing popularity of email, it is possible to keep dialogue journals with each student electronically. If you opt for an electronic version of the notebook, make sure you keep a record of all journal entries by simply adding to the message rather than starting a new message every time. The advantage of the paper notebook is that you have a record of the errors, the pencil marks, the scratches, and the corrections that the student made. These give you insight into the process that the student is using when he or she writes. You can also detect general patterns of errors or difficulties that individual students have in writing and you can pay special attention to those errors when

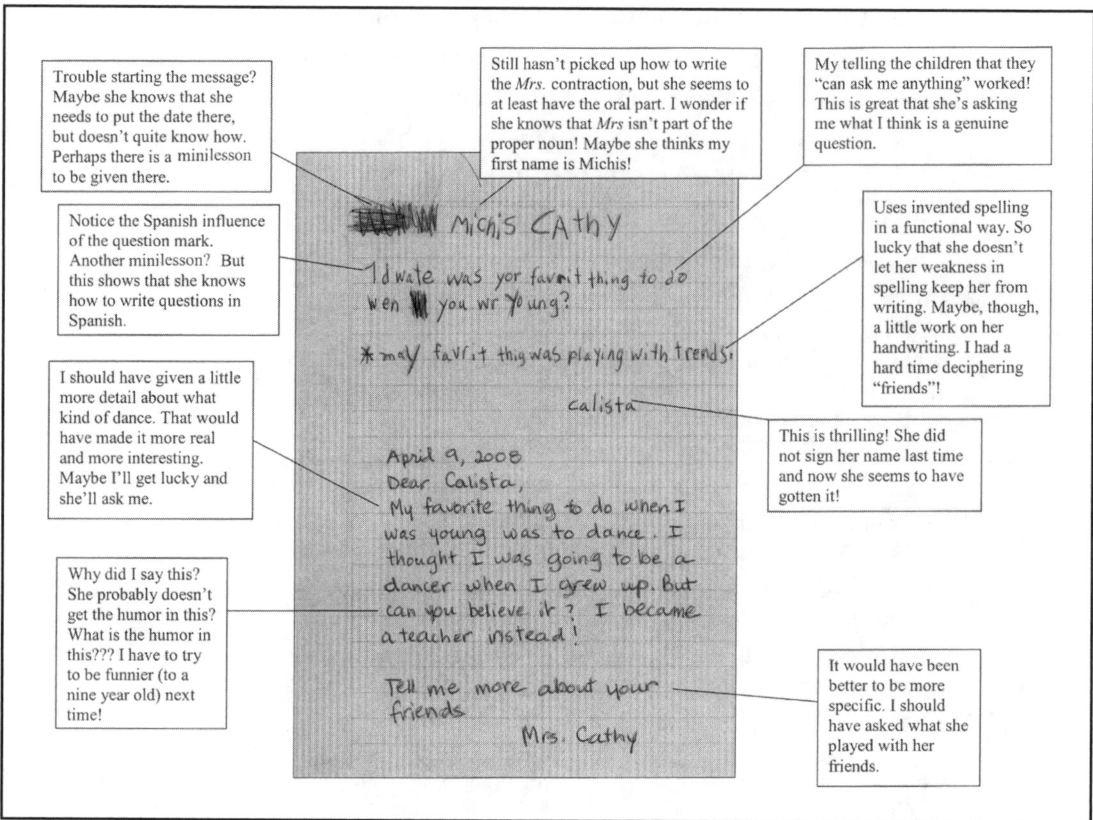

Figure 5.4 Example of Dialogue Journal Entry

writing your response. With the increasing use of automatic spell checks on computers, the information about hesitations and corrections is often lost, or sometimes one ends up with strange "corrections" that make it hard to understand the message.

Dialogue journals are not for everyone. It is difficult to get some students interested in writing to the teacher in a notebook. But when reluctant students see how thrilling it is for their classmates to read the teacher's response to their message, they are likely to become engaged. Using notebooks is more likely to produce visible enthusiasm in the classroom, as reluctant students observe others picking up their notebooks, reading, laughing as they read, and as they rush to write a response.

One last issue with dialogue journals is that sometimes students may bring up sensitive topics in their written conversations with the teacher. While this is not a likely event, it is always advisable to have thought about it and to be prepared to respond in the best way possible. Always be aware of the possibility that a student might start writing about something that is very personal and of a sensitive nature. In these cases, think carefully about the implications in each of your responses and try to stay away from issues that that are best avoided. If a student should introduce a sensitive topic and you are not sure what to do about it, consult a colleague or the social worker for advice, all the time respecting the child's confidentiality and anonymity.

Beginning Steps in Using Dialogue Journals

1. Have a stack of notebooks ready to be distributed to anyone who gets interested in keeping a dialogue journal.
2. When the opportunity arises, tell students (or a small group of them who get curious about the stack of notebooks that you keep bringing out and putting on your desk!) that you would like to have written conversations with them.
3. Explain the rules:
   a. They can write about anything they want.
   b. Whatever they or you write about remains between the two of you. If anything is shared with a third person, permission has to be granted by the person whose writing is being shared.
4. Have each student write his or her name in a notebook.
5. Collect the notebooks and write a message to each of the students.
6. Return the notebooks to their owners and invite them to write back to you.
7. Display great enthusiasm around these mysterious notebooks; more students will eventually want to join the project.

Variations on the classic model of dialogue journals

We have just described the classic model for doing dialogue journals. There are many variations on this model.

- Dyad or small-group correspondents. Instead of having the written conversation with a single student, you can invite pairs or small groups of no more than four students to be the correspondents. This model is particularly useful if you have many students who want to participate, as it will save you time. This format may also be appealing to those students who are reluctant, for whatever reason, to do journals individually.

- Learning logs. These are journals that focus on schoolwork that students are doing; they do not include personal matters. You do not need to respond to every journal entry, but it is still important for students to keep these logs on a regular basis. For these, as well as reading logs, described later, students need to see models of what these logs look like. You may want to keep a log from a past year to show students. It is also a good idea for you to keep a learning log and show students how you make entries.
- Reading logs. Students record their thoughts and reactions to books they are reading. These logs can also be a place where students record phrases or words that they find particularly interesting. You do not need to respond to these journals frequently.

Strategies for Intermediate Advanced and Advanced Supported Stages

Once students have reached a certain level of oral and written proficiency in English where they can get meaning out of written language and can convey ideas through their own writing, they can begin to develop a more critical approach to reading and they can focus on more sophisticated aspects of writing. They can pay attention to how meaning is conveyed in a text, and they can begin to develop an awareness of the nuances that different expressions convey. They can do this with both fiction and nonfiction and can then use that knowledge to fine-tune their own writing. Thus, they would be reading in order to learn about how people write and they would be using what others have written as a model for their own writing.

To help students look at text critically, we can teach them to use the characteristics or traits that define good writing as guides.

Using the Traits Model to Edit Students' Own Writing

Most writing experts agree that good writing is well organized, communicates ideas effectively, uses varied vocabulary and phrasing, carries the writer's voice, and reflects the accurate use of mechanics (Culham 2003). Many experts define these generally agreed upon characteristics of good writing as "traits." Currently, many teachers use six traits to define effective writing: ideas, organization, voice, word choice, sentence fluency, and conventions. Those who subscribe to a traits-based approach view the "conventions" trait as part of the editing process and not part of the writing process itself; that is, conventions are simply acceptable ways of presenting written text (Culham 2003, 2005; Spandel 2008, 2009). Some teachers also focus on the writer's presentation of the piece (Culham 2003, 2005). But it is important to note that the act of writing as communication involves the first five traits, and that to enhance their written communication writers learn to edit and present the piece using standard conventions. In some writing classrooms, students are led to believe that the mechanics of the piece outweigh the content and they are taught to focus on "correctness" and "accuracy." This can occur especially with ELLs and so we remind you that the emphasis in teaching reading and writing should always remain on communication over mechanical correctness, particularly during the early stages.

Several writing rubrics and descriptions of traits are available. One of the popular tools is the *6+1 Traits* model developed at the Northwest Regional Educational Laboratory (www.nwrel.org; also, see the Additional Resources section at the end of this chapter for more information on the traits model). Using traits as guides for writing is very useful for looking at a text critically because it provides students and teachers with a common language that they can use to talk about writing. ELLs of all ages can talk about their writing and the writing of others using this language. The six traits are:

- Ideas/Content. Any text must have clear content, presented through specific ideas. Without these, a text becomes meaningless. Ideas should be presented clearly and developed in a way that makes sense to the reader.

- Organization. Ideas should be presented in a sequence that is easy to follow and the writing should be organized in a way that makes sense to the reader.
- Word Choice. Words must convey ideas precisely and effectively, conveying the mood and perspective of the writer.
- Sentence Fluency. When read aloud, a text should flow smoothly. Short, artificial-sounding sentences stand in the way of comprehensibility. Sentences should also be varied.
- Voice. The personality of the text must correspond to the content.
- Conventions. Spelling, mechanics, usage, and agreement must be appropriate to the content of the text.

The additional trait is:

- Presentation. The way the text looks must be clear and the format must be regular and appropriate to the content.

Many of the resources that use the traits model for writing come with tools for teaching and rubrics for assessment. Some even have "student-friendly" rubrics that can be used by young students. However, we must make it clear that most of the rubrics that are available do not account for second-language forms or spellings. Thus, they do not account for special types of miscues made by ELLs, such as guesses they make about spelling or sentence constructions based on how things work in their home language. (See Chapter 6 for an example of how to conduct a traits assessment with ELLs.) The best way for students to use traits to edit their own writing is to go through the whole text, focusing on one trait at a time. It is suggested that conventions be left to the last, and presentation, if used at all, is left until the piece is ready for publishing.

Learning About How Other People Write

Another way to get students to make the connection between reading and writing is to get them to look critically at other people's writing, preferably authors who have written books that the students are excited about. You can use children's literature to model the traits of effective writing. As you read a book with the students, you can show examples of effective writing in that book or you can have the students discover specific aspects of a book that are good examples of various traits of good writing. This enhances the connections between reading and writing further. Many of the books presented in Additional Resources for Teachers section describe and demonstrate how to use published books to model the traits to students.

Another way of learning about how other people write can be done by hearing from published authors, preferably ones that the students know. Students need to hear from these authors as they talk about what they go through when they write as well as their reading habits. Of course, having an author come and talk to the students in person is the best option, but that is not always possible. So, the next best choice is to bring videos or audio recordings of interviews with authors. Some audio and video resources available are listed in the Additional Resources for Teachers section at the end of this chapter.

The following activities help ELLs become aware of how they, as well as others, write. The goal is to develop an awareness of the "tricks" of writing well, and, as the following section describes, to learn how to follow the criteria and the standards for good writing when students do their own writing.

Activities That Focus on the Nature of Writing

Working with Text That Others Have Written

1. Select two books on the same theme, one fiction and the other nonfiction. For example, if you have a theme like learning about Africa, pick a social studies text that gives information about Kenya and one of our pancake books—*Mama Panya's Pancakes*. What can you learn about Kenya from both books? How is that information presented in each book? What's different? What's the same?
2. Pick three or four books by the same author. How are they similar? How are they different? Is there a common pattern of writing that the author uses? Why do you think he or she uses that pattern?
3. Have students pick a favorite paragraph, section, or sentence from a book that they recently read. What makes the chosen segment interesting?

4. Engage in word study: Find interesting or highly descriptive words to use in a future composition; study figurative language; see how a particular sentence is constructed so that it flows. This advanced language study is perfect for students in later stages of English proficiency development.

Working with Text That You or the Students Have Written

1. Share with students an essay you have written. Focus their attention on a paragraph or a sentence or two that does not sound right. In small groups, let them identify what makes the excerpt weak. Let students discuss how it can be improved. Share the suggestions offered by the different groups.
2. Look at a piece of writing that the students had written in the past. Show students how far they have come. What makes the later piece better?
3. Have students choose a favorite paragraph or sentence that they have written. Why do they like it?

Using Text to Master Different Aspects of Writing

Once students have become comfortable looking at text critically, as suggested in the previous section, they can begin to focus on detailed aspects of writing. Using the traits of good writing, we can have students focus specifically on word choice in a text that they are familiar with. Let us use one of our pancake books, introduced in Chapter 2, *Pancakes, Pancakes!* by Eric Carle, as an example. Take the sentence "He gave Jack a flail and spread the wheat onto the ground" and have students in small groups discuss what the word *spread* indicates and whether it could be replaced with the word *put,* for example. Notice that we didn't choose the word *flail,* which is a word that occurs with much lower frequency. Rather, we chose a word that is more likely to be part of the students' underlying language competencies, one for which students are likely

"... research suggests that ELLs need more exposure to and instruction relevant to complex genres of literacy."

(Riches & Genesee 2006, 83)

to know possible substitutions, and one that can be used in different contexts.

Students can then examine a piece of writing that they have produced themselves and look up synonyms for words they have used. They can then decide whether a synonym might be a better choice for what they want to express, and what slight variation of meaning is conveyed by each word. Another exercise might be to have students focus on organization and rewrite the book starting from the end of the story and moving on to the beginning. The class can be divided into two groups and each can argue for one type of organization; a comparison and contrast chart can be made to illustrate the points. Through these exercises, students get a sense of what it is like to read what one writes and how to improve what we write in order for text to read better.

Summing Up

Clearly, language skills are connected with one another. Reading and writing in any language depend on having an adequate oral language base. Reading picture and chapter books to students builds their listening comprehension (receptive) and expressive language skills. Talking about books and "author's craft" creates awareness of what it is that accomplished writers do to make their writing connect better with the reader. It gives learners ideas, phrasing, and special words to use when speaking and when writing. Being in the Author's Chair and doing silent rereading helps students appreciate something they have done well and find aspects to revise to strengthen a piece of writing. The interaction among the language skills is clear—one aids and extends the other. With careful planning, you can take advantage of these interconnections and really promote the growth of literacy as well as the underlying language competencies of your ELLs.]

Additional Resources for Teachers

Books for the theme: Pancakes, Pancake Day, or Pancakes Around the World

Pancakes, Pancakes!
Written and illustrated by Eric Carle
Knopf (New York, 1970)
By cutting and grinding the wheat for flour, Jack starts from scratch to help make his breakfast pancake.

The Runaway Tortilla
by Eric A. Kimmel, Randy Cecil (Illustrator)
Winslow Press (Delray Beach, FL, 2000)
In Texas, Tia Lupe and Tio Jose make the best tortillas—so light that the cowboys say they just might jump right of the griddle. One day, a tortilla does exactly that.

Resources for the Trait Model of writing

Culham, R. 2003. *6 +1 Traits of Writing: The Complete Guide Grades 3 and Up.* New York: Scholastic.

Fletcher, R. 1996. *A Writer's Notebook: Unlocking the Writer Within You.* New York: Harper Trophy.

Fletcher, R., & J. Portalupi. 1998. *Craft Lessons: Teaching Writing K–8.* Portland, ME: Stenhouse.

———. 2001. *Writing Workshop: The Essential Guide.* Portsmouth, NH: Heinemann.

Portalupi, J., & R. Fletcher. 2001. *Nonfiction Craft Lessons: Teaching Information Writing K–8.* Portland, ME: Stenhouse.

Spandel, V. 2001. *Books, Lessons, Ideas for Teaching the Six Traits: Writing in the Elementary and Middle Grades.* Wilmington, MA: Great Source Education.

———. 2008. *Creating Young Writers: Using the Six Traits to Enrich Writing Process in Primary Classrooms,* Second Edition. Boston: Allyn & Bacon.

———. 2009. *Creating Writers Through 6-Trait Writing Assessment and Instruction,* Fifth Edition. Boston: Allyn & Bacon. (has a student checklist in Spanish in Appendix 4)

Wood Ray, K. 1999. *Wondrous Words: Writers and Writing in the Elementary Classroom.* Urbana, IL: National Council of Teachers of English.

———. 2002. *What You Know By Heart: How to Develop Curriculum for Your Writing Workshop.* Portsmouth, NH: Heinemann.

Classroom products

- Northwest Regional Educational Laboratory: www.nwrel.org/assessment
- Carson-Dellosa Publishing Company: www.carsondellosa.com
- Culham, R. 2004. *Using Picture Books to Teach Writing with the Traits.* New York: Scholastic. ISBN 0-439-55687-2
- Culham, R., & A. Wheeler. 2003. *40 Reproducible Forms for the Writing Traits Classroom.* New York: Scholastic. ISBN 0-439-55684-8

Websites

- National Staff Development Council: www.nsdc.org/midbook/trait.pdf
- Norwest Regional Education Laboratory: www.nwrel.org/assessment; www.nwrel.org/assessment/scoring.php
- Madison Metropolitan School District: www.madison.k12.wi.us/tnl/langarts/
- Wired Instructor: www.wiredinstructor.net/TraitsLinks.html
- 6 Traits Resources on Teachers.net: http://teachers.net/gazette/FEB03/hoover.html

Resources for authors talking about their writing

- Carter, J. 1999. *Talking Books Children's Authors Talk About the Craft, Creativity and Process of Writing.* Milton Park, UK: Routledge. This product comes in both a paper and electronic format and can be ordered through any of the book distributors on the web. ISBN: 978-0-415-19417-4 (paperback); 978-0-415-19416-7 (hardback); 978-0-203-02517-8 (electronic).
- www.learnoutloud.com/Podcast-Directory/Literature/Authors-Reading: This website offers podcasts of authors talking about their work.
- www.readingrockets.org: Often features special events that include interviews with children's authors. Another wonderful feature of the Reading Rockets website is the Books and Authors section.
- Also check this website: http://thejoyofchildrensliterature.blogspot.com/2008/03/new-features-from-reading-rockets.html. You can also find a Spanish version of the website at www.colorincolorado.org

CHAPTER

6

Assessment

What is assessment? *186*

Classroom assessment and ELLs *194*

Assessment tools *219*

Summing up *220*

Additional resources for teachers *221*

THERE IS GENERAL AGREEMENT THAT ASSESSMENT IS CRITICAL FOR EFFECTIVE INSTRUCTION. CLASSROOM TEACHERS ENGAGE IN ASSESSMENT ALL THE TIME AS THEY GO ABOUT THEIR DAY-TO-DAY BUSINESS OF TEACHING. A LOT OF TEACHER ASSESSMENT IS NOT OBVIOUS, EVEN TO TEACHERS, BECAUSE IT IS INFORMAL, AND IT IS SELDOM GIVEN AS MUCH CREDIT AS IT DESERVES.

District- and state-mandated tests are often the only forms of assessment that are fully valued. And yet, it is teachers' day-to-day informal assessments that play the biggest and most important role in student learning—for example, when teachers assess whether students are on track with group work that has been assigned, to determine whether Antonio and Jennifer are paying attention during "circle time," to be sure that Maria understands what she is supposed to do during the visit to the school library, to determine if Miguel and Machid understand the story that the class is studying together, and to see if the new student in the class is fitting in with the others. These kinds of assessment, and other forms of teacher assessment, are so important because they shape classroom decisions—about what to teach, how to teach it, and when to teach certain topics. Teacher assessments make it possible to individualize instruction—a critical feature of effective teaching for ELLs. Every decision you make in class every day is based on your assessment of what is most appropriate at that time given what you know about your students and what you think you need to do to advance their learning. In this chapter, we want to hone your assessment skills to ensure that they are as sensitive and useful as possible for teaching literacy to your ELL students.

Research Finding

Many studies have pointed out the benefits of using student achievement data to shape and/or monitor program effectiveness (August & Hakuta 1997, Berman et al. 1995, Slavin & Calderón 2001).

What Is Assessment?

This might seem like a trivial question because, as we just said, teachers are assessing all the time. However, a great deal of classroom assessment is done without conscious awareness and without explicit planning. Moreover, the results of your assessments are often not recognized outside the classroom. For classroom-based assessment to be maximally effective and appropriate, you should be consciously aware of what assessment in the classroom entails and, in particular, the goals of your assessment. Assessment, in fact, is not one thing. It is not just about whether students get the right answer, understand the story, or are paying attention to your instructions. It is also about what you do in response to the results of your assessments. In fact, useful assessment is a cycle of activities that provides you with information that you can use to plan instruction. In this sense, it is as much about you the teacher as it is about your students. It is useful to think of assessment as a cycle of activities, as depicted in Figure 6.1.

To better understand the cycle of classroom assessment, refer back to the literacy development framework we proposed in Chapter 1 (see Chart 1.1). Such a framework is useful in helping you decide the level or stage of literacy development of your ELLs. In other words, you can devise assessment activities and interpret the results from those activities with reference to the descriptors contained in the framework. Our framework describes milestones that students go through as they learn to read and write in English, from the earliest emergent literacy stage (*beginning*) to an advanced level (*advanced supported*). This framework could apply to native English-speaking students, in which case the stages would align roughly with different grade levels, from kindergarten to grade five or six. However, it does not necessarily align with grade level when applied to ELLs for two reasons: (1) ELLs can begin their education in English in any grade, from kindergarten to grade six; and (2) when they begin schooling in English, they speak another language as a native language and they have different levels of

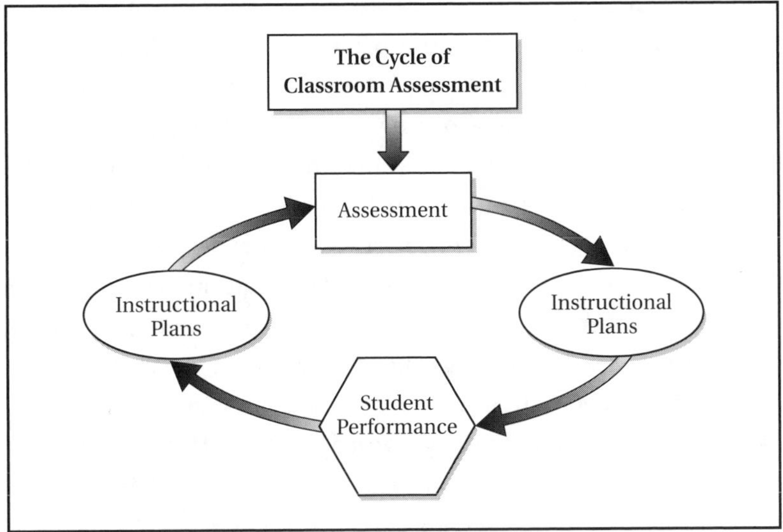

Figure 6.1 Cycle of Classroom Assessment

exposure to and competence in their native language as well as English, from none to lots. This means that the *beginning* stage described in Chart 1.1 could be equally appropriate for an ELL who begins schooling in English in kindergarten or an ELL who begins schooling in English in grade five or six. However, the goals and learning needs of a beginning-level ELL in kindergarten versus grade three would be quite different because the level and kinds of language competence as well as the literacy and academic objectives for these students are very different.

Remember, we included a framework in Chart 1.1 on pages 24–25 to illustrate the kinds of stages or benchmarks for literacy development that have been devised by school districts, and states, in some cases. They are intended as guides to developing curriculum and instruction. You should familiarize yourself with the ESL framework in your school or district.

What is important about the cycle of classroom assessment is the idea that assessment provides information that is critical for devising instructional plans, including literacy objectives for the class as a whole and for individual ELLs. Your plans also include activities that will promote literacy development. Assessment during specific instructional activities or units of instruction provides information as to whether your activities are working as you intended (e.g., Do students understand the activity? Are they engaged?) and that students are learning content, language, and literacy objectives as you intended.

Observing students during planned activities is the primary and most powerful means of assessment. It is important that you observe individual students—especially your ELLs, and not just the whole class—to see if the activities are working for them as you want. It is also important that you learn to distinguish to what extent students are acquiring the content objectives independently of language and literacy objectives when you assess ELLs' acquisition of content, or vice versa; otherwise your assessment of content learning will also be an assessment of ELLs' language and literacy skills. If you want to focus on what content objectives they have learned, it is important to devise assessments that reduce the language load for ELLs. Here are some suggestions for assessment that can help you distinguish between acquisition of language/literacy and content objectives:

- ❑ When assessing language or literacy skills, be sure to use content that is familiar to students and is within their range of cognitive development; using content that is unfamiliar or too complex will give you an underestimation of their language and literacy skills.
- ❑ When assessing language and reading skills, if ELLs are having difficulty expressing themselves, assess their comprehension skills by using closed-ended or limited-response formats that make minimal demands on their expressive skills. This will permit you to see if their difficulty is primarily an expressive problem or if it is also a comprehension problem. For example, after students have read a sentence or short paragraph, show them pictures of alternative answers to questions pertaining to what they have just read and ask them to select the one they think is best; or let them draw, demonstrate, or act out their responses. These kinds of response formats can indicate if students understand what they have read even though they can not express their understandings orally or in writing.
- ❑ When assessing content knowledge, be sure the oral or written language you use in your assessment is appropriate for the students' level of English language proficiency; otherwise you will be assessing their language and literacy skills as well as their content knowledge.
- ❑ When assessing content knowledge, if ELLs have difficulty expressing what they know using English, use close-ended or limited-response formats that do not call for productive language skills; for example, and as above, provide pictorial or oral alternative answers that they can choose from, or let them draw, demonstrate, or act out their responses. These kinds of responses indicate what content skills or knowledge ELLs have learned without calling for extensive oral or written productive language skills they do not have.
- ❑ You can also ask students to respond in the native language and ask a speaker of that language to translate for you to see if they have learned the content and simply cannot express themselves well in English.

If your observations during literacy instruction indicate that the activities are not working as you had intended, you need to modify them so that they work as you want. Modifications may be needed for the whole class or just for individual students. The modifications may need to focus on the language, literacy, or content objectives, or some combination of these.

As you approach the end of a unit, assessment is critical for determining if the unit had its desired effects—are your ELL students advancing in their literacy skills in the ways that you want? ELL students may be following the same unit of instruction and be involved in the same instructional activities as the whole class, but they can have different, individualized learning objectives; for example, they are learning new vocabulary or grammatical forms in English that native speakers can be assumed to know. Thus, it is important that assessment is individualized. If you are not satisfied that individual students have progressed with respect to specific literacy objectives as a result of instruction as you had wanted, then you may decide to individualize instruction further for those students or to reinforce the same objectives again in the next unit. The process is cyclical because assessment of student growth as a result of your initial instructional plans starts the whole cycle over again.

Classroom Versus High-Stakes Assessment

NOTE TO ADMINISTRATORS

To get a complete and valid picture of your ELL students, it is critical that you not rely solely on results of standardized tests since such tests give an incomplete view of what they know and can do, and moreover, they fail to provide important background information that can be obtained from other sources (current teachers' assessments, previous school records and teachers, interviews with parents). Classroom teachers are a valuable source of information about ELLs since they observe them in class and, thus, can provide information that is simply not available from standardized tests. This kind of information is useful for placement, planning instruction, and promotion.

Before we get into detail about classroom assessment, it is important that we talk about high-stakes mandatory testing and whether the latter is useful for instructional planning in your classroom. Some school districts, states (or provinces), and even national governments in some places require that all students be administered specific tests in certain subjects (such as language arts and mathematics) at certain grades and at virtually the same time of the school year. These are called high-stakes tests because the results are used to make important decisions about students, such as promotion to the next grade, retention in the current grade, or referral to special services. In some districts, the results of these tests are also used to decertify teachers and/or take control of schools if student performance consistently falls below some specified level.

Such high-stakes tests are not very useful for planning instruction for ELLs for a number of reasons. Most important, high-stakes tests take a one-size-fits-all approach. They treat all students as if they have the same language, educational, cultural, and social backgrounds.

Important differences among ELLs and between ELL and mainstream students are ignored by high-stakes tests. ELLs are different from one another and from most mainstream students because: They join your class with different levels of exposure to and competence in English; they have had different levels and quality of prior education; they can begin their education in English at any grade level;

and because they have varied cultural backgrounds. ELLs are not included in the standardization groups that are used to devise high-stakes tests, and, thus, all of this variation is ignored. As a result, their results on high-stakes tests can make them look deficient even though they are not, because the test does not consider their backgrounds and the skills they bring to the test.

> "High-stakes tests as currently constructed are inappropriate for ELLs, and most disturbing is their continued use for high-stakes decisions that have adverse consequences."
>
> (Solórzano 2008, 260)

As well, high-stakes tests are not sensitive to the curriculum and instructional goals that are the focus of your attention. Again, the reason for this is that high-stakes tests take a one-size-fits-all approach—this time with respect to curriculum. They assume that all students are following essentially the same curriculum at each grade level and, as a result, that all students will achieve the same learning outcomes at the same time. The specific curriculum and instructional goals that guide your instruction are not reflected in the content of high-stakes tests, and, certainly, high-stakes tests that must be administered according to a mandatory schedule do not reflect the pacing or sequencing of your instruction. In short, the performance of ELLs on high-stakes tests cannot indicate whether your instructional plans for them are working because your plans for them differ from the one-size-fits-all curriculum that underlies the tests.

High-stakes tests make it impossible for classroom teachers to control their own instruction and, in particular, they make it especially difficult to individualize instruction for students who do not match the one-size-fits-all student profile. In fact, another pernicious and damaging side effect of high-stakes testing is that they diminish and devalue the role of teachers in student assessment and give teachers the impression that classroom assessment is unimportant and inconsequential. This is a formula for academic failure, not success, as was found by Solórzano (2008). For instruction to be effective for all students, including ELLs, you need to use classroom assessment to guide instruction. It is important that you are skilled, confident, and actively engaged in assessing the performance of your students in the

Research Finding

Assessment data are most effective in improving programs when schools use assessment measures that are aligned with the school's vision and goals, the curriculum, and district and state standards (Montecel & Cortez 2002).

NOTE TO ADMINISTRATORS

The results of classroom assessments of the type we discuss in this chapter can also be used to supplement standardized test results if a few extra steps are taken: (a) Be systematic and keep records whenever collecting information about student performance when using any of the procedures described in this chapter; (b) be sure to include all students; and (c) quantify results when possible—for example, running record reports can be quantified according to how error-free student performance is.

classroom as they learn with you. The remainder of this chapter is intended to help you do that.

As you will see in the following sections of this chapter, classroom assessment is primarily concerned with collecting information that allows you to plan differentiated instruction. This is the chief difference between classroom and high-stakes assessment. Classroom assessment can be thought of as a triangle (see Figure 6.2). At the base are assessment activities that tell you what individual ELL students know and can do with reference to your framework for literacy development. Your assessment activities should also include collecting background and personal information about each student (such as interests, hobbies, and prior schooling experiences) that you can use to devise instruction. This information can be obtained from talking with the students, interviewing their parents, or discussing them with former teachers in some cases. The apex of the classroom assessment triangle represents the instructional decisions and plans that you devise using assessment information that you gather. Your instructional plans should be aligned with your school's literacy framework, taking into account what your ELLs can already do and what they already know.

In contrast, high-stakes testing is like a one-way street with the outcome being a simple judgment of whether ELLs measure up to some arbitrary standard without consideration of individual differences in background or instructional objectives for literacy development.

Nevertheless, sometimes it is necessary to assess ELLs using standardized tests. Most experts agree that if the focus of the test is to assess students' knowledge of academic content (such as science or mathematics), then it is important to make accommodations to ensure that ELLs demonstrate what they know and can do in the content areas in ways that are not masked by their developing language and lit-

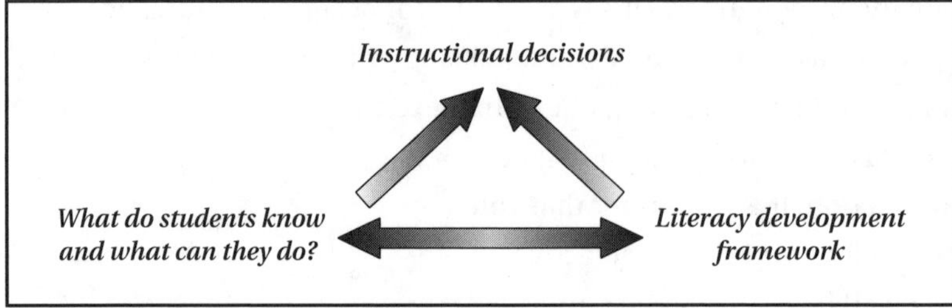

Figure 6.2 The Classroom Assessment Triangle

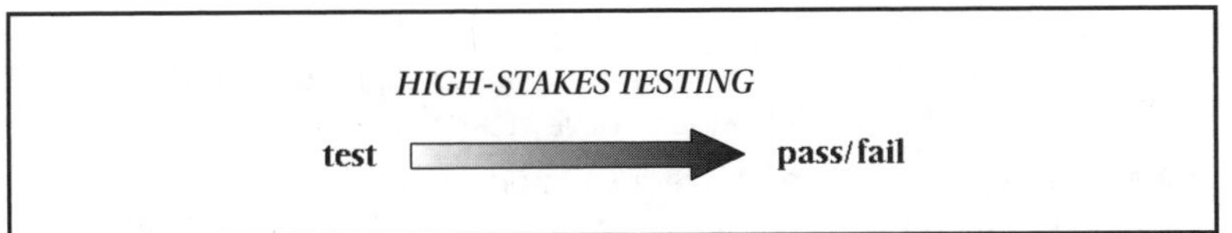

Figure 6.3 High-Stakes Testing Assessment

eracy abilities in English. As we noted before, for ELLs, a test of academic knowledge is also a test of English. Thus, it may be necessary to reduce the influence of language and literacy skills when assessing ELLs' content knowledge; this is especially true for beginning-level ELLs. Otherwise, you risk getting invalid and unreliable indicators of what ELLs have actually learned in the content areas.

"Appropriate accommodations enable English learners to show what they know and can do on content tests administered in English (e.g., a math test) by reducing the interference of English language demands on the test."

(Wolf et al. 2008, 6)

Wolf et al. (2008), following a review of research on assessment for ELLs, reported that "direct linguistic support is crucial for ELL students" in order to ensure accurate assessment of what they know and can do in the content areas. This means that the language of the test should be adjusted so that it does not interfere with ELLs' expression of what they know. Short (2007) provides a comprehensive list of the kinds of accommodations to consider—see below. Research indicates further that, to be effective, accommodations should correspond to ELLs' individual learning needs and profiles, such as their level of proficiency in English, their prior schooling, and the proximity of their home culture to the mainstream culture of the school (Kopriva, Emick, Hipolito-Delgado, & Cameron 2007).

Research Question

To assess what your ELL students have learned following a social studies lesson or unit, try assessing some ELLs using the same procedure you would use with native speakers of English and assess some ELLs using an adapted version of the native-speaker test in which you simplify the language of the test and you allow the ELL students to respond using alternative methods (e.g., in the native language, drawing, pointing to pictures). See if student performance in response to these different procedures differs. Which procedure results in more responding and which produces more evidence of learning?

SUGGESTIONS FOR ASSESSMENT ACCOMMODATIONS FOR ELLS (FROM SHORT 2007)

Guidelines for Language Simplification

Replace low-frequency words with common words.

Replace culturally biased words and contexts with culturally neutral words.

Use familiar (universal) contexts and settings.

Research Question

Research indicates that accommodations for ELLs during subject matter testing are most effective when they are tailored according to individual learner profiles, taking into account factors such as the student's level of proficiency in English, prior schooling, and proximity of the home culture to mainstream culture. To examine which language accommodations are most effective for ELLs who differ with respect to proficiency in English, try using simplified instructions in English and the kinds of instructions you would use with native speaker to see which ones allow ELLs to perform optimally; remember, these kinds of accommodations are appropriate when assessing ELLs' content-based skills and knowledge.

Repeat nouns. Avoid indefinite pronouns (e.g., *some, any*) and synonyms. Check that all pronouns have clear antecedents.

Make presentation more concrete and personal.

Remove unnecessary expository material.

Replace conditional clauses with separate sentences.

Replace verbs in the passive voice with verbs in the active voice.

Reduce the number of words in a sentence or separate long sentences into shorter ones.

Use bulleted lists instead of paragraphs wherever possible.

Reduce number of modifiers in a noun phrase.

Replace complex question phrases with simple question words.

Remove or recast relative clauses.

Rephrase negatives in a positive form.

Rephrase sentences that can confuse the order of math operations to eliminate reversal errors.

Other Accommodations to Make Assessments More Comprehensible for ELLs

Use graphic organizers.

Provide on-page glosses or a glossary (English or key terms in the text).

Break tasks into smaller steps.

Provide graphic organizers or note-taking sheets.

Change the task product to suit the language proficiency level but still meet standards.

Illustrate with visuals and other graphics.

Include more white space on the page and use larger font size.

Include a checklist of items to be included in the response to the task prompt, in the written response portion of the project, or in the oral presentation.

Classroom Assessment and ELLs

In this section, we talk about best practices when it comes to assessment of ELLs and their literacy development. Classroom assessment for ELLs as well as for mainstream students can serve multiple purposes, as summarized in Chart 6.1.

Purposes of Classroom Assessment

(a) To devise an initial individualized literacy plan for a student based on what he or she already knows and can do relative to your literacy development goals.

(b) To monitor student progress following reading and writing instruction in order to plan follow-up instruction.

(c) To plan reading and writing instruction that reflects students' individual learning styles; their preferred learning strategies, interests, attitudes, and motivations; and background factors that might influence their acquisition of reading and writing skills.

(d) To engage students in self-assessment so that they can take an active role in planning their own literacy development.

(e) To demonstrate to parents and other educators what students can do and that they are on track in learning to read and write.

Chart 6.1 Purposes of Classroom Assessment

Assessment of ELLs is different from that for mainstream students:

1. Assessment of ELLs must distinguish between students' proficiency in language and literacy and their achievement in the content areas.
2. Assessment of ELLs must monitor students' proficiency in language and literacy for both academic and social purposes since ELLs may need support learning language and literacy for both whereas native English-speaking students have acquired language and literacy skills for social purposes.
3. Assessment of ELLs must also assess students' sociocultural competence with respect to both language and literacy.
4. Assessment must be culturally appropriate for individual ELLs.

The following observation by Martha Crago during a study of language development in Inuit children in Northern Quebec provides a dramatic example of how different mainstream teachers' cultural expectations of students can be from those of parents of minority language children:

CULTURAL MISMATCHES: AN INUIT EXAMPLE FROM QUEBEC (FROM CRAGO 1988, 12)

An Anglo-Canadian teacher's report about an Inuit child:

"Does not talk in class."

An Inuit parent's reaction:

"These Qallunaat (non-Inuit) teachers never seem to learn that well-raised Inuit children never talk in class. They learn by looking and listening."

Cloud, Genesee, and Hamayan (2000, 145) have identified the following culture-specific factors to consider when assessing ELLs:

CULTURE-SPECIFIC FACTORS	IMPLICATIONS FOR ASSESSMENT
• **Wait time**. Some second-language learners and students from some cultural groups require longer wait times than many native English-speaking students from majority-group backgrounds.	Give ELLs more time to respond than you would other students.
• **Individual or group response**. Students from some cultural backgrounds prefer to respond to teachers' questions or calls for displays of knowledge as part of a group; they are uncomfortable responding as individuals because it sets them apart from their peers. Some students also prefer to work with their fellow students to formulate a response to teachers' questions. This is frowned on by Anglo-American culture, which highly values individual displays of competence but is not valued by other cultural groups.	Do not assume that an ELL student who does not jump up to respond to questions put to the whole class does not know the correct answer. Give ELLs plenty of opportunity to show what they know—for example, let them work with a small group to formulate their answers.
• **Feedback**. Whereas many students from the majority English-speaking group like to receive individual and public praise from the teacher, students from some groups may be deeply embarrassed by such praise; they do not expect public or explicit praise from the teacher.	If you feel that an ELL is not comfortable with public praise, make sure to praise him or her privately and to praise his or her parents for the work their child has done.
• **Eye contact**. In contrast to students from the dominant Anglo-American culture who are taught to look directly at adults when being spoken to, children from many cultures are taught that direct eye contact with adults is inappropriate and is a sign of impertinence.	Do not expect all ELLs to look you in the eye when you address them. If you are giving directions using gestures, draw students' attention to what you are showing them so that they do not miss important information.

continued

CULTURE-SPECIFIC FACTORS	IMPLICATIONS FOR ASSESSMENT
• **Guessing**. Some students will not give the answer to a question unless they are certain that they are accurate; language-majority students are generally comfortable with guessing.	Teach ELLs the strategies involved in guessing and let them know that they can use them to their advantage.
• **Question-and-answer format**. Many students may not have had prior experience with the question-and-answer format you are using; for example, do they understand what to do with multiple-choice questions that are presented with blank bubbles?	Spend time explaining, in language that ELLs can understand, the formats that you are using in your tests. Give students opportunity to practice.
• **Volunteering**. Students from many cultural groups are uncomfortable showing what they know by volunteering a response or initiating interaction with the teacher–they believe that it is appropriate to respond only when called up on to do so.	Use choral or group responding to circumvent this preference.

The most effective classroom assessments are highly individualized—what you assess, how you assess, and when you assess depends on each learner. Therefore, we have organized this chapter around a number of case studies: an ELL student in grade one (José); one in grade four (Ludmila); and one in grade seven (Ping), with different kinds of educational and personal backgrounds. We devote two cases to Spanish-speaking ELL students because the vast majority of ELLs in the United States are of Hispanic backgrounds. But, it is important to remember that there are students from many other ethnolinguistic groups among this population. Therefore, our last case, Ping, is a grade seven student who speaks Chinese (Mandarin), but she could just as easily have been Russian, Haitian, or Pakistani.

We recommend that you read all of these case studies even if they are not at your grade level because there is something to learn from each one. Moreover, even a case about a student in the primary grades is relevant to upper elementary and middle school teachers because ELL students entering those grades may be at only the beginning level of literacy development, much like many primary school ELLs.

Mrs. Oliver and José

Mrs. Oliver has been teaching grade one in the same urban school in a district located in the southwestern United States for fifteen years. It is the start of a new year and Mrs. Oliver is meeting her students for the first week of school, a very important week since this is when she needs to finalize her curriculum and start to devise individualized instructional plans for her students. In the past, the majority of students in her class were monolingual English-speaking. In the last ten years, she has noticed that there are more students each year who speak a language other than English at home—often Spanish. Some of them know quite a bit of English when they join her class, and some seem to know very little at all. She has also noticed that some have been exposed to lots of reading and writing at home, and others have not had many opportunities to engage in reading and writing activities in either English or the home language.

José is a new student in Mrs. Oliver's class. All new students are seen by intake personnel in the district who collect basic information about new students, including information about their previous schooling, when available. Mrs. Oliver has checked the intake form for José. The record indicates that he was born in the southwestern United States and that he has two sisters, one who is older than him and one who is younger. José lives with both parents, both of whom have a college education from Mexico. The primary language used in the home is Spanish, although José's *parents report that they both speak some English. When she met with the parents, Mrs. Oliver learned that both parents are highly literate and they engage in many reading and writing activities as a family at home. These experiences are usually in Spanish because they want José to maintain his Spanish, both because they see it as a long-term occupational advantage and in case he visits relatives in Mexico.*

This case illustrates a critical purpose of classroom assessment: *to determine what individual ELLs know and can do in literacy when they join your classroom* (see Chart 6.1 on page 195 for a complete list of the important goals of classroom assessment.). This information is important so you can plan an individualized program of literacy instruction for each ELL when he or she joins your class. Let's take a closer look at what such an initial assessment might look like in the case of Mrs. Oliver and José.

Mrs. Oliver wants to know which of the beginning-level competencies José has already acquired (see Chart 1.1 in Chapter 1). She focuses on beginning-level literacy skills because José would be expected to be at this level. She sets aside a thirty-minute slot during the second week of class when she can sit down with José to assess how advanced he is with respect to beginning-level literacy skills. Mrs. Oliver sometimes meets with two or three new students at one time because she has discovered that many students, especially those who have just arrived, are more comfortable and engaged if they are with other students rather than being alone with her. In contrast, some students are outgoing and highly engaged in one-on-one interactions with her.

During her conference with José, Mrs. Oliver lays out a number of books that he can choose from; some are in English and some are in Spanish and some include only pictures, while others include pictures and written language. As José makes his choice, Mrs. Oliver observes whether he flips through the books from front to back, whether he looks carefully at the pictures before making his choice, whether he is enthusiastic or reluctant as he makes his choice, and so on. This is all important information for Mrs. Oliver because it indicates to her how knowledgeable José is about print and books and his confidence as a beginning reader.

Before her individual session with José, Mrs. Oliver observed that he had some conversational skills in English since he was able to play and get along with other students well, although he was somewhat shy. This impression is reinforced when she meets with him—he responds appropriately to her "Hello" and "How are you?", although he provides limited responses to her other questions about how he is feeling. Mrs. Oliver knows that this is quite typical of Hispanic children who tend to be less assertive as a sign of respect in their conversations with adults than many mainstream American children. She also notes that he avoids direct eye contact with her and speaks only when spoken to.

Mrs. Oliver wants to observe the full range of José's English skills—she has seen he can use English with his peers, but can he use English in more "academic" ways? When she first started teaching ELLs, she often mistook their fluent conversational skills with other students as evidence that ELLs could manage curriculum instruction easily. However, she found that many ELLs could converse in English quite well but had difficulty when she expected them to talk in complex and precise ways about school topics. They often lacked depth and breadth in their vocabulary in English and had difficulty expressing complex thoughts. To assess José's English skills more closely, therefore, she asks him to choose one of the wordless picture books and to tell her the story in the book. She offers him books with different themes, some of which depict culturally diverse children and situations as well as typical mainstream scenarios, so he can choose one that is of interest to him. José chooses a wordless book about a birthday party. She listens patiently as he "talks his way through the book."

As José tells his "story," Mrs. Oliver makes lots of mental notes about what he says—for example, does he have the words and grammar skills to describe the characters and objects depicted in the book; does he describe how the characters relate to one another; does he sequence the events in the story using temporal connectives (*then, after, now*); what kinds of connectives does he use; and does his story have a beginning and an end. When he is finished, she asks him questions to see if he can relate the characters or events in the story to his own life ("Can you tell me what you do when you have a birthday party?"); if he can infer why the characters are doing what they are doing (e.g., "Why did the mother hide the candy?"; whether his interpretations and inferences are different from mainstream students and if these interpretations help explain his other reading and writing behaviors; and what the consequences of their actions are ("What do you think will happen when José finds the candy?"). If he doesn't answer a question or answers reluctantly, she tells him he can use Spanish because even though she does not understand Spanish very well, she can guess from how long and fluent his answers in Spanish are how much he seems to understand. She knows also that she could call on a Spanish-English bilingual student from her class to help her interpret what he is saying. Allowing José to use Spanish also gives her an opportunity to see how talkative he can be in a language that he knows well, and this gives José a chance to show that he knows Spanish well so he can feel proud of knowing another language. When he does not respond to a specific question or gives a very limited response, she asks him "yes-no questions" to test if he understands and is shy or simply has trouble giving complex verbal answers, for example "Is the mother hiding the candy because she is mean?"

Even though Mrs. Oliver has not asked José to actually read or write anything, her conference with him reveals a lot about his underlying language competencies. These are important in learning to read and write because the storybooks, social studies texts, and other written materials that José will be working with in school all call on these kind of language competencies: labeling, sequencing, understanding cause-effect relationships, inferring consequences, predicting, and so on. Children who can produce or comprehend complex language of this sort have acquired important building blocks of literacy; children who have not acquired these kinds of language skills need enrichment so that they can acquire them. All children need these kinds of language abilities to advance in literacy beyond simply decoding and writing single words. Many students, mainstream and ELL alike, may not have had the chance to acquire these skills prior to beginning schooling, and it is the responsibility of classroom teachers to help students who have not acquired skills to acquire them. This is such an important responsibility that all teachers, including classroom teachers, must share in making this happen. As a classroom teacher, you also have the important responsibility to ensure that ELLs have the background and sociocultural knowledge they need to acquire literacy skills in English.

Mrs. Oliver goes one step further and asks José to choose one of the books with words in it and to read it to her. As he does, she keeps a running record of what he does (see guidelines on pages 202–3). Finally, when their session is almost finished, Mrs. Oliver asks José to do one more thing for her: to take the wordless book he chose to read and to write her a story about it once he gets back to his desk. She tells him he can use pictures or words to tell his story, and he can use Spanish words or English words if he wants. By examining what José can write using any and all resources, Mrs. Oliver is able to assess José's ability to handle pencil and paper, his penmanship, his emergent spelling skills, the range of his vocabulary, his ability to sequence events (either in words or pictures), his knowledge of how English works, and so on. She plans to schedule time for a writing conference with José the following week.

Research Question

To see if the reading material you select to assess students' reading makes a difference, do a running record using different book selections—use a book that you choose with some ELLs and a book that they choose with others. See if the students' reading behavior changes with these two different books. Focus especially on their level of engagement, their self-corrections, and their comprehension.

Running Records

WHY?

(a) To determine a student's instructional reading level.

(b) To monitor ongoing student progress in reading.

(c) To find out which particular skills and strategies students are using to read.

(d) To establish specific needs of individual students.

(e) To group together students with similar needs.

(f) To choose books at an appropriate level for students.

TIPS:

(a) This method is most useful with ELLs at the *beginning intermediate* level of reading proficiency.

(b) The first time you do a running record, familiarize students with the procedure by giving them a book to read that you are sure they can read and enjoy.

(c) As the student reads, mark each word he/she reads with a checkmark and, if any words are omitted, inserted, mispronounced, or substituted, make a note of this. If the student hesitates or repeats a word, part of a word, or a phrase, mark this as well.

(d) Avoid giving corrections or evaluative comments so that the student does not feel like this is a test.

(e) Do not intervene except to help the student with problem words or pronunciations; this should not be instructional—that comes later.

(f) Before helping students with words they cannot read, give them plenty of wait time to try to figure it out themselves.

(g) Be sure to use a recording form to record your observations as the student is reading.

(h) Use either a blank record or, preferably, a formatted record with rubrics of skills and behaviors you want to observe (self-corrections, semantic errors, phonological errors, etc.). Always note whether "the error" contributes to a change in meaning that would affect comprehension.

(i) Include a symbol that denotes influences from the home language so that you can see if there is a pattern of transfer from that language to English.

Mrs. Oliver scheduled reading and writing conferences with José during the first two weeks of school so she could devise an individualized literacy plan for him. Later on, she and José can continue their conversation using a dialogue journal or learning log. In a learning log, José can let Mrs. Oliver know how he is doing in school, what he likes, what he has learned, and so on (see the following guidelines for more details about dialogue journals and learning logs).

Guidelines for Dialogue Journals

WHY?

a. To assess vocabulary skills—range of vocabulary and spelling skills when writing about personal topics.

b. To assess grammar skills—use of varied sentence types and complex grammar to write about personal and social topics in interesting and focused ways.

c. To assess organization skills when writing—is information presented in a logical sequence; is there a sense of purpose; is there a personal voice?

d. To assess the range of topics and subjects students can write about.

e. To identify students' interests, likes and dislikes in general.

f. To learn more about students' backgrounds with a view to using this information in individualized literacy plans.

TIPS:

a. Most useful for students who are at least at the *beginning intermediate* level of proficiency in English.

b. Have students write in journals and collect them on a regular and relatively frequent basis so you can monitor progress regularly.

c. Avoid direct critical correction; make notes of what students do well and have difficulty with in a separate notebook for your own reference purposes.

d. Devise a checklist of specific aspects of writing to monitor: vocabulary, grammar, organization; mechanical skills (spelling, punctuation, paragraphing, use of quotations) and of specific features of each (e.g., vocabulary: range of vocabulary; appropriate use of specific words; use of less frequent words); you can use a proficiency framework like the one we presented in Chapter 1.

e. When students make mistakes or their usage is not native-like try to figure out if the student has transferred knowledge from the home language—this would be an indication that the student understands what he or she is doing but has not learned the correct English form.

f. Note common patterns of errors that occur in more than one student's writing and devise minilessons focusing on those patterns.

g. Note improvements in problem areas over time; in particular, note if students incorporate correct usage of aspects of English that you have focused on in class or in minilessons.

Dialogue journals and learning logs are useful assessment tools for a number of reasons: (1) They give ELLs the opportunity to practice their language skills in a safe environment, and teachers can use students' entries to monitor their linguistic strengths and weaknesses; (2) they allow students to let the teacher know what interests them and what they enjoy doing; and (3) students can identify learning obstacles or challenges. All of this information can be useful to a teacher for instructional planning. If students agree, a learning log or journal can also be used to show José's parents what he can do and how he has progressed. Dialogue journals and learning logs can even be done using audio recordings to monitor students' progress in oral language and literacy development.

You can see from this case study that assessing literacy skills, especially for devising initial literacy plans for a student, involves looking at more than just reading and writing as we traditionally think of

Guidelines for Learning Logs

WHY?

a. To assess how well students can write about academic content.

b. To assess use of academic language, especially written forms of academic language.

c. To determine if ELLs understand complex academic language in their textbooks and other instructional materials.

d. To identify self-identified areas of student success and difficulty so that you can reinforce successes and support student development in areas of difficulty.

e. To better understand students' goals, likes, and dislikes with a view to designing instructional activities that reflect individual student profiles.

f. To give students opportunities to use English for personally relevant purposes—to communicate about their own school experiences.

g. To encourage student self-assessment.

h. To collect samples of student writing for assessment purposes.

i. To monitor progress in writing over time.

TIPS

a. Most useful when ELLs are at least at the *beginning intermediate* level of proficiency in English.

b. Keep running notes of information about students' self-identified successes, difficulties, etc., in a separate notebook so that you can monitor progress over time.

c. Devise a checklist of specific aspects of English writing to be assessed: vocabulary, grammar, organization, mechanical skills, etc.

d. Keep in mind that while your long-term objective is for ELLs to attain the same literacy objectives as mainstream students, short-term objectives for ELLs should be adjusted to reflect their individual learning profiles.

e. Let students use the home language, if possible, so that you can figure out what kinds of writing skills they might have in the home language.

them. It involves collecting information about a host of skills—some involve written language directly, such as word-decoding skills or the ability to understand written text—but many are related to literacy indirectly. We have called these abilities underlying language competencies because they are not specific to written language. These competencies include children's knowledge of the structure of stories, their comprehension of complex grammar to describe events in time or cause-effect relationships, and their knowledge of how words are interrelated—you can add the sound / *-ly*/ to the end of a noun to turn it into an adjective: *friend* → *friendly*. Learning to read and write successfully is also critically dependent on students' interest or enthusiasm about reading and writing, their confidence as readers and writers, and their access to or experiences with written language outside school. In other words, learning to read and write is not only about cognitive skills. All of these factors should be addressed in a comprehensive plan of instruction and all have to be assessed.

Of course, the specific skills and knowledge that are important for assessing individual children are guided by the framework for literacy development that your school adheres to. We presented one such framework in Chapter 1 and use it here to illustrate classroom assessment. Since these frameworks, including our own, are often very detailed and sometimes difficult to grasp easily, for this chapter, we have prepared a list of the different kinds of skills, knowledge, and learner attributes (with some examples) that are important to consider when assessing ELLs in Chart 6.2. Most of these are the same kinds of things that guide assessment of mainstream students' literacy development. They take on special significance, however, in the case of students who are learning English at the same time as they are learning to read and write in English. It is important to recall here that acquisition of these kinds of skills, knowledge, and predispositions in the home language gives ELLs a head start in learning to read and write in English because many of them transfer to English, as discussed in Chapter 1.

So far we have illustrated how assessment is valuable for collecting information in order to devise initial individualized literacy plans for ELLs, and we have suggested how ongoing conferences with students as well as dialogue journals and learning logs can be useful in learning about your students on a continuous basis. Another important and common purpose for classroom assessment is *to monitor*

Elements of Literacy Development in English and the Home Language

- Familiarity with books and other printed materials
- Experiences with or access to written language outside school
- Penmanship
- Familiarity with and competence using computers
- Interest in and enthusiasm for reading and writing
- Confidence as a reader or writer
- Underlying language competencies: breadth and depth of vocabulary related to academic subjects, comprehension of or ability to use complex sentence patterns to express complex ideas, and ability to organize ideas, events, and details logically and sequentially
- Word-level skills and knowledge: the ability to read and write words accurately, fluently, and with meaning; knowledge of how words are interrelated and organized semantically and grammatically
- Sentence-level skills: the ability to read and write grammatically and to comprehend complex sentences; ability to use varied sentence patterns to good effect and appropriately
- Text-level skills: the ability to read, write, and comprehend text-length passages that conform to the conventions of different genres and to comprehend written text of different genres
- Reading and writing strategies for monitoring comprehension and comprehending new or unfamiliar words and complex text

Chart 6.2 Elements of Literacy Development in English and the Home Language

student progress in literacy development as a result of instruction. Here, it is a matter of assessing whether your instructional plans are successful in meeting your objectives.

Continuing with José's case, based on her initial assessment, Mrs. Oliver determined that while José has relatively good social communication skills in English, he has relatively limited academic vocabulary and storytelling skills. As a result, his story was largely descriptive rather than narrative—that is to say, while he was able to identify key people and elements in the story, he had difficulty narrating how they related to one another; also his story did not have a beginning or an end. Mrs. Oliver also realized that José had relatively limited decoding skills in English: When asked to read the book with words, he could not read single words easily and read with some reluctance in English.

Taking all this information into account, along with what she had read in José's school file, Mrs. Oliver devised an instructional plan to work on all of these areas: expanding his vocabulary, story grammar, organization, and decoding skills in English; and, at the same time, making sure that he enjoyed reading and writing. She decided that the best way to do this and keep José working with the rest of the students in the class was to integrate her plans for José in the social studies unit on My Community, a unit that all students were going to work on together. She also asked the ESL specialist to work closely with José on his vocabulary and decoding skills with words and themes taken from the unit. In fact, she gave the ESL teacher the reading materials and unit so that what José was doing with her would help him to work along with the other students as quickly as possible. This left her more time to work on bigger skills and issues—his understanding of story structure, his enjoyment of reading and writing, and the development of his underlying language competencies.

The most powerful assessment tool Mrs. Oliver and all teachers have to monitor a student's literacy development is observation: observing what José does, or does not do, as he is engaged in activities that you plan for them. This is a form of assessment that all teachers use all the time, so we have provided guidelines for observation of

Guidelines for Observation

WHY?

a. To assess students' comprehension and production of academic language when reading or writing during classroom activities.

b. To assess appropriacy of activities or materials that call for reading and writing by monitoring ELLs' engagement in and comprehension during tasks that involve reading and writing.

c. To assess social language competencies by observing ELLs' use of language with classmates during nonacademic periods.

d. To assess development of reading and writing skills following instruction that focuses directly and explicitly on specific skills by observing students' use of target language skills during follow-up and extension activities.

TIPS

a. Observation can be used when ELLs are at any level of proficiency in English.

b. To ensure that observation is focused, identify which reading and writing skills and behaviors you want to focus on beforehand, for example, engagement in reading, comprehension of written text, and so on; otherwise, your observations will be unfocused and less useful.

c. To facilitate recording observational information, prepare a checklist of specific reading and writing skills and behaviors to be observed based on your literacy objectives.

d. For particularly important literacy objectives, devise an activity that requires use of the targeted skills so that you can systematically observe if students are learning them.

e. In order to assess specific aspects of ELLs' literacy development in English when they are in the beginning stages, provide closed-ended response alternatives that students can choose from, rather than requiring them to produce the correct answer; for example, after the student reads a short sentence, ask him or her to point to one of several pictures that are possible answers to questions about the sentence.

f. Keep a journal of your observations of individual student performance in order to monitor students' literacy development; this will reduce the chances of forgetting; or always have available small sticky notes so that you can jot down comments and add them to your journal later.

ELLs' literary skills. Observation is a particularly important tool when assessing the progress of ELLs because they may not be performing in exactly the same ways as native English-speaking, mainstream students. Therefore, it is important to observe individual ELLs carefully and note what each can do given their individual starting points and your instructional plans for them. ELL students, while working on the same long-term goals as mainstream students, often are working on different short-term goals, so you need to observe them as individual learners with individualized goals.

As Mrs. Oliver works through the unit and observes José, she will probably want to make accommodations so that he can demonstrate what he is learning. For example, if she observes that he has difficulty naming different kinds of habitats and buildings in his community,

Research Finding

Abedi and his colleagues have conducted a series of studies examining various types of accommodations on the performance of ELLs. They found that most accommodations helped both ELLs and mainstream students and that ELLs performed substantially higher under the accommodated conditions than under the standard conditions. The greatest score improvements for ELLs resulted from accommodations that allowed them to use a glossary and extra time. The accommodation that narrowed the performance gap between ELL and other students the most was use of simplified English in the test (Abedi et al. 2001).

she might scaffold his response by asking him to label pictures of different kinds of buildings that she has posted on the classroom walls; or she might give him word choices in English and ask him to choose the best one for each building and then write them down in his word book. During writing assignments ELLs might be taught to use the Word Wall or "word book" that they have built up over time in the classroom; or, if tests are used, ELLs might be given a version that uses simplified English. Mrs. Oliver will probably expand her wait time so he has more time to answer—it often takes longer to respond in a second language than a first language. She will also want to give him more opportunities to practice using new words and sentence patterns to encourage him to use new terms, and, certainly, she will want to praise his every attempt to use the new language he is learning.

This case study was about a young ELL who started English schooling in grade one, around the time when most children start school. But the same scenario could pertain to ELLs who have recently immigrated and are beginning school in English for the first time in a higher grade. ELLs who have had little, interrupted, or no formal schooling prior to attending an English school and especially if they have had little exposure to English could be at the same stage of literacy development as young José even though they start schooling in English in a higher grade. Certainly, the kind of initial assessment activities that Mrs. Oliver used with José would also be appropriate for older ELLs with limited prior schooling. In the next case study, we describe a teacher working at the grade four level.

LESSONS FROM JOSÉ AND MRS. OLIVER

- Classroom assessment is critical for collecting information about individual students that can be used to plan instruction and monitor its effectiveness.

- Standardized and classroom-based tests provide a limited range of information about ELLs; it is necessary to go beyond test information and use a variety of alternative assessment tools to plan effective instruction for ELLs.
- A variety of sources of information should be consulted when getting to know your ELLs and planning appropriate instruction for them, including intake records, previous teachers, report cards from previous schools, ESL specialists, parents, and students themselves during conferences.
- In addition to the above sources of information, observation of students with other students and in class along with reading/writing conferences (and running records) can provide valuable information about what individual ELLs know and can do.
- Permitting ELLs to use their home language during assessment activities and using the assistance of other ELLs who are relatively proficient in other languages can provide insights about what ELLs know and can do in the home language. This, in turn, reveals the kinds of skills and knowledge that ELLs have in their reservoir of abilities that they can apply to learning to read and write in English.

Mrs. Bartlett and Ludmila

Mrs. Bartlett teaches grade four in the same school as Mrs. Oliver and has been teaching in the school for two years. She used to teach in a suburban school in the Midwest. She had few ELLs in her classroom there; virtually all of the students spoke English. Ludmila joined Mrs. Bartlett's class in December. When Mrs. Bartlett checked Ludmila's intake file, she learned that Ludmila was born in the United States, but her parents had been born in Guatemala. The primary language spoken at home is Spanish, although her parents report that some English is used, especially among the children themselves and, of course, they watch TV in English. Neither parent completed high school and both work in the service sector where they use Spanish most of the time.

Fortunately, a report from Ludmila's previous school was also part of her file. From this, Mrs. Bartlett also learned that Ludmila had been in an English-only school program; she had little or no educational support (bilingual education) in Spanish; and her ESL support seems to have been inconsistent. Ludmila's grades, especially in reading and writing, were well below grade level, but Mrs. Bartlett is not sure what this really means because it is possible they reflect inadequate or inconsistent instruction and not an underlying reading problem on Ludmila's part. In order to devise an instructional plan for Ludmila, Mrs. Bartlett carried out an initial assessment conference with her to determine what she knows and can already do with respect to reading and writing in English.

Mrs. Bartlett carried out an initial reading and writing assessment with Ludmila in December, shortly after Ludmila joined the class.

Guidelines for Reading/Writing Conferences

WHY?

a. To assess students' insights or self-reports about their reading and writing skills by questioning them during a reading and writing activity.

b. To probe ELLs' reading and writing strategies by asking probe questions about why students did what they did when they had difficulty or made a mistake.

c. To assess students' meta-communication skills about reading and writing—that is, their ability to talk about their reading, writing, and oral academic language skills.

d. To give students an opportunity to identify difficulties, successes, and goals for learning to read and write in English so that you can devise instruction that supports them.

TIPS

a. Reading and writing conferences can be used when ELLs are at any level of proficiency in English.

b. Prepare a checklist of specific reading and writing skills and strategies you want to inquire about during the conference.

c. Record students' responses in your journal in order to monitor individual student progress over time and to identify common problematic areas that deserve more focused instruction.

d. If students are having trouble responding to your probes, provide response alternatives from which they can choose in order to describe the strategies they use when they encounter obstacles (e.g., unfamiliar words or grammatical patterns) during reading and writing.

e. Give students credit for using the home language and try to figure out when they make "mistakes" or use non-nativelike forms if it is transfer from the home language.

The assessment conference that Mrs. Bartlett conducted with Ludmila was a lot like Mrs. Oliver's, except that Mrs. Bartlett is guided by the *beginning intermediate* descriptors in the literacy development framework. Mrs. Bartlett chose this level because Ludmila had had some schooling in the United States since kindergarten and, therefore, she might be expected to be at this level of development.

There are other differences in the way Mrs. Bartlett conducts the assessment conference with Ludmila: (a) She does not offer Ludmila wordless picture books because she has been in an English school and, therefore, should have some literacy skills in English; (b) she offers her storybooks at different levels of difficulty to see if she can select an appropriate level for herself; and (c) she asks Ludmila to bring a book that she really likes, either in English or in Spanish.

When they meet, Mrs. Bartlett asks Ludmila to read one of the books out loud to her so she can observe how accurate and fluent her reading skills are; she pays particular attention to how she reads irregular or infrequent words and whether she can use story context to figure out the meaning of the words that she cannot read easily. Mrs. Bartlett does a running record while Ludmila reads. Although Mrs. Bartlett assumes that Ludmila knows how to handle books, she casually observes how she interacts with the books to see if she is comfortable and confident with them; this would be a sign that she has had lots of experiences with books. After she reads the book, Mrs. Bartlett asks Ludmila questions that are intended to probe her understanding of story structure and more inferential aspects of the story: Who is the main character, what is the book about, what is the significance of the ending, and so on. Finally, she asks Ludmila if she liked the story and why. They then turn to the book(s) that Ludmila brought herself, and Mrs. Bartlett uses them to probe Ludmila's interest in books—does she talk enthusiastically and in detail about them or is she casual and disinterested; does she demonstrate that she reads them in depth; why does she like this book; and so on.

Finally, before she finishes off her conference with Ludmila, Mrs. Bartlett asks Ludmila to write a short story once she gets back to her desk and before they meet again about the best gift she ever had. Mrs. Bartlett gives her some guidelines so that Ludmila has some idea of what Mrs. Bartlett expects. We use Ludmila's "story" about her pink skates to illustrate how to assess ELLs' writing skills; we use the 6+1 Traits Model that we introduced in Chapter 5 because we think it captures the features of writing that deserve attention. As you review our comments on Ludmila's writing sample (see Figure 6.4), which appear in the boxes surrounding her story, there are a number of important things to notice. First of all, notice that the focus is on language and using language to communicate. Feedback concerning the mechanics or conventions of language is kept to a minimum. It is critical when assessing the writing skills of beginning ELL writers that you resist the temptation to focus on spelling, punctuation, and paragraphing. These are easy features of writing to focus on because you can simply circle errors. But this is a misguided focus since excessive emphasis on the mechanics of writing highlights what students have not yet mastered and can discourage them. It is far more motivating to students when you focus on the ideas expressed in the piece, the student's varied use of vocabulary to express those ideas, and the voice they project in their writing. In other words, focus on the communicative features of writing; what was identified in Chapter 1 (Chart 1.1) as top-level skills. This does not mean ignoring the bottom-level skills, but avoid taking the easy route and simply correcting spelling, punctuation, and other technical errors. Also, look for influences from ELL students' home languages as they express themselves in writing—what might at first look like an error is really a student's best attempt to write in English using knowledge from the home language.

Based on this assessment conference and Mrs. Bartlett's assessment of Ludmila's writing, she devised an individual instructional plan that focused on:

(a) Expanding Ludmila's academic vocabulary and knowledge of words

(b) Enhancing her reading fluency

(c) Boosting her enthusiasm for reading and writing

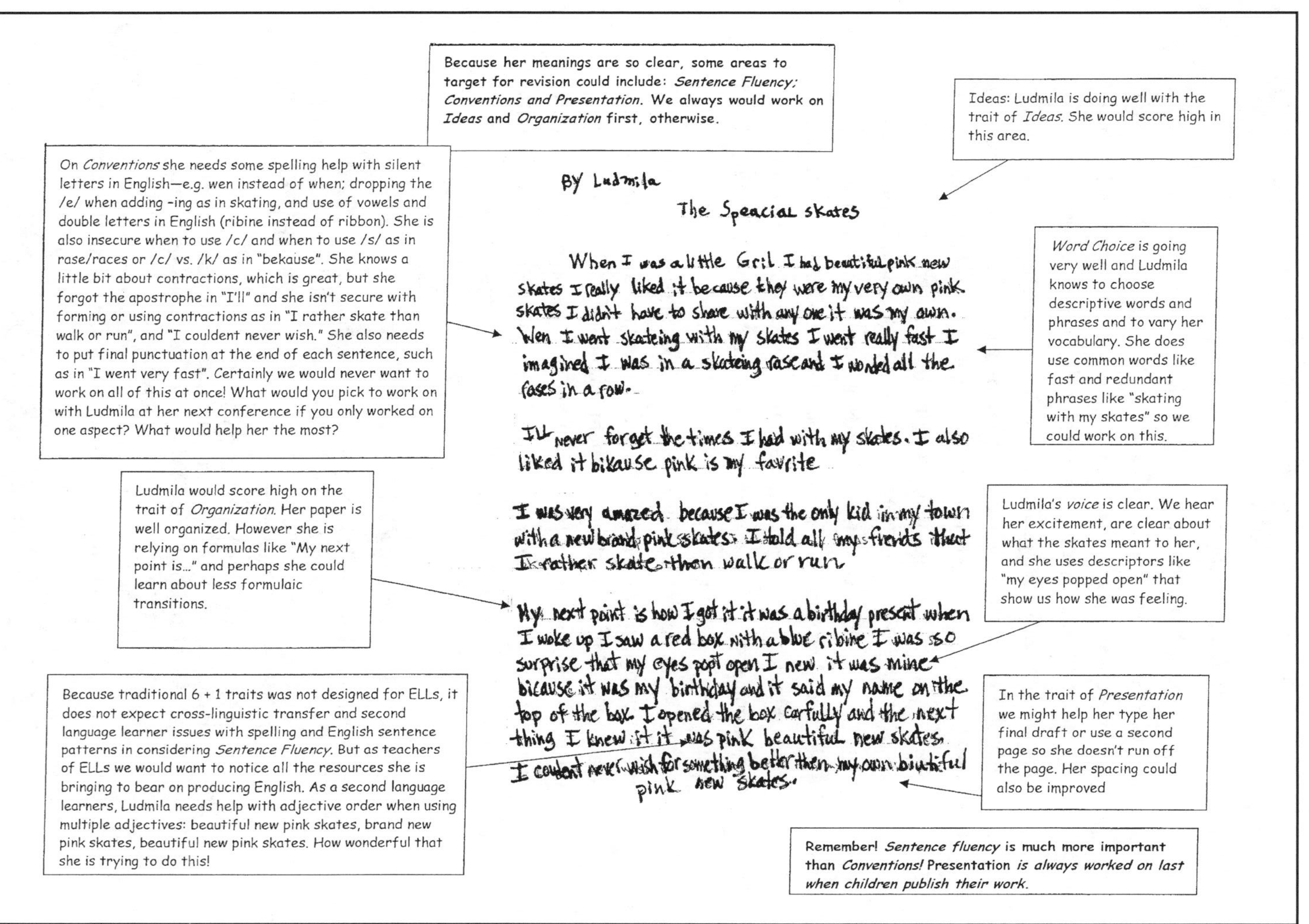

Figure 6.4 Writing Analysis for Ludmila

(d) Expanding her knowledge of different genres of text (expository as well as narrative)

(e) Improving her writing skills

Mrs. Bartlett works with the ESL specialist to share responsibility for teaching these objectives because they benefit from small-group and one-on-one attention that the specialist can provide easily, while Mrs. Bartlett works on the other objectives. She decides that using a combination of guided reading and writing conferences along with a learning log focusing on books that Ludmila is reading is a good way to give Ludmila both practice reading different genres of text and practice writing about what she is reading. Hopefully, this will also help Ludmila enjoy reading and writing more because she will also be sharing her logs about reading with the teacher during conferences. Through guided reading minilessons Mrs. Bartlett can model skills and strategies that Ludmila needs to learn and practice. She can also give Ludmila emotional support and encouragement so that she feels successful and supported and wants to learn to read and write even better.

Mrs. Bartlett also decides to put Ludmila in partner-writing tasks during writer's workshop with students who are somewhat above her level of literacy so she can benefit from what they know as they create stories together. While the students are spending time in writer's workshop, Mrs. Bartlett is careful to observe Ludmila working with the other students to see if and how she is contributing.

LESSONS FROM LUDMILA AND MRS. BARTLETT

- ❑ ELLs' level of proficiency in reading and writing in English and the home language may not line up with their grade-level placement because they have had no prior education, interrupted education, or inappropriate education.
- ❑ The same assessment procedures and tools can be used with ELLs at different levels of proficiency and grade levels, but adjustments need to be made to reflect their individual learner profiles. Some assessment tools work well with students at all levels (like observation), but others require a certain minimum level of proficiency in English reading and writing before they can be useful (like running records).
- ❑ A number of tools can serve both instructional and assessment purposes (e.g., dialogue journals, learning logs, conferences). It is important to avoid using these tools explicitly for assessment

purposes if you want to use them for instruction purposes or to give students opportunities to use English for authentic communication; explicit feedback could stifle their enthusiasm to use English.

- ❑ Sharing responsibility for collecting assessment information and for co-planning instruction in response to assessment information with ESL and other specialists benefits everyone. There is no reason for classroom teachers to work alone; collaborate with the reading and/or ESL specialist to design, carry out, and interpret assessments. Of course, it also makes sense that you share assessment information so that you can co-plan complementary instruction.

Mr. Samuelson and Ping

Mr. Samuelson, the English teacher on the seventh-grade team, was told that he would receive a new student, Ping, who had never been to school in the United States but had gone to school in China. He knew that it would be very important to review Ping's school records from China so that he could get an idea of her level of general education and how well she had done in school before emigrating. To his relief, Ping's parents had given the school extensive school records. Mr. Samuelson asked a Chinese colleague who had been educated in China to help interpret Ping's report card results for him. From these, they both could see that Ping had been in the appropriate grade level for someone her age and that she had done well in school. They could also see that she had studied English as a second language and had done quite well; as a result, they expected that she probably had rudimentary reading and writing skills in English as well as basic oral language skills.

When he first met her in September, Mr. Samuelson greeted Ping in English and saw that she was able to respond quite fluently. Mr. Samuelson decided to enlist the help of a native Chinese speaker the district had on contract to assess Ping's actual reading and writing levels in Chinese. He thought this would be useful because he had found with previous ELLs that those who had good reading and writing skills in their home language were able to learn reading and writing in English quite quickly, even when the writing system in their home differed from English. Working with the Chinese-speaking resource person, he learned that Ping was on or above grade level in reading and writing in Mandarin, the language of instruction in China. Because of Ping's strong literacy skills in Mandarin, they knew that there were skills and predispositions that Ping could transfer to English, including:

- ❏ *Self-confidence as a reader/writer*
- ❏ *Knowledge that symbols correspond to words and that there is a system to the written code*
- ❏ *A range of strategies for uncovering meaning from text, from using text formatting features (bold, italics) to the use of illustrations to detect meaning, to asking for assistance or using a bilingual dictionary when meaning is unclear. All of these skills were skills she could build on.*

Mr. Samuelson and the ESL teacher were able to conduct their own assessment of Ping's reading and writing skills in English using the same kinds of techniques as Mrs. Bartlett and Mrs. Oliver, but they had to adjust them to be suitable for Ping. Their assessments of Ping's English indicated that she was at an intermediate advanced *level in oral English and at a* beginning intermediate *level in reading and writing English.*

The main difference between this case and the others is that Ping has advanced literacy skills in her home language, and this bodes well for her acquisition of reading and writing in English. If Mr. Samuelson had not made the extra effort to check Ping's previous school records and if he had not worked with a Chinese speaker to directly assess her reading and writing skills in Mandarin, he would not have know this. Taking Ping's level of literacy in Mandarin into account, Mr. Samuelson thought it best to focus on developing Ping's academic language skills in English, with a focus on the development of her academic language skills in oral English and at the same time to focus reading instruction on word-decoding skills in English so that she could transfer her decoding skills from Chinese to English as quickly as possible. He did not plan to spend much time on decoding, however, since Ping already had fluent reading skills in Mandarin and understood the basics of the English writing system. This gave him more time to begin to introduce her to grade-appropriate reading material in the content areas, focusing on building background knowledge and text-level skills in English.

LESSONS FROM PING AND MR. SAMUELSON

- Because a student has just started their education in English does not mean that he or she cannot read or write. Whenever possible, draw on all the resources you have to assess or find out about ELLs' literacy skills in the home language.
- It can also be useful to "assess" the family's literacy skills by interviewing parents or visiting the home to see if parents can readily engage in home-based literacy activities or if they need support from the school to engage their children in home-based reading and writing activities.
- Students themselves, especially at the age of Ping, can be a good source of information about their own reading and writing—ask them what they can read and write, or simply ask them to write about themselves in their home language. Even if you do not know how to read and write the language yourself, you can still probably make a number of useful observations about the students' abilities.

Assessment Tools

Throughout this chapter, we have referred to a number of different assessment tools.

1. Observation
2. Reading and writing conferences
3. Running records
4. Dialogue journals
5. Learning logs

You may already be using some or all of these. Our focus of attention here is on why and how they can be used effectively with ELLs for literacy-assessment purposes. Dialogue journals and learning logs were discussed in Chapter 5 as instructional activities. Additional general resources on assessment tools are listed in the Additional Resources for Teachers section at the end of the chapter.

Summing Up

In this chapter, we learned that classroom assessment is substantially different from high-stakes testing, which has become so commonplace in U.S. schools. In contrast to high-stakes testing, classroom assessment gives classroom teachers control and responsibility for designing and carrying out literacy assessments that reflect their school's, district's, or state's standards and benchmarks for achievement in reading and writing. Also, classroom assessment is primarily about determining what students know and can do so that teachers can plan literacy instruction that is fine-tuned to their individual levels of reading and writing in English and that moves them to the next stage. In short, a primary goal of classroom assessment is to develop instructional plans that will advance ELLs' development of reading and writing skills in English, as well as the home language wherever possible. We illustrated how classroom assessment is cyclical using a number of case studies of ELLs in the primary, elementary, and middle school grades. Many of the assessment tools that are useful with mainstream students are also useful for assessing ELLs—for example, running records, reading and writing conferences, learning logs, and dialogue journals. However, modifications are necessary to allow ELLs to fully demonstrate their reading and writing skills as well as what they have learned in the content areas if reading and writing are involved—for example, simplifying instructions in English, allowing ELLs more time, and permitting them to use the home language. The key to successful use of classroom assessment to promote literacy development is to tailor assessment activities to the individual learners and groups of learners you have. As a result, classroom teachers should use their own judgment and, at the same time, adopt a reflective, critical approach to examine which assessment techniques work best and under what conditions and with what kinds of ELLs. In other words, to be really effective classroom assessment calls on teachers to also engage in informal action research to assess their own assessment procedures.

Additional Resources for Teachers

Books on assessment in ESL contexts

- Brantley, D. K. 2007. *Instructional Assessment of English Language Learners in the K–8 Classroom.* Boston: Pearson/Allyn and Bacon.

  Differentiates between formal and alternative assessments, then discusses oral language and vocabulary assessment strategies, word identification, comprehension and reading-fluency assessment strategies (including assessment of concepts of print, phonemic awareness, and the alphabetic principle), written language and spelling assessment methods (including a developmental assessment of orthographic knowledge), and classroom-based strategies for assessment in the content areas. Appendices provide a running record sheet, narrative story-retelling assessment, and writing assessment form.

- Cheng, L. L. 1991. *Assessing Asian Language Performance: Guidelines for Evaluating Limited English-Proficient Students.* Second Edition. Oceanside, CA: Academic Communications Associates.

  Provides information about the cultural and linguistic characteristics of Vietnamese, Cantonese, Mandarin, Japanese, Khmer, Korean, and other Asian Pacific Island languages. Also provides a sample background information questionnaire that can be useful in gathering information about the home language when working with Asian and Pacific Island families. The book includes critical cultural information about these groups and gives important information about the linguistic systems of these languages as contrasted to English, which can be helpful to teachers in identifying potential cross-linguistic influences they may see in children's oral and written production.

- Gottlieb, M., & D. Nguyen. 2007. *Assessment & Accountability in Language Education Programs: A Guide for Administrators and Teachers.* Philadelphia: Caslon.

  Designed to address the accountability assessment concerns of teachers and administrators serving ELLs, this resource book addresses both formative and summative assessment. It has a chapter on using pivotal portfolios—portfolios that includes oral language proficiency, literacy, and academic learning assessments. It also includes chapters on assessment strategies for dual language and transitional bilingual programs.

- Hamayan, E., B. Marler, C. Sanchez-Lopez, & J. Damico. 2007. *Special Education Considerations for English Language Learners: Delivering a Continuum of Services.* Philadelphia: Caslon.

  Although this book is oriented to ELLs who are having difficulties in school, there are useful instruments for gathering information about all ELLs in Chapters 6 to 11.

- ❑ Law, B., & M. Eckes. 2007. *Assessment and ESL: An Alternative Approach.* Second Edition. Winnipeg, Manitoba, Canada: Portage & Main Press.

  Designed by two seasoned ESL classroom teachers, one Canadian and one American, this highly practical book concentrates on classroom-based assessment strategies for initial placement, emerging literacy, and beyond. Chapters are dedicated to the topics of observational strategies for the assessment of oral language and literacy and use of checklists, anecdotal records, and conferences. It also discusses the thorny issues associated with grading ESL students. Many classroom examples are provided.

- ❑ O'Malley, J. M., & L. Valdez Pierce. 1996. *Authentic Assessment for English Language Learners: Practical Approaches for Teachers.* Reading, MA: Addison-Wesley.

  A classic assessment book for teachers of ELLs, this book discusses authentic assessment, portfolio assessment, and methods of conducting classroom-based assessment of oral language, reading, writing, and content area subjects. Filled with practical tools and step-by-step procedures designed by teachers, a very helpful book to assist with informal assessment of students.

- ❑ Genesee, F., & J. A. Upshur. 1996. *Classroom-Based Evaluation in Second Language Education.* New York: Cambridge University Press.

  This book provides a useful overview of different types of classroom-based assessment with second-language learners. The authors emphasize the use of "alternative assessment" information to design effective instruction. They provide detailed and comprehensive guidelines for conducting assessment using both tests and alternative assessment methods, such as conferencing, learning logs, observation, dialogue journals, and observation.

- ❑ Valdez-Pierce, L. 2003. *Assessing English Language Learners.* Washington, DC: National Education Association.

  A succinct book that discusses the use of standardized tests and performance-based assessments with ELLs. The chapter on performance-based assessment provides guidelines for assessment accommodations by language proficiency level, while the chapter on scoring tools discusses checklists, scoring rubrics and rating scales, and formats for recording teacher observations. Many examples are provided.

Guidance for using running records

- ❑ Clay, M. M. 2000. *Running Records for Classroom Teachers.* Portsmouth, NH: Heinemann.

  An explanation of running records; why and how to use them.

Appendix A

Checking for Quality of Books in Languages Other than English

In translated books:

- ❑ The translation represents the original justly
- ❑ The language contains no errors of any sort
- ❑ The language is not too formal
- ❑ The language is not artificial sounding
- ❑ The cultural context is authentic to the story
- ❑ Words or phrases in the illustrations are in the appropriate language
- ❑ Photographs or illustrations are embedded in a cultural context that is appropriate for the story so that there is a good fit of pictures to text

In monolingual books:

- ❑ The quality of the type is adequate (especially with non-roman alphabet scripts)
- ❑ The print quality is adequate; the colors and images and words are sharp and well defined
- ❑ The binding can withstand classroom use

In addition, in bilingual books:

- ❑ The status of the two languages are equally represented (one language does not take precedence)
    - The two languages are printed in the same size and quality font
    - The writing in the illustrations is in both languages
    - The names of the characters are appropriate to both languages
    - The directionality of the book is appropriate to both languages, even if the other language goes from right to left
- ❑ One culture does not take precedence over the other; the language other than English is not nested in the English-dominant culture, as in, for example a story titled *Mr. McGillicutty se va a McDonald's,* where the language is translated but there is no effort to ground the story in one of the appropriate cultural contexts of Spanish.

Appendix B

Quick Guide to ELL Literacy Strategies

Quick Guide to ELL Literacy Strategies

This guide is meant to provide only general recommendations. You may find that other ways of carrying out a strategy fit your context and needs better.

STRATEGY[1] & LEVEL OF PROFICIENCY	DESCRIPTION	GRADE LEVEL	SUGGESTED TIME FRAME/LIMIT	INDIVIDUAL OR GROUP	POTENTIAL FOR HOME/COMMUNITY CONNECTIONS (IF PARENTS ARE ALSO ELLS)	COMPATIBLE ASSESSMENT APPROACHES
BOOTSTRAPPING FROM HOME LANGUAGE LITERACY						
B, BI, IA, AS[2]	Use of knowledge and skills in home language literacy to develop literacy in English (p. 96)[3]	K–8	Every opportunity you get	Individual or same home language groups	Extensive	Observation; writing sample analysis
COLLABORATIVE TEXT WRITING						
B, BI	A text produced by ELLs collaboratively based on a story that was read or a topic that was studied (pp. 63–64)	K–3	Once every week or two	Group	Extensive	Dialogue journals; learning logs; writing sample analysis
DIALOGUE JOURNALS						
BI, IA	A written conversation that goes back and forth, usually between teacher and student (p. 171)	3–8	5 minutes, every two days	Individual	Extensive	Observation during the journal writing; process writing conference; writing sample analysis
EDITING OWN WORK						
BI, IA, AS	Students use traits of good writing as guidelines to edit their own writing (p. 177)	1–8	Any time students complete a writing assignment	Individual or small group	Limited	Writing conferences; observation
FOCUSING ON THE WRITING OF OTHERS						
BI, IA, AS	Students use traits of good writing as guidelines to analyze published works (p. 178)	2–8	15–30 minutes, once every two to four weeks	Small group	Depends on texts selected	Class discussion; dialogue journals

[1]The list here is by no means exhaustive. Rather, it includes strategies that are most prominently discussed in this book. Some of these strategies, such as dialogue journals, are particular to teaching students for whom English is a second language. Others, such as guided reading, are used with the general population; however, the way they are used with ELLs differs slightly from the way they are used with the mainstream population.

[2]English Proficiency Levels, as described in our framework: B = Beginning, BI = Beginning Intermediate, IA = Intermediate Advanced, AS = Advanced Supported, LFS = Limited Formal Schooling

[3]Page numbers where the strategy is discussed in this book.

(continues)

STRATEGY[1] & LEVEL OF PROFICIENCY	DESCRIPTION	GRADE LEVEL	SUGGESTED TIME FRAME/LIMIT	INDIVIDUAL OR GROUP	POTENTIAL FOR HOME/COMMUNITY CONNECTIONS (IF PARENTS ARE ALSO ELLS)	COMPATIBLE ASSESSMENT APPROACHES
FRONTLOADING (VOCABULARY, GRAMMATICAL STRUCTURES THROUGH CLASS ACTIVITIES, SONGS, CHANTS, POEMS)						
B, BI	Teaching vocabulary and grammatical structures specific to text that will be read or written (p. 45)	1–8	Every time text to be taught contains language that is unfamiliar to ELLs	Group	Limited	Observation; writing samples analysis; reading/writing conferences
GRAPHIC ORGANIZERS & SIGNAL WORDS						
B, BI, IA	Visual summaries of important information in a text using key words (p. 140–42)	K–8	Whenever a text contains concepts and words unknown to ELLs	Whole class	Limited	Observation; writing sample analysis; learning logs
GUIDED READING						
BI	Modeling efficient reading behaviors for ELLs, introducing and practicing helpful decoding and text comprehension strategies, showing how language and text features function (pp. 61 and 143)	3–8	One to three times per week during reading workshop	Small groups	Not an appropriate home activity	Running records; observation
GUIDED WRITING						
BI	Introducing writing strategies to ELLs, showing how known strategies apply to English (pp. 63 and 142–43)	3–8	Two to three times a week during writer's workshop	Individual or small groups	Not an appropriate home activity	Writing sample analysis
HANDWRITING PRACTICE						
B, LFS (only needed for beginning students and students new to English orthography)	Practice in forming letters and writing words and phrases (pp. 41 and 50)	K–8	Limit to 5 minutes (combined with mimic writing), once or twice a week unless student is in kindergarten or grade 1	Individual	Limited	Dialogue journals; writing smples analysis; observation

[1]The list here is by no means exhaustive. Rather, it includes strategies that are most prominently discussed in this book. Some of these strategies, such as dialogue journals, are particular to teaching students for whom English is a second language. Others, such as guided reading, are used with the general population; however, the way they are used with ELLs differs slightly from the way they are used with the mainstream population.

[2]English Proficiency Levels, as described in our framework: B = Beginning, BI = Beginning Intermediate, IA = Intermediate Advanced, AS = Advanced Supported, LFS = Limited Formal Schooling

[3]Page numbers where the strategy is discussed in this book.

JIGSAW AND PAIRED READING (COOPERATIVE LEARNING)						
BI, IA	ELLs are divided into pairs, triads, or small groups to read different sections of a text (p. 146)	4–8	Two to three times per week	Small groups	Extensive	Observation; learning logs
LABELS, CAPTIONS, LISTS						
B, LFS	ELLs create labels, make captions and write lists—all with a functional purpose (pp. 54 and 158)	1–8	Combined with Mimic Writing	Individual or small groups	Extensive for messages sent home; otherwise limited	Limited assessment potential
LANGUAGE EXPERIENCE APPROACH						
B, BI	Based on an activity that students shared, a group story is dictated to the teacher or written by the students; this story is then used for reading and editing (p. 66)	1–8	40 minutes to weeks	More group in beginning level, more individual in intermediate	Extensive	Writing sample analysis; observation; learning logs
LEARNING LOGS						
BI, IA, AS	Written text that summarizes the most important things being learned in class (pp. 142 and 146)	1–8	5–10 minutes every two or three days	Individual	Limited	Analysis of learning logs
MIMIC WRITING						
B, LFS (only earliest stage)	ELLs copy a short message, lists, or labels that they can read, for aspecific functional purpose (p. 158)	1–8	No more than 5 minutes, twice or three times a week	Individual	Extensive	Writing sample analysis
MINI SHARED READING						
B	Teacher does shared reading in small groups of 3–5 ELLs for at least 30 minutes (p. 61)	K–3	30 minutes, at least once a week	Small groups	Extensive	Observation; running records

(*continues*)

STRATEGY[1] & LEVEL OF PROFICIENCY	DESCRIPTION	GRADE LEVEL	SUGGESTED TIME FRAME/LIMIT	INDIVIDUAL OR GROUP	POTENTIAL FOR HOME/COMMUNITY CONNECTIONS (IF PARENTS ARE ALSO ELLS)	COMPATIBLE ASSESSMENT APPROACHES
MODELING AFTER PUBLISHED BOOKS						
BI, IA	ELLs use a book they have read as a model for a text they write themselves (p. 168)	1–6	Spread over days, as long as it takes to complete writing	Individual or small group	Dependent upon texts selected	Writing conferences; writing sample analysis; dialogue journals
READ-ALOUD						
B, BI	Books are read by a proficient reader, either in person or on tape/DVD (p. 45)	K–8	Once or twice a week; more frequently in lower grades	Individual or group	Extensive	Observation
STORYTELLING AND RETELLING						
B, BI	ELLs tell stories of wordless books or after picture books are read (p. 45)	K–8	Once or twice a week; more frequently in lower grades	Individual or group	Extensive	Observation
SUPPORTING HOME LANGUAGE LITERACY AT HOME						
B, BI, IA, AS	Actively encouraging family members to keep literacy in the home language alive (p. 94)	K–8	On a regular basis	Group	Extensive	Reading logs; dialogue journals
USING BILINGUAL TEXT						
B, BI, IA, AS	Reading bilingual books or books in the home language; writing bilingual texts (p. 98)	K–8	Once a week	Individual or small group	Extensive	Observation; reading logs (list of books read)
USING MULTICULTURAL LITERATURE (READ-ALOUD; MODEL FOR WRITING, ETC.)						
B, BI, IA, AS	Using books that revolve around cultures other than those of the mainstream population (p. 106)	K–8	Every other book that is read in class	Individual or group	Dependent upon books and activities selected	Observation

[1]The list here is by no means exhaustive. Rather, it includes strategies that are most prominently discussed in this book. Some of these strategies, such as dialogue journals, are particular to teaching students for whom English is a second language. Others, such as guided reading, are used with the general population; however, the way they are used with ELLs differs slightly from the way they are used with the mainstream population.

[2]English Proficiency Levels, as described in our framework: B = Beginning, BI = Beginning Intermediate, IA = Intermediate Advanced, AS = Advanced Supported, LFS = Limited Formal Schooling

[3]Page numbers where the strategy is discussed in this book.

WRITING STORIES BASED ON PHOTOGRAPHS AND VIDEOS						
B, BI	Use of digital pictures and captions to stimulate earliest writing and genuine communication (p. 164)	K–8	Once a month	Individual or group	Limited; dependent upon photographs available	Writing sample analysis; observation
WORD STUDY						
B, BI, IA, AS	Cognates, Word Walls, word sorts, and word notebooks (pp. 50 and 136)	1–8	Whenever the opportunity arises, in context	Group	Except for cognates; not appropriate	Observation; written products
WRITING SCRIPTS; WRITING FRAMES						
IA, AS	Useful phrasing for introductions, conclusions, transitions; templates for planning a piece of writing (p. 171)	3–8	Once a week	Individual	Limited	Observation during the journal writing process; writing conference; writing sample analysis

References

Abedi, J., C. Lord, C. Hofstetter, & E. Baker. 2001. "Impact of Accommodation Strategies on English Language Learners' Test Performance." *Educational Measurement: Issues and Practice* 19 (3): 16–26.

Ada, A. F. 1988. "The Pajaro Valley Experience: Working with Spanish-Speaking Parents to Develop Children's Reading and Writing Skills in the Home Through the Use of Children's Literature." In *Minority Education: From Shame to Struggle*, edited by T. Skutnabb-Kangas & J. Cummins, 223–38. Clevedon, UK: Multilingual Matters.

———. 2003. *A Magical Encounter: Latino Children's Literature in the Classroom.* Second Edition. Boston: Allyn and Bacon.

Ada, A. F., V. J. Harris, & L. B. Hopkins, 1993. *A Chorus of Cultures: Developing Literacy Through Multicultural Poetry.* Carmel, CA: Hampton Brown.

Ammar, A., & N. Spada. 2006. "One Size Fits All? Recasts, Prompts, and L2 Learning." *Studies in Second Language Acquisition* 28: 543–74.

Asher, James J. 1982. *Learning Another Language Through Actions.* Los Gatos, CA: Sky Oaks Productions.

August, D. 2006. "How Does First Language Literacy Development Relate to Second Language Literacy Development?" In *English Language Learners at School: A Guide for Administrators*, edited by E. Hamayan & R. Freeman, 71–72. Philadelphia: Caslon.

August, D., & K. Hakuta, Eds. 1997. *Improving Schooling for Language Minority Children: A Research Agenda.* Washington, DC: National Academy Press.

August, D., & T. Shanahan, eds. 2006. *Developing Literacy in Second Language Learners: Report of the National Literacy Panel on Minority-Language Children and Youth.* Mahwah, NJ: Lawrence Erlbaum.

———. 2008. *Developing Reading and Writing in Second-Language Learners: Lessons from the Report of the National Literacy Panel on Minority-Language Children and Youth*, 7–8. New York: Routledge.

August, D., & M. Vockley. 2002. *From Spanish to English: Reading and Writing for English Language Learners Kindergarten Through Third Grade.* Pittsburgh: National Center on Education and the Economy and the University of Pittsburgh New Standards Project.

Avalos, M. A., A. Plasencia, C. Chavez, & J. Rascón. 2007. "Modified Guided Reading: Gateway to English as a Second Language and Literacy Learning." *The Reading Teacher* 61 (4): 318–29.

Ayers, W. 1988. "Fact or Fancy: The Knowledge Quest in Teacher Education." *Journal of Teacher Education* 39: 24–29.

Baker, C. 2006. *Foundations of Bilingual Education and Bilingualism*, Fourth Edition. Clevedon, UK: Multilingual Matters.

Bassano, S., & M. A. Christison. 1995. *Drawing Out: Creative, Personalized, Whole Language Activities.* Burlingame, CA: Alta.

Bear, D. R., L. Helman, S. Templeton, M. Invernizzi, & F. Johnston. 2007. *Words Their Way with English Learners: Word Study for Phonics, Vocabulary and Spelling Instruction.* Upper Saddle River, NJ: Pearson, Merrill/Prentice Hall.

Beck, I. L., M. G. McKeown, & L. Kucan. 2002. *Bringing Words to Life: Robust Vocabulary Instruction.* New York: Guilford.

Beeman, K., & C. Urow. (in press). *Teaching Spanish Literacy in the United States: A Practitioner's Handbook.* Philadelphia: Caslon.

Berman, P., C. Minicucci, B. McLaughlin, B. Nelson, & K. Woodworth. 1995. *School Reform and Student Diversity: Case Studies of Exemplary Practices for English Language Learner Students.* Santa Cruz, CA: National Center for Research on Cultural Diversity and Second Language Learning, and B. W. Associates.

Bialystok, E. 2007. "Acquisition of Literacy in Bilingual Children: A Framework for Research." *Language Learning* 57: 45–77.

Biber, D., S. Johansson, G. Leech, S. Conrad, & E. Finegan. 1999. *Longman Grammar of Spoken and Written English.* London: Longman.

Blumenfeld, S. 1994. "How Should We Teach Our Children to Write? Cursive First, Print Later!" *Blumfenfeld Education Letter* 9 (9). Available at www.howtotutor.com/cursive.htm.

Bouchard, M. 2005. *Comprehension Strategies for English Language Learners: 30 Research-Based Reading Strategies That Help Students Read, Understand and Really Learn Content from Their Textbooks and Other Nonfiction Materials (Grades 4 & Up).* New York: Scholastic (Teaching Resources Series).

Boyd-Batstone, P. 2006. *Differentiated Early Literacy for English Language Learners: Practical Strategies.* Boston: Pearson.

Brice-Heath, S. 1983. *Ways with Words.* Cambridge: Cambridge University Press.

Cappellini, M. 2005. *Balancing Reading and Language Learning: A Resource for Teaching English Language Learners, K–5.* Portland, ME: Stenhouse.

Carle, Eric. 1970. *Pancakes, Pancakes!* New York: Knopf.

Carlisle, J. F., & L. A. Katz. 2005. "Word Learning and Vocabulary Instruction." In *Multisensory Teaching of Basic Language Skills,* Second Edition, edited by J. Birsch. Baltimore: Paul H. Brookes.

Carrasquillo, A., & P. Segan. 1998. *The Teaching of Reading in Spanish to the Bilingual Student.* Second Edition. Mahwah, NJ: Lawrence Erlbaum.

Carrell, P. L. 1984. *Facilitating Reading Comprehension by Teaching Text Structure: What the Research Shows.* ERIC Document Number ED 243311.

———. 1985. "Facilitating ESL Reading by Teaching Text Structure." *TESOL Quarterly* 19 (4): 727–52.

Chamot, A. U., S. Barnhardt, P. B. El-Dinary, & J. Robbins. 1999. *The Learning Strategies Handbook.* White Plains, NY: Longman.

Chamot, A. U., & J. M. O'Malley. 1994. *The CALLA Handbook: Implementing the Cognitive Academic Language Learning Approach,* Second Edition. Reading, MA: Addison-Wesley.

Christison, M., & S. Bassano. 1982. "Drawing Out: Using Art Experience in ESL." *TESL Talk* 13 (2): 33–40.

Clandinin, D. 1986. *Classroom Practice: Teacher Images in Action.* London: The Falmer Press.

Cloud, N., F. Genesee, & E. Hamayan. 2000. "Chapter 7: Assessment." In *Dual Language Instruction: A Handbook for Enriched Education.* Boston: Heinle & Heinle.

Coelho, E. 1982. "Language Across the Curriculum." *TESL Talk* 13: 56–70.

———. 1991. *Caribbean Students in Canadian Schools: Book 2.* Markham, ON: Pippin.

Coiro, J. 2001. *Using Expository Text Patterns to Enhance Comprehension.* Available at www.Suite 101.com; downloaded September 26, 2001 from http://www.suite101.com/article.cfm/1411/68477

Comrie, B., S. Matthew, & M. Polinsky. 1996. *The Atlas of Languages: The Origin and Development of Languages Throughout the World.* London: Quatro Publishing Plc.

Corallo, C., & D. H. McDonald. 2002. *What Works with Low-Performing Schools: A Review of Research.* Charleston, WV: AEL, Regional Educational Laboratory, Region IV Comprehensive Center.

Crago, M. 1988. *Cultural Context in Communicative Interaction of Young Inuit Children.* Unpublished doctoral dissertation, McGill University, Montreal, Canada.

Crandall, J. A., ed. 1987. *ESL in Content Area Instruction.* Englewood Cliffs, NJ: Prentice Hall Regents.

Cruger Dale, D. 2002. *Bilingual Children's Books in English and Spanish/Los Libros Bilingues para Los Muchachos en Espanol: An Annotated Bibliography, 1942–2001/Una Bibliografia con Anotaciones,* 1942–2001. Jefferson, NC: McFarland & Company.

Culham, R. 2003. *6+1 Traits of Writing: The Complete Guide Grades 3 and Up.* New York: Scholastic.

———. 2004. *Using Picture Books to Teach Writing with the Traits: An Annotated Bibliography of More Than 200 Titles with Teacher-Tested Lessons.* New York: Scholastic.

———. 2005. *6+1 Traits of Writing: The Complete Guide for the Primary Grades.* New York: Scholastic.

Cummins, J. 2000. *Language, Power and Pedagogy: Bilingual Children in the Crossfire.* Clevedon, UK: Multilingual Matters.

———. 2006. "How Long Does It Take for an English Language Learner to Become Proficient in English?" In *English Language Learners at School: A Guide for Administrators,* edited by E. Hamayan & R. Freeman. Philadelphia: Caslon.

Cummins, J., V. Bismilla, P. Chow, S. Cohen, F. Giampapa, L. Leoni, P. Sandhu, & P. Sastri. 2005. "Affirming Identity in Multilingual Classrooms." *Educational Leadership* 63 (1): 38–43.

Dale, T. C., & G. J. Cuevas. 1987. "Integrating Language and Mathematics Learning." In *ESL Through Content Area Instruction: Mathematics, Science, Social Studies. [Language in Education/Theory & Practice Series of the ERIC Clearninghouse on Languages and Linguistics-ERIC/CLL],* edited by J. Crandall. Englewood Cliffs, NJ: Prentice Hall.

Day, F. A. 2003. *Latina and Latino Voices in Literature for Children and Teenagers: Lives and Works (Updated and Expanded).* Westport, CT: Greenwood.

Dickson, S. V., D. C. Simmons, & E. J. Kameenui. 1995. "Text Organization and Its Relation to Reading Comprehension: A Synthesis of the Research." *ERIC Document # ED 386 864.* Technical Report #77. Eugene, OR: University of Oregon, College of Education.

Drake, S. M. 2007. *Creating Standards-Based Integrated Curriculum: Aligning Curriculum, Content, Assessment and Instruction.* Thousand Oaks, CA: Corwin Press.

DuFour, R., & R. Eaker. 1998. *Professional Learning Communities: Best Practices for Enhancing Student Achievement.* Bloomington, IN: National Education Service.

Echevarria, J., M. E. Vogt, & D. J. Short. 2004. *Making Content Comprehensible for English Language Learners: The SIOP Model,* Second Edition. Boston: Pearson/Allyn & Bacon.

———. 2008. *Making Content Comprehensible for English Language Learners: The SIOP Model,* Third Edition. Boston: Allyn & Bacon.

Edelsky, C. 2006. *With Literacy and Justice for All: Rethinking the Social in Language and Education,* Third Edition. Hillsdale, NJ: Lawrence Erlbaum.

Edelsky, C., & K. Jilbert. 1985. "Bilingual Children and Writing: Lessons for All of Us." *The Volta Review* 87 (5).

Ellis, R., S. Loewen, & R. Erlam. 2006. "Implicit and Explicit Corrective Feedback and the Acquisition of L2 Grammar." *Studies in Second Language Acquisition* 28: 339–68.

Ernst-Slavit, G., & M. Mulhern. 2003. "Bilingual Books: Promoting Literacy and Biliteracy in the Second-Language and Mainstream Classroom." *Reading Online* 7 (2). Available at www.readingonline.org/articles/art_index.asp?HREF=ernst-slavit/index.html.

Flaitz, J. 2006. *Understanding Your Refugee and Immigrant Students: An Educational, Cultural, and Linguistic Guide.* Ann Arbor: The University of Michigan Press.

Flores, B. M. 2008. *Teaching to the Potential: Mini Shared Reading as a Bridge to Proficient Reading in L1 and L2.* Presentation made at the Pre-Conference Dual Language Institute at the *37th Annual International Bilingual/Multicultural Education Conference,* sponsored by the National Association for Bilingual Education, Tampa, FL, February 6, 2008. (Various handouts developed by B. Flores, Ph.D., CSU San Bernardino [1992–1997], bflores@csusb.edu).

Frayer, D. A., W. D. Frederick, & H. J. Klausmeier. 1969. *A Schema for Testing the Level of Concept Mastery* (Working Paper No. 16). Madison: Wisconsin Research and Development Center for Cognitive Learning.

Freeman, D. 1998. *Doing Teacher Research: From Inquiry to Understanding.* Boston: Heinle & Heinle.

Freeman, D. E., & Y. S. Freeman. 2006. *Teaching Reading and Writing in Spanish in the Bilingual Classroom,* Second Edition. Portsmouth, NH: Heinemann.

Freeman, Y. S., D. E. Freeman, & S. Mercuri. 2002. *Closing the Achievement Gap: How to Reach Limited Formal Schooling and Long Term English Language Learners.* Portsmouth, NH: Heinemann.

Friend, M., & L. Cook. 2000. *Interactions: Collaboration Skills for School Professionals.* Third Edition. New York: Longman.

Fry, E. B., & J. E. Kress. 2006. *The Reading Teacher's Book of Lists.* Fifth Edition. San Francisco: Jossey Bass.

Gallimore, R., & C. N. Goldenberg. 1993. "Activity Settings of Early Literacy: Home and School Factors in Children's Emergent Literacy." In *Contexts for Learning: Sociocultural Dynamics in Children's Development,* edited by E. Forman, N. Minick, and C. A. Stone, 315–35. Oxford: Oxford University Press.

Galindo, R. 1993. "The Influence of Peer Culture on Mexican-Origin Bilingual Children's Interpretations of a Literacy Event." *The Bilingual Research Journal* 17: 71–99.

Genesee, F., & E. Geva. 2006. "Cross-Linguistic Relationships in Working Memory, Phonological Processes, and Oral Language." In *Developing Literacy in Second Language Learners: Report of the National Literacy Panel on Language-Minority Children and Youth,* edited by D. August & T. Shanahan, 175–84. Mahwah, NJ: Lawrence Erlbaum.

Genesee, F., K. Lindholm-Leary, W. Saunders, & D. Christian. 2006. *Educating English Language Learners: A Synthesis of Empirical Evidence.* New York: Cambridge University Press.

Genesee, F., J. Paradis, & M. Crago. 2004. *Dual Language Development and Disorders: A Handbook on Bilingualism and Second Language Learning.* Baltimore: Paul H. Brookes.

Genesee, F., & C. Riches. 2006. "Literacy: Instructional Issues." In *Educating English Language Learners: A Synthesis of Research Evidence,* edited by F. Genesee, K. Lindholm-Leary, W. M. Saunders, and D. Christian, 109–76. New York: Cambridge University Press.

Genesee, F., & J. Upshur. 1996. *Classroom-Based Evaluation in Second Language Education.* New York: Cambridge University Press.

Gibbs, W. 2002. "Saving 'Dying Languages.'" *Scientific American* August: 78–85.

Goldenberg, C. 2008. "Teaching English Language Learners: What the Research Does—and Does Not—Say." *American Educator* 32 (2): 8–44.

Gonzalez, N., L. C. Moll, & C. Amanti. 2005. *Funds of Knowledge: Theorizing Practices in Households, Communities and Classrooms.* Mahwah, NJ: Lawrence Erlbaum.

Gorrell, J., C. Tricou, & A. Graham. 1991. "Children's Short- and Long-Term Retention of Science Concepts via Self-Generated Examples." *Journal of Research in Childhood Education* 5: 100–08.

Gottlieb, M. 2006a. "How Should You Assess the Language Proficiency of English Language Learners?" In *English Language Learners at School: A Guide for Administrators,* edited by E. Hamayan & R. Freeman. Philadelphia: Caslon.

———. 2006b. *Assessing English Language Learners: Bridges from Language Proficiency to Academic Achievement.* Thousand Oaks, CA: Corwin Press.

Graham, C. 1998. *Singing, Chanting, Telling Tales: Arts in the Language Classroom.* McHenry, IL: Delta Systems.

Graves, M. 2006. *The Vocabulary Book: Learning and Instruction.* New York: Teachers College Press (IRA and NCTE).

Graves, D., & J. Hansen. 1983. "The Author's Chair." *Language Arts* 60 (2): 176–83.

Haghighat, C. 2003. *Language Profiles. Vols. I–III.* Toronto, ON: World Languages Publishing House. Available at http://alphaplus.ca.

Halliday, M. A. K., & R. Hassan. 1989. *Language, Context, and Text: Aspects of Language in a Social-Semiotic Perspective* Second Edition. Oxford: Oxford University Press.

Hamayan, E. 1994. "Language Development of Low-Literacy Students." In *Educating Second Language Children: The Whole Child, the Whole Curriculum, the Whole Community,* edited by F. Genesee, 278–300. Cambridge, MA: Cambridge University Press.

Hamayan, E., B. Marler, C. Sanchez-Lopez, & J. Damico. 2007. *Special Education Considerations for English Language Learners: Delivering a Continuum of Services.* Philadelphia: Caslon.

Haynes, J. 2007. "Collaborative Teaching: Are Two Teachers Better Than One?" *Essential Teacher* 4 (3): 6–7. Alexandria, VA: Teachers of English to Speakers of Other Languages.

Herrell, A. L., & M. Jordan. 2008. *50 Strategies for Teaching English Language Learners,* Third Edition. Upper Saddle River, NJ: Pearson/Merrill/Prentice Hall.

Hiebert, E. H. 2005. "In Pursuit of an Effective, Efficient Vocabulary Curriculum for Elementary Students." In *Teaching and Learning Vocabulary: Bridging Research to Practice,* edited by E. H. Hiebert and M. Kamil, 243–63. Mahwah, NJ: Lawrence Erlbaum.

Hiebert, E. H., Z. A. Brown, C. Taitague, C. W. Fisher, & M. A. Adler. 2004. "Texts and English Language Learners: Scaffolding Entrée to Reading." In *Multicultural and Multilingual Literacy and Language Practices,* edited by F. B. Boyd, C. H. Brock, and M. S. Rozendal, 32–53. New York: The Guilford Press.

Inger, M. 1993. "Teacher Collaboration in Secondary Schools." *CenterFocus Number 2.* Berkeley, CA: National Center for Research in Vocational Education, University of California at Berkeley.

Iwai, Y. 2007. "Developing ESL/EFL Learners' Reading Comprehension of Expository Texts." *The Internet TESL Journal* XIII (7). Available at http://iteslj.org/Techniques/Iwai-ExpositoryTexts.html.

Jacobs, H. H. 1997. *Mapping the Big Picture: Integrating Curriculum and Assessment K–12.* Alexandria, VA: Association for Supervision and Curriculum Development.

Jalongo, M. R., D. Dragich, N. K. Conrad, & A. Zhang. 2002. "Using Wordless Picture Books to Support Emergent Literacy." *Early Childhood Education Journal* 29 (3): 167–77.

Jimenez, R. T. 2000. "Literacy and the Identity Development of Latina/o Students." *American Educational Research Journal* 37 (4): 971–1000.

Jimenez, R., G. E. Garcia, & P. D. Pearson. 1996. "The Reading Strategies of Bilingual Latina/o Students Who Are Successful English Readers. Opportunities and Obstacles." *Reading Research Quarterly* 31: 90–112.

Kagan, S. 1995. "We Can Talk: Cooperative Learning in the Elementary ESL Classrooms." *Elementary Education Newsletter* 17 (2): 3–4.

Kessler, C., & M. E. Quinn. 1987. "ESL and Science Learning." In *ESL Through Content-Area Instruction: Mathematics, Science, Social Studies. Language in Education. Theory & Practice,* edited by J. Crandall, 54–87. Englewood Cliffs, NJ: Prentice Hall Regents. [A publication of the ERIC Clearinghouse on Languages and Linguistics, Center for Applied Linguistics.]

Kopriva, R. J., J. E. Emick, C. P. Hipolito-Delgado, & C. A. Cameron. 2007. "Do Proper Accommodation Assignments Make a Difference? Examining the Difference of Improved Decision Making on Scores for English Language Learners." *Educational Measurement: Issues and Practice,* 11–20.

Langer, J. A., L. Barolome, & O. Vasquez. 1990. "Meaning Construction in School Literacy Tasks: A Study of Bilingual Students." *American Educational Research Journal* 27 (3): 427–71.

Law, B., & M. Eckes. 2007. *Assessment and ESL: An Alternative Approach.* Second Edition. Winnipeg, Manitoba, Canada: Portage & Main Press.

Leeman, J. 2003. "Recasts and Second Language Development." *Studies in Second Language Acquisition* 25: 37–63.

Lesaux, N. K., & E. Geva. 2006. "Synthesis: Development of Literacy in Language-Minority Students." In *Developing Literacy in Second Language Learners: Report of the National Literacy Panel on Language-Minority Children and Youth,* edited by D. August and T. Shanahan, 53–74. Mahwah, NJ: Lawrence Erlbaum.

Lesaux, N. K., with K. Koda, L. S. Siegel, & T. Shanahan. 2006. "Development of Literacy." In *Developing Literacy in Second Language Learners: Report of the National Literacy Panel on Language-Minority Children and Youth,* edited by D. August and T. Shanahan, 75–122. Mahwah, NJ: Lawrence Erlbaum.

Lightbown, P. M., & N. Spada. 2006. *How Languages Are Learned,* Third Edition. Oxford, England: Oxford University Press.

Lindholm-Leary, K., & G. Borsato. 2006. "Academic Achievement." In *Educating English Language Learners: A Synthesis of Research Evidence,* edited by F. Genesee, K. Lindholm-Leary, W. Saunders, & D. Christian, 176–222. New York: Cambridge University Press.

Lindholm-Leary, K. J., & R. Molina. 2000. "Two-Way Bilingual Education: The Power of Two Languages in Promoting Educational Success." In *The Power of Two Languages 2000: Effective Dual-Language Use Across the Curriculum,* edited by J. V. Tinajero & R. A. DeVillar, 163–74. New York: McGraw Hill.

Lively, T., D. August, M. Carlo, & C. Snow. 2003. *Vocabulary Improvement Program for English Language Learners and Their Classmates.* Baltimore, MD: Paul H. Brookes Publishing Co.

Lyster, R. 2004. "Differential Effects of Prompts and Recasts in Form-Focused Instruction." *Studies in Second Language Acquisition* 26: 399–432.

McDonough, K., & A. Mackey. 2006. "Responses to Recasts: Repetitions, Primed Production, and Linguistic Development." *Language Learning* 56: 693–720.

McKeown, M. G., I. L. Beck, R. Omanson, & M. T. Pople. 1985. "Some Effects of the Nature and Frequency of Vocabulary Instruction on the Knowledge and Use of Words." *Reading and Research Quarterly* 20: 522–35.

Mackey, A. 2006. "Feedback, Noticing and Instructed Second Language Learning." *Applied Linguistics* 27: 405–30.

Martin, J. R. 1992. *English Text.* Philadelphia: John Benjamins.

Melber, L. M. 2007. *Informal Learning and Field Trips: Engaging Students in Standards-Based Experiences Across the K–5 Curriculum.* Thousand Oaks, CA: Corwin Press.

Mohan, B. A. 1986. *Langauge and Content.* Reading, MA: Addison-Wesley.

Moll, L. C. 2000. "Inspired by Vygotsky: Ethnographic Experiments in Education." In *Vygotskian Perspectives on Literacy Research,* edited by C. D. Lee & P. Smagorisky, 256–68. Cambridge: Cambridge University Press.

Moll, L. C., C. Amanti, D. Neff, & N. González. 1992. "Funds of Knowledge for Teaching: Using a Qualitative Approach to Connect Homes and Classrooms." *Theory into Practice* 31 (2): 132–41.

Montecel, M. R., & J. D. Cortez. 2002. "Successful Bilingual Education Programs: Development and the Dissemination of Criteria to Identify Promising and Exemplary Practices in Bilingual Education at the National Level." *Bilingual Research Journal* 26.

Mora, J. K. 2007. *Metalinguistic Transfer in Spanish/ English Biliteracy: Theory, Research & Practice.* Presentation at the Two-Way CABE Conference, Burlingame, CA, July 10–13, 2007. Available at http://coe.sdsu.edu/people/jmora/MoraModules/

Nagy, W., G. Garcia, A. Durgunoglu, & B. Hancin-Bhatt. 1993. "Spanish-English Bilingual Students' Use of Cognates in English Reading." *Journal of Reading Behavior* 25 (3): 241–59.

Nakanishi, A. 1990. *Writing Systems of the World: Alphabets, Syllabaries, Pictograms.* Tokyo and Rutland, VT: Charles E. Tuttle.

Nathenson-Mejia, S. 1989. "Writing in a Second Language: Negotiating Meaning Through Invented Spelling." *Language Arts* 66 (5): 516–26.

National Clearinghouse for English Language Acquisition and Language Instruction Educational Programs. 2006. *NCELA FAQ: How has the English language learner (ELL) population changed in recent years?* Available at http://www.ncela.gwu.edu/expert/faq/08leps.html.

National Reading Panel. 2000. *Teaching Children to Read: An Evidence-Based Assessment of the Scientific Research Literature on Reading and Its Implications for Reading Instruction (Executive Summary).* Washington, DC: National Institute of Child Health and Human Development (NICHD) and U.S. Department of Education.

O'Malley, J. M., & L. Valdez Pierce. 1996. *Authentic Assessment for English Language Learners: Practical Approaches for Teachers.* Reading, MA: Addison-Wesley.

Ontario Ministry of Education. 2005. *Many Roots, Many Voices: Supporting ELLs in Every Classroom: A Practical Guide for Ontario Educators.* Toronto: Ontario Ministry of Education. Available at www.edu.gov.on.ca.

Peyton, J. K., & J. Staton. 1993. *Dialogue Journals in the Multilingual Classroom: Building Language Fluency and Writing Skills Through Written Interaction.* Norwood, NJ: Ablex.

Quaglio, P., & C. Lauth. 2006. *Corpus-Based Research and ESOL Materials Development.* 36th Annual NYS TESOL Conference, Saratoga Springs City Center, November 17–18, 2006.

Ragan, A. 2005. "Teaching the Academic Language of Textbooks: A Preliminary Framework for Performing a Textual Analysis." *The ELL Outlook.* Available at www.coursecrafters.com/ELL-Outlook/2005/nov_dec/ELLOutlookITIArticle1.htm.

Railsback, J. 2002. *Project-Based Instruction: Creating Excitement for Learning.* Portland, OR: Northwest Regional Education Laboratory.

Reese, L., H. Garnier, R. Gallimore, & C. Goldenberg. 2000. "Longitudinal Analysis of the Antecedents of Emergent Spanish Literacy and Middle-School English Reading Achievement of Spanish-Speaking Students." *American Educational Research Journal* 37: 633–62.

Reyes, P., J. D. Scribner, & A. Paredes Scribner, eds. 1999. *Lessons from High-Performing Hispanic Schools: Creating Learning Communities.* New York: Teachers College Press.

Riches, C., & F. Genesee. 2006. "Crosslinguistic and Crossmodal Issues." In *Educating English Language Learners: A Synthesis of Research Evidence,* edited by F. Genesee, K. Lindholm-Leary, W. Saunders, & D. Christian, 64–108. New York: Cambridge University Press.

Routman, R. 2000. *Conversations: Strategies for Teaching, Learning and Evaluating.* Portsmouth, NH: Heinemann.

Samway, K. D. 2006. *When English Language Learners Write: Connecting Research to Practice, K–8.* Portsmouth, NH: Heinemann.

Schleppegrell, M. J. 2001. "Linguistic Features of the Language of Schooling." *Linguistics and Education* 12 (4): 431–59.

Schon, D. A. 1983. *The Reflective Oractitioner.* New York: Basic Books.

Shanahan, T., & I. L. Beck. 2006. "Effective Literacy Teaching for English-Language Learners." In *Developing Literacy in Second Language Learners: Report of the National Literacy Panel on Language-Minority Children and Youth,* edited by D. August and T. Shanahan, 415–88. Mahwah, NJ: Lawrence Erlbaum.

Sharp, A. 2004. "Strategies and Predilections in Reading Expository Text: The Importance of Text Patterns." *RELC Journal* 35 (3): 329–49.

Short, D. J. 1993. "Integrating Language and Culture in Middle School American History Classes." *Center for Research on Education, Diversity & Excellence. NCRCDSLL Educational Practice Reports.* Paper EPR08. Available at http://www.ncela.gwu.edu/pubs/ncrcdsll/epr8.htm.

———. 2007. *Designing Comprehensive Course Assessment Prompts, Portfolio Tasks and Exhibition Projects for ELLs.* Paper presented at Secondary ESL Institute, Pawtucket, RI, December 2007.

Short, D., & S. Fitzsimmons. 2007. *Double the Work: Challenges and Solutions to Acquiring Language and Academic Literacy for English Language Learners.* Washington, DC: Alliance for Excellent Education. (A Report to the Carnegie Corporation of New York.)

Showers, B., and D. Hansen. 2006. *Professional Development Model Training Manual* (Part 4: Tools and Resources). Available at www.iowa.gov/educate/content/view/232/637/. State of Iowa, Department of Education.

Slavin, R. E., & M. Calderón. 2001. *Effective Programs for Latino Students.* Mahwah, NJ: Lawrence Erlbaum.

Snow, M. A., & D. Brinton, eds. 1997. *The Content-Based Classroom: Perspectives on Integrating Language and Content.* White Plains, NY: Longman.

Solórzano, R. W. 2008. "High Stakes Testing: Issues, Implications and Remedies for English Language Learners." *Review of Educational Research* 78 (2): 260–329.

Spandel, V. 2008. *Creating Young Writers: Using the Six Traits to Enrich Writing Process in Primary Classrooms,* Second Edition. Boston: Allyn & Bacon.

———. 2009. *Creating Writers Through 6-Trait Writing Assessment and Instruction,* Fifth Edition. New York: Allyn & Bacon.

State of Wisconsin. 2004. *English Language Proficiency Standards for English Language Learners in Kindergarten Through Grade 12.* Madison: WIDA Consortium.

Swan, M., & B. Smith, eds. 2001. *Learner English: A Teacher's Guide to Interference and Other Problems,* Second Edition. Cambridge: Cambridge Handbooks for Language Teachers.

Teachers of English to Speakers of Other Languages. 2006. *PreK–12 English Language Proficiency Standards [an augmentation of the WIDA English Language Proficiency Standards].* Alexandria, VA: TESOL.

Templet, C. D., S. Squires, & S. Stickler. 1999. "Finding Time for Collaboration." *NAESP "Here's How"* 17 (4): 1–4. [National Association of Elementary School Principals].

Tovani, C. 2004. *Do I Really Have to Teach Reading? Content Comprehension, Grades 6–12.* Portland, ME: Stenhouse.

U.S. Department of Education. 2007. *National Assessment of Educational Progress, Writing Assessments.* Washington, DC: U.S. Department of Education.

Vygotsky, L. S. 1978. *Mind in Society: The Development of Higher Psychological Processes.* Cambridge, MA: Harvard University Press.

Walker, B. J. 1992. *Supporting Struggling Readers.* Scarborough, Ontario: Pippin.

Wein, C. A. 1995. *Developmentally Appropriate Practice in "Real Life."* New York: Teachers College Press.

Weinstein, G., ed. 1999. *Learners' Lives as Curriculum: Six Journeys to Immigrant Literacy.* McHenry, IL: Delta Systems.

———. 2004. "Moving Toward Learner-Centered Teaching with Accountability." *CATESOL Journal* 16 (1): 97–110.

Wolf, M. K., J. L. Herman, L. F. Bachman, A. L. Bailey, & N. Griffin. 2008. *CRESST REPORT 37: Recommendations for Assessing English Language Learners: English Language Proficiency Measures and Accommodation Uses.* UCLA: National Center for Research on Evaluation, Standards and Student Testing. Available at www.cse.ucla.edu/products/reports/R737.pdf.

Zehler, A. 1994. *Working with English Language Learners: Strategies for Elementary and Middle School Teachers.* Washington, DC: NCBE Program Information Guide Series, Number 19.

INDEX

Abedi, J., 210
Abuela (Dorros), 69, 76
academic language, 116–55. *See also* content area instruction and discourse
building, 127–28
challenges of, 125–26
communicative functions of, 126, 128
defined, 117–18
grammatical structure of, 126, 127
mathematics, 127, 131
registers, 126
science, 127, 129
social language *vs.*, 117, 125–26
social studies, 127, 130
technical terms, 125
text structure, 125
vocabulary, 125
academic literacy, 124–26
accommodations for ELLs, 136
classroom assessment, 207–8, 220
standardized tests, 193–94
acting out stories, 57–58
active voice, 128
Ada, Alma Flor, 58, 59, 60, 77, 95, 99, 115
Adler, M. A., 48
administrators
classroom assessment and, 190, 192
competence in ELL language and culture, 92
cultural learning and, 11
standardized tests and, 190, 192
advanced supported proficiency level, 23–25
reading/writing strategies for, 176–81
affective filter, 145
Alpers, J., 115
alphabet books, 58
alphabetic home languages, 85–86
Amigo Means Friend (Everett), 69, 76
Ammar, A., 172
Anaya, R., 95, 115
Asher, James J., 48, 58
Assessing Asian Language Performance: Guidelines for Evaluating Limited English-Proficient Students (Cheng), 221
Assessing English Language Learners (Valdez-Pierce), 222
assessment, 185–222. *See also* classroom assessment; standardized testing
benchmark books for, 91–92
classroom-based, 11–12, 33, 190–94
of content knowledge, 189
of content versus language, 189, 192–93
cultural factors and, 196–97
defined, 186–90
formal, 11, 21, 91, 186
high-stakes, 190–93
home language, 90–93, 189, 211
importance of, 185
individualized instruction and, 186, 190, 192
informal, 21, 91, 186
literacy assessment, in home language, 90–93, 218–19
of language proficiency, 21, 40–41
motivation and, 214
of reading comprehension, 189
of special needs, 31, 32
standardized, 190–94
Assessment & Accountability in Language Education Programs: A Guide for Administrators and Teachers (Gottlieb and Nguyen), 221
Assessment and ESL: A Handbook for K–12 Teachers (Law and Eckes), 222
assessment conferences, 213
assessment tools, 219
dialogue journals, 203–4, 219
learning logs, 205, 219
observation, 207–8, 219
reading and writing conferences, 212–13, 219
running records, 202–3, 219
atypical backgrounds, students with, 35
August, D., 11, 15, 18, 22, 39, 41, 50, 83, 84, 85, 87, 113, 125, 186
Authentic Assessment for English Language Learners: Practical Approaches for Teachers (O'Malley and Valdez Pierce), 222
Author's Chair, 168, 181
Avalos, M. A., 61
Ayers, W., 4

background characteristics of learners
prior/previous schooling, 26–27, 38
extent of literacy skills in home language or home language skills, 22–26
literacy in English, 21–22
literacy environment in the home and community, 28–29
background knowledge
acquisition of, by ELLs, 14
for content learning, 128, 132
cultural, 61, 68
experiential, 117
home language and, 17
importance of, 42
preteaching, 49
reading and, 13
second-language and, 15, 17
for texts, 51, 134
Baker, C., 105
Balancing Reading and Language Learning: A Resource for Teaching English Language Learners, K–5 (Cappellini), 77–78
Barolome, L., 85
Bassano, S., 167
Batalova, Jeanne, 34
Bear, D. R., 23, 51, 53, 55, 63, 77, 85, 86, 92, 113
Beck, I. L., 52, 137
Beeman, K., 113, 157
beginning intermediate proficiency level, 23–25
reading/writing connection activities, 161–76
beginning proficiency level, 23–25
grade level and, 187–88
reading/writing connection activities, 161–76
benchmark books, 91–92
Berman, P., 186
"best practices," 3
Bialystock, E., 86
Biber, D., 127
bilingual books
activities with, 102–4
community and, 108
metalinguistic awareness and, 102–3
quality of, 223
selecting, 99–100
sources of, 115
for storytelling, 101
student-produced, 100–101, 105
types of, 99–101
using, 47, 98–104, 228
value of, 98
Bilingual Books: Promoting Literacy and Biliteracy in the Second-Language and Mainstream Classroom (Ernst-Slavit & Mulhern), 99
Bilingual Children's Books in English and Spanish, An Annotated Bibliography, 1942–2001 (Cruger Dale), 99
bilingual-education programs, 93
bilingual teachers, 2, 111
professional books for, 113–14
biliteracy, 80–115
community and, 108–10
as goal, 33
identity and, 104–7
levels of, 88–93
social aspects of, 104–10
teachers and, 110–12
value of, 37, 81, 82, 83
Blumenfeld, S., 53
books. *See also* bilingual books; multicultural books; student-made books; texts; text sets; wordless picture books
alphabet, 58
benchmark, 91–92
for classroom assessment, 199, 209–10
home language, 99–100
letter name, 58
modeling, using, 168–69, 228
monolingual, quality of, 223
multicultural, 69–71
rewriting activities, 181
student-made, 165
theme, 66

translated, quality of, 223
word, 207
bootstrapping
activities, 96–98
defined, 9, 84
guidelines for, 225
on home language, 9, 10, 18, 84–85, 96–98
Borsato, G., 9, 11, 82
bottom-up processes, 15, 41
defined, 14
themes or topics and, 42
Bouchard, M., 142
Boyd-Batstone, P., 23, 77
Boyle, O. F., 79
Brantley, D. K., 221
Bread Is For Eating (Gershator and Gershator), 153, 154
Brice-Heath, Shirley, 105
Brigance Assessment of Basic Skills–Revised, Spanish Edition, 91, 92
Brinton, D., 121
Brown, Z. A., 48
Bruner, Jerome, 2
Bunting, Eve, 69, 76

Cairns, Julia, 49, 74
Calderón, M., 11, 186
Calkins, L., 57
Cameron, C. A., 193
Campoy, F. I., 95, 99, 115
Cappellini, M., 59, 60, 78
captions
for digital photographs, 55–56, 164
guidelines for, 227
for illustrations, 67
Carle, Eric, 47, 53, 75, 155, 164, 169, 182
Carlisle, J. F., 136
Carlo, M., 87
Carrasquillo, A., 114
Carrell, P. L., 62
Carter, J., 183
Center for Research on Educational Diversity and Excellence, 15
Chamberlin, Mary, 49, 74
Chamberlin, Richard, 49, 74
Chamot, A. U., 21, 118, 121, 144
Chandra, Deborah, 74
Chavarría Cháriez, B., 115
Chavez, C., 61
Cheng, L. L., 221
Chinese language, 85, 86, 92, 217–19
Chinese-speaking English language learners
classroom assessment of, 217–19
choice
in pictures for storytelling, 128
word, in traits model, 177–78
choral reading, 63
Chorus of Cultures, A (Ada), 58
Christian, D., 15, 82
Christison, M. A., 167
Clandinin, D., 4
classroom assessment, 33. *See also* assessment
accommodations for ELLs, 193–94, 208, 220
assessment tools, 219
books for, 199, 201, 213
case studies, 197–215
conferences: reading, writing, 201, 203, 212–13, 219
of Chinese-speaking ELLs, 217–19
cycle of, 187–88
dialogue journals for, 203
effectiveness of, 186–87, 197
of ELLs, 194–215
English-as-a-second-language teachers and, 212
individualized, 186, 190, 192, 197
instructional plans and, 188, 192, 207, 214–15
learning logs and journals for, 203
observation, 208–9
purposes of, 195, 198, 206–7
running records, 201–3
shared responsibility for, 217
of Spanish-speaking ELLs, 197–217
standardized testing and, 190–94
teacher skills for, 206
triangle, 192
of underlying language competencies, 201, 203
value of, 11–12, 192, 220
wordless picture books for, 200, 201
Classroom-Based Assessment activities, 66–67
Classroom-Based Evaluation in Second Language Education (Genesee and Upshur), 222
classroom libraries
evaluating, 72
student-made books in, 166
tips for multicultural books, 107
Closing the Achievement Gap (Freeman, Freeman, and Mercuri), 69
Cloud, N., 196
cloze assessment, 91, 92*n*
Coelho, E., 113, 127
cognates
defined, 87
helping students recognize, 127
notebooks, 137–38
recognition of, 88
strategies for learning, 137–38
Word Walls, 137–38
Coiro, J., 62, 141
collaborative instruction planning, 122, 123–24
collaborative learning, 145
collaborative texts, 63, 225
collaborative text writing procedure (Flores), 63–64, 67
Colorin Colorado for Families: What You Can Do at Home (website), 114
communication
academic language, 126, 128
language for, 210–11
school/home notebooks, 159–60
writing as, 178, 214
community connections
bilingual books, 102, 103–4
biliteracy, 108–10
intergenerational, 170–71
literacy activities, 59–60
literacy block schedule, 65
literacy events, 109
literacy practices, 39–40
reading/writing activities, 163–64
community explorations, 148
complex noun phrases, 46
compound words, 61
Comrie, B., 113
connections. *See also* reading/writing connection activities
with community, 65, 102, 103–4, 163–64, 170–71
with home, 59–60, 65, 72, 170–71
with home language, 9, 72
intergenerational, 170–71
reading/writing, 170–71
Conrad, N. K., 47
content area instruction. *See also* academic language
academic language and, 117–18, 127–28
background knowledge and, 128, 132
cultural background and, 117
dictionaries for, 138
field trips, 148–49
frontloading for, 132
guided reading and writing in, 142–43
home language and, 126
linguistic demands of, 117, 126–28
literacy development in, 116–55, 117
objectives for, 134
preparing students for, with bilingual books, 102, 103
project-based learning, 147
reading specialists and, 118
reading/writing connections and, 157
specialized language in, 125
student experience and, 117
teacher collaboration for, 122–24
teaching strategies, 133–47
text sets for, 134
content knowledge
assessment of, 189
in traits model, 177–78
conventional writing, 57
conventions, in traits model, 177–78
Cook, L., 122
cookbooks, student-written, 169
cooperative learning, 144–46
cooperative reading, 227
Cooter, R., 91
co-planning, 123–24
copying writing, 158–61
Corallo, C., 11
Cortex, J. D., 11, 191
Crago, Martha, 31, 32, 195–96
Crandall, J. A., 121
cross-cultural literature, 69–71. *See also* multicultural books
cross-linguistic transfer
defined, 84
promoting metalinguistic awareness with, 86–88
value of, 84–86
cross modal interactions, 38
Cruger Dale, D., 99

cuaderno de communicacion, El, 160
cueing systems, 63, 87
Cuevas, G. J., 127
Culham, R., 177, 182
cultural background knowledge. *See also* background knowledge
  content area instruction and, 117
  text analysis, 61
cultural identities
  confirming, 105
  home language literacy and, 83
cultural learning
  language learning and, 10–11, 36
  by mainstream students, 11
  in second- and native-language literacy, 17
cultural values, 30–31, 70
culturally responsive instruction, 36
cultures
  contexts, 68–69
  language development and, 195–97
  learning about, 34
  literature about, 58–59
  norms, 30
  referents, 61
  valuing, 83
Cummins, J., 9, 21, 31, 100, 105, 169
Curious George Makes Pancakes (Rey), 70, 71, 74
curriculum design, 71–73
curriculum mapping, 122
cursive writing, 53
cycle of classroom assessment, 187–88

Dale, T. C., 127
Damico, J., 11, 31, 32, 33, 221
Dargan, P. B., 78
Day, F. A., 107
Day It Snowed Tortillas, The (Hayes), 115
decoding skills
  defined, 41
  in emergent literacy instruction, 49–50
  in home language and English, 214
  identifying and reinforcing, 52
  sight words, 53–54
  teaching, for texts, 51
  text analysis, 61
deep (opaque) orthography, 50–51
definition(s), student-developed, 138, 140
DePaola, Tomie, 45, 75
dialogue journals, 171–76, 219
  for classroom assessment, 204
  engagement and, 174
  errors in, 172, 173–74
  example, 172, 174
  goals of, 172
  guidelines for, 173, 203–4, 225
  sensitive topics in, 174–75
  steps in, 175
  teacher responses to, 172, 173
  value of, 172
  variations on, 175–76
Dickson, S. V., 141
dictionaries, 138
Differentiated Early Literacy for English Language Learners: Practical Strategies (Boyd-Batstone), 77
digital photographs
  storytelling with, 164–65
  writing captions for, 55–56, 164
directionality of print, 85
discourse, content area, 117, 126–28
discourse style, 126
Dorros, A., 69, 76
Dragich, D., 47
Drake, S. M., 122
dramatic performance activities, 67
drawings
  as early writing, 166–68
  "Draw a Story: Stepping from Pictures into Writing" (NCTE), 167
  "drawing out," 167
  labeling objects in, 168
  vocabulary development and, 138
dual-language learning, 110
  programs, 93
  special needs and, 31–32
DuFour, R., 4
Durgunoglu, A., 88

Eaker, R., 4
early literacy practices, 40
Eating The Alphabet (Ehlert), 58, 76
Echevarria, J., 121
echo reading, 62
Eckes, M., 23, 222
Edelsky, C., 57, 156
editing guidelines, 225
education
  in other countries, 26–27
  prior schooling, of ELLs, 26–27
Education at a Glance, 93
Ehlert, L., 58, 76
Ellis, R., 172
email
  for dialogue journals, 173
  writing, 40
emergent literacy instruction, 43–60
  background knowledge and, 49
  books on, 77–79
  daily schedules, 64–65
  decoding/encoding skills, 49–50
  direct, 43, 48–50, 52
  guided reading methods, 61–63
  guided writing methods, 63–64
  literacy block schedule sample, 64–65
  meaningful activities, 43, 44–45, 50
  modeling reading and writing, 48–50
  opportunities for reading and writing, 54–57
  oral language and, 43, 45–48, 49, 51, 52
  phonological awareness, 49–50
  principles of, 43–44
  promoting literacy growth, 60–67
  reading strategies, 50
  reading/writing connections, 54, 158–61
  in a second language, 35–73
  sound-symbol correspondence, 50–54
  student observation, 62
  templates, 49–50
  unit plans, 66–67
  wordless picture books and, 46–47
  word play in, 50
  writing development stages, 57
Emick, J. E., 193
encoding skills
  defined, 41
  in emergent literacy instruction, 49–50
  teaching, for texts, 51
engagement
  activities for, 45
  dialogue journals and, 174
  encouraging own, 144
  home language use and, 126, 140
  in pantomime, 57–58
  parents and, 59, 101
  second-language literacy development and, 15–16
  writing activities, 55–57
English as a second language
  academic language and, 117–18
  classroom assessment and, 216
  describing proficiency in, 21–22
  ELL students and, 7–8
  goals of, 117
  mainstream teachers as, 118–20
  roles of, 120–21
English-Español Reading Inventory for the Classroom (Flynt/Cooter), 91
English language
  bootstrapping into, 9, 10, 18
  cross-linguistic transfer, 84–86
  deep (opaque) orthography in, 50–51
  home language connections to, 9, 38–39, 63, 88, 93–104
  home language similarities, 29–31, 84, 97–98
  importance of, 36–37
  introducing literacy, 36–37
  letter-sound correspondences in, 52
  orthography, 96–97
  real-life usage, 48
  sequencing events in, 13
English Language Proficiency (ELP) standards, 120
English-only instruction, 82, 211
environmental print, 158
Erlam, R., 172
Ernst-Slavit, G., 99, 102
errors
  in dialogue journals, 172, 173–74
  first- and second language literacy skills and, 18
  home language transfer and, 29–30, 97
  learning from, 12
  reading and writing strategies for, 98
  in writing, 214
  spelling, 63
Evaluación del Sesarrollo de Lectura (EDL), 91
event sequencing, 13
Everett, L., 69, 76
Expected Home Language Literacy (EHL) ELLs
  bilingual books for, 102–3
  bootstrapping on home language by, 96
  defined, 89–90
  evaluating literacy in, 90
  student-written bilingual books for, 100
experts, students as, 148

explicit instruction, 52, 142
expository texts, 19
eye contact, 196

fables, 58
families. *See also* parents
  home language literacy, 94–95
  language experience activities, 95
  literacy environment, 108–9
  literacy practices, 39–40
  reading/writing activities, 163–64
Fearnley, Jan, 70, 75
feedback, 196
field trips, 148–49
figurative language, 61
finger plays, 95
First Tortilla, The (Anaya), 95, 115
Fisher, C. W., 48
Fitzsimmons, S., 125
Flaitz, J., 34, 93
Fletcher, R., 182
Flores, B. M., 62, 63
fluency, 41
Flynt, E., 91
folktales, 58
foundational skills, 42, 46
Frayer, D. A., 139–40
Frayer method, 139–40
Frederick, W. D., 140
Freeman, D. E., 4, 69, 78, 114, 133
Freeman, Y. S., 69, 78, 114, 133
Friend, M., 122
From Cotton to Blue Jeans (Thomas), 155
From Spanish to English: Reading and Writing for English Language Learners, Kindergarten through Third Grade (August and Vockley), 113
frontloading
  for content area instruction, 132
  guidelines for, 226
  for pancakes theme, 46
  for producer/consumer unit, 138–40
  vocabulary and concepts, 136–41
  with wordless picture books, 46
Fry, E. B., 53
functional literacy, 2, 41
"funds of knowledge," 28, 117, 132

Galindo, R., 171
Gallimore, R., 39, 82, 105
Garcia, G. E., 39, 86, 88
Garnier, H., 39, 82
Genesee, F., 15, 22, 29, 30, 31, 32, 39, 44, 50, 52, 82, 84, 125, 142, 180, 196, 222
genres
  learner's stage of development and, 19
  variety in, 57–58
Gershator, D., 150, 154
Gershator, P., 150, 154
Geva, E., 39, 42, 82
Gibbs, W., 81
GIST technique, 143
Going Home (Bunting), 69, 76
Goldenberg, C., 39, 82, 105, 137
Gorrell, J., 138
Gottlieb, M., 88, 91, 221
grade level, ELLs and, 27–28, 187–88, 218
Graham, A., 138
Graham, C., 48
grammatical structure
  in academic language, 125–26, 127
  directly teaching, 127
  repetitive sentence patterns, 48
graphic organizers
  guidelines for, 226
  online copies, 142
  for signal words, 141
  for text structure, 141
  uses of, 140–43
graphophonic cueing systems, 63
Graves, D., 57, 136, 168
Graves, M., 87, 137
Great Pancake Escape, The (Many), 70, 74
Griego, M. C., 95, 115
guided reading, 61–63
  activities, 67
  benefits of, 215
  guidelines for, 226
  mini lessons, 62
  shared portion of, 62
  steps in, 61
  strategies for content area instruction, 142–44
  text analysis in, 61–62
guided writing, 63–64
  in content area instruction, 128, 143–45
  guidelines for, 226

Hadaway, N. L., 76, 78
Haghighat, C., 34, 113
Hakuta, K., 11, 186
Halliday, M. A. K., 126
Hamayan, E., 11, 31, 32, 33, 159, 172, 196, 221
Hancin-Bhatt, B., 88
hands-on activities, 147
handwriting, 41, 44, 53
  cursive writing, 53
  guidelines for, 226
  practice with, 52
Handwriting Without Tears, 53
Hansen, D., 122
Hansen, J., 168
Hassam, R., 126
Hayes, J., 115
Haynes, J., 122
Helman, L., 77
Herrell, A. L., 144
Hiebert, E. H., 48, 51, 52, 53, 54, 85
high-frequency words, 61
  difficulties reading, 54
  practice writing, 53
  as sight words, 53–54
high-stakes testing. *See* standardized testing
Hipolito-Delgado, C. P., 193
Hohston, F., 77
home connections
  intergenerational, 171–72
  with literacy at school, 59–60, 72
  literacy block schedule, 65
  literacy development, 12
home culture
  learning about, 30–31
  similarity to mainstream culture, 29–31
  volunteer participation and, 30
home language
  assessment and, 189, 210–11
  benchmark books, 91–92
  books, 99–100
  bootstrapping on, 9, 10, 18, 84–85, 96–98
  characteristics, 38
  community and, 108–9
  connections with, 9, 72
  in content area instruction, 126
  cross-linguistic transfer, 84–86
  curriculum development and, 72
  engagement and, 126, 140
  English language development and, 17–18, 81, 93–104, 111–12
  errors and, 29–30, 63, 97
  field trips and community explorations, 148
  homework in, 111
  investigating student skills in, 38–39
  literacy evaluation in, 90–93, 214–15
  literacy instruction and, 86
  literacy skills and, 18
  literacy skills in, 22–26, 36, 83–84
  in mainstream classrooms, 120
  mainstream language similarities, 29–31, 84, 97–98
  NHL students and, 94–95
  orthography, 96–97
  parental preferences about, 37
  predictable texts in, 36
  print-related experience in, 12
  reading to children in, 59
  reading wordless picture books in, 47
  role of, 82–88
  sharing knowledge of, with mainstream students, 88
  spelling systems, 85–86
  teacher learning about, 30, 31, 96, 110–11
  texts, student-created, 100–101
  transferring knowledge from, 29, 38–39, 63
  websites about, 114–15
  writing assessment and, 214
Howlett, Bud, 69, 76
How-To Guide for Teaching English Language Learners in the Primary Classroom (Dargan), 78
humor, 173

ideas, in traits model, 177–78
identity, biliteracy and, 104–7
identity texts, 169–70
  bilingual, 100–101
  defined, 100, 105
  social aspects of, 105–6
idioms, 45
If You Give a Pig a Pancake (Numeroff), 45, 61, 74
I Hate English (Levine), 69, 76
I'm New Here (Howlett), 69, 76
independent reading activities, 67
individual/group response, 196
individualized instruction, 186, 190, 192, 197
informal assessments
  of home language literacy, 91
  value of, 186

informational texts, 134
Inger, M., 122
initial literacy, 43–60
Instructional Assessment of English Language Learners in the K–8 Classroom (Brantley), 221
instructional collaboration, 121–24
planning, 123–24
as professional development, 122
scheduling, 123
strategies for, 133–46
support for, 124
technology and, 123
text selection for, 134
instructional plans, classroom assessment and, 188, 192, 207–8, 214–15
intake assessment, 198
interactive lessons, 44
interactive writing, 171–76
intermediate advanced proficiency level, 23–25
reading/writing strategies for, 176–81
inventive spelling, 63
Invernizzi, M., 77
Iwai, Y., 140

Jacobs, H. H., 122
Jalongo, M. R., 47
Jazz Chant (Graham), 48
jazz chants, 48
Jigsaw Reading, 146, 227
Jilbert, K., 57
Jimenez, R., 39, 86, 171
Jordan, M., 143

Kagan, S, 144
Katz, L. A., 136
Kessler, C., 127
Kimmel, Eric A., 75, 115, 168–69, 182
Kimmelman, Leslie, 45, 75
Klausmeier, H. J., 140
Koda, K., 60
Kopriva, R. J., 193
Korean language, 92
Kress, J. E., 53
Kucan, L., 137

labels
for classroom objects, 158–59
guidelines, 227
Langer, J. A., 85
Language Assessment Scales Reading/Writing, 92
language experience activities (LEAs), 66, 161–63
guidelines for, 227
language experience texts, 161–63
language learning
cultural learning and, 10–11, 36
familiarity and, 10
giving students opportunities for, 119
promoting in mainstream classrooms, 119–20
Language Profiles (Haghighat), 34
language
for communication, 214, 216
detectives, 119
learning about, 34
resources, books on, 113
simplification, for standardized tests, 193–94
Latina and Latino Voices in Literature for Children and Teenagers: Lives and Works (Updated and Expanded) (Day), 107
Latino Children's Literature in the Classroom (Ada), 99
Lauth, C., 127
Law, B., 23, 222
learners
diversity of, 117
resourceful, 9, 29, 63
viewing self as reader and writer, 161
learning
extra time for, 8–9
familiarity and, 10
from "mistakes," 12
learning disabilities, 31–32
Learning Disabilities Quarterly, 33
Learning in Two Languages: Questions Parents Ask (website), 114
learning logs and journals, 176, 215
for classroom assessment, 203
for content area instruction, 146
guidelines for, 205, 227
learning stages
second-language literacy development and, 18–19
stage-appropriate instruction, 40–43
learning strategies, 142–43
Lesaux, N. K., 42, 60
Lessac, F., 69, 76
lesson planning
classroom assessment and, 188
framework for, 134
template, 135
letter formation, 41, 44. *See also* handwriting
presentation order, 53
letter name books, 58
letters
introducing, 53
recognizing, 41
letter-sound correspondences, 42, 44, 50–54, 51
cross-linguistic transfer, 84
in Spanish and English, 52
spelling inconsistencies and, 52
steps in teaching, 52
Levine, E., 69, 76
libraries, 72, 109. *See also* classroom libraries; school libraries
life experiences, writing about, 69
Lightbown, P. M., 118
limited formal schooling (LFS), 27
notes for teachers, 94, 162
working with students with, 69
Lindholm-Leary, K. J., 9, 11, 15, 82
linguistic goals, 127
lists, 40, 227
literacy block schedules
planning, 64–67
sample, for emergent literacy students, 64–65
literacy development
bottom-up processes, 14, 15, 41
in content area classes, 116–55
cross-linguistic transfer, 84–86
cultural factors, 195–97
curriculum development and, 72
early literacy practices, 40
elements of, 207
in ELLs, 14–19
general, 10–14
at home, 12, 94–95
home language literacy and, 83–84, 88
as integrated process, 13–14
models of, 22–26
prior literacy experience and, 29
proficiency levels, 23–25
promoting growth from one stage to the next, 60
research on, 12–14
stages of, 72, 73
student attitudes and, 204–7
top-down processes, 14, 15, 41
literacy instruction
home language and, 86
oral language and, 45–48
stage-appropriate, 40–43
literacy practices, 39, 59
literacy skills
cognitive abilities and, 2
of communities, 39–40
components, component skills, 41–43
of families, 39–40
learner's stage of development and, 18–19
prior, 22–26
strategies, 225–29
targeting, 124
Literature-based Instruction with English Language Learners K–12 (Hadaway, Vardell, and Young), 78
Lively, T., 87
Loewen, S., 172
logographic home languages, 85–86
low-incidence languages, 37
Lyster, R., 172

Mackey, A., 172
Magda's Tortilla (Chavarría Cháriez), 115
Magical Encounter, A: Latino Children's Literature in the Classroom (Ada), 77
mainstream classrooms, language and literacy development in, 118–21
mainstream culture, similarity of home culture to, 29–31
mainstream students
cultural learning by, 11
home literacy development, 12
homogeneity of, 20
sharing knowledge of home language with, 88
mainstream teachers. *See also* teachers
ELL students and, 7–8
home languages of students and, 88
interconnecting instruction of, 121–24
as language models, 119
as second-language teachers, 118–20

Mamá Goose: A Latino Nursery Treasure (Ada and Campoy), 95, 99, 115
Mama Panya's Pancakes: A Village Tale From Kenya (Chamberlin, Chamberlin, & Cairns), 49, 68, 70, 74, 97
mandated testing. *See* standardized testing
Many, Paul, 70, 74
Marler, B., 11, 31, 32, 33, 221
Martin, J. R., 126
mathematics, 127, 131
Matthew, S., 113
McDonald, D. H., 11
McDonough, K., 172
McKeown, M. G., 137
meaning
  getting from texts, 41
  negotiation of, 145
meaningful activities
  for emergent literacy instruction, 43, 44–45, 50
  messages to parents, mimic writing, 159
  for reading/writing connections, 157
  for teaching sight words, 50–54
  for teaching sound-symbol correspondence, 50–54
Melber, L. M., 148
Mercuri, S., 69, 133
metalinguistic awareness
  cross-linguistic transfer and, 86–88
  promoting, with bilingual books, 102–3
mimic writing, 158–61
  advantages of, 161
  guidelines, 160, 227
  for school/home communication, 159–60
  topics for, 160
minilessons
  in guided reading, 62
  home language, 97
mini shared reading (Flores), 62–63, 227
Miss Mabel's Table (Chandra and Grover), 74
mistakes. *See* errors
"Mix a Pancake" (Rossetti), 58
Mohan, B. A., 121
Molin, R., 11
Moll, L. C., 105, 132
Montecel, M. R., 11, 191
Mora, J. K., 87
motivation
  bilingual books and, 98
  cooperative learning and, 145
  writing assessment and, 214, 216
Mr. Wolf's Pancakes (Fearnley), 70, 71, 75
Mulhern, M., 99, 102
multicultural books
  community and, 108
  cross-cultural learning through, 70
  cross-cultural literature, 69–71
  guidelines for using, 228
  publishers, 6, 58–59, 76
  selecting, 107
  sources of, 68–69, 76, 106
  tips for classroom and school libraries, 107
Multiliteracy Project, 100, 105
multimedia resources, 76
multisensory teaching methods, 127
music, 48
My Community unit, 206
My Little Island (Lessac), 69, 76

Nagy, W., 88
Nakanishi, A., 113
Nathenson-Mejia, S., 113
National Clearinghouse for English Language Acquisition and Language Instruction Educational Programs, 34
  website, 6
National Literacy Panel on Minority-Language Children and Youth, 15, 41, 42, 52, 60
National Reading Panel, 41
NCTE, 167
newsletters, in multiple languages, 104
Nguyen, D., 221
No Home Language Literacy (NHL) ELLs
  bilingual books and, 99
  bootstrapping on home language by, 96
  defined, 89
  promoting home language literacy in, 94–95
notebooks
  cognates, 137–38
  for dialogue journals, 173
  for school/home communications, 159–60
Notes for Administrators
  classroom assessment, 190, 192
  competence in ELL language and culture, 92
  cultural learning, 11
  special education, 33
  standardized tests, 190, 192
Notes for Bilingual Teachers
  student storytelling, 165
Notes for School Psychologists, 169
Notes for Upper Grade Teachers
  selecting motivating materials, 54
note-taking, 143
Numeroff, Laura, 45, 74
nursery rhymes, 40

observation, 215
  for classroom assessment, 208–9
  guidelines for, 208–9
older students, motivating, 54, 69
O'Malley, J. M., 21, 23, 92*n*, 118, 121, 222
Omanson, R., 137
online groups, 123
Ontario Ministry of Education, 118, 125
opaque (deep) orthography, 50–51
oral language
  curriculum development and, 72
  development activities, 66–67
  emergent literacy instruction and, 43, 45–48, 49, 51, 52
  language experience activities, 161–63
  literacy block schedule, 64
  proficiency in, 124
  reading/writing connections and, 158
  student-made books and, 168
  text analysis and, 61
oral reading, 145
oral storytelling. *See* storytelling
organization, in traits model, 177–78
paired reading, 227
Pair Share, 145
Pancakes, Pancakes! (Carle), 47–48, 53, 54, 75, 155, 164, 169, 182
Pancakes for Breakfast (DePaola), 45, 68, 70, 71, 75, 168
pantomime, 57–58
Paradis, J., 31, 32
paraprofessionals, 111
Paredes Scribner, A., 11
parents. *See also* families
  communicating with, 159–60
  engagement and, 59, 101
  guidance to, 37
  inviting participation by, 72
  literacy of, 59
  messages to, mimic writing for, 159
  objections to instruction in home language, 37
  questions asked about multilingual children, 6
  regard for learning by, 59
  skills of, 29
  wordless picture books and, 47
parent-teacher nights, 95
Partner Reads, 145
Partner Writes, 145, 212
patterned language, 168
Paulsen, Gary, 95, 99, 115, 155
Pearson, P. D., 39, 86
peer support, 145
  Author's Chair, 168
  encouraging, 120
Peregoy, S. F., 79
Perfect Pancakes If You Please (Wise), 50, 75
personal stories
  opportunities for, 169–70
  sensitive topics, 169, 170, 174–75
Peyton, J. K., 172
phonemic awareness, 41
phonetic patterns, 61
phonetic writing, 57
phonological awareness, 41, 42, 43, 49–50, 87
  in second- and native-language literacy, 17
photographs
  personal *vs.* outside, 164
  storytelling based on, 164–65, 229
  writing captions for, 55–56, 165
picture books. *See also* wordless picture books
  repetitive text structure in, 47–48
  value of, 58
  wordless, 47–48
picture-sequencing activities, 48
picture walks, 62
¡Pío Peep!: Tradition Spanish Nursery Rhymes (Ada, Campoy, and Schertle), 99, 115
Plasencia, A., 61
PM Colección, 91
poetry, 40, 57, 95
Polinsky, M., 113
Pople, M. T., 137
Portalupi, J., 182
predictable texts, 36

prefixes, 87
Pre-K–12 English Language Proficiency Standards (Teachers of English to Speakers of Other Languages), 120
pre-phonetic writing, 57
prereading
  for content area instruction, 143
  unfamiliar cultural contexts and, 68
presentation, in traits model, 178
pretend writing, 57
prewriting
  for content area instruction, 143
  defined, 57
  unfamiliar cultural contexts and, 68
print-related experience
  in home language, 12
  in second- and native-language literacy, 17
prior schooling, 26–27, 38
professional development, instructional collaboration as, 122
project-based learning, 147
prompts, for dialogue journals, 174
public libraries, 109

Quaglio, P., 127
question-and-answer format, 197
questioning self, 143
Quinn, M. E., 127

Ragan, A., 125
Railsbach, J., 145
Rascón, J., 61
read-alouds
  activities, 67
  literacy block schedule, 64
  theme books, 66
  wordless picture books for, 47
reading
  background knowledge and, 13
  cultural context of, 68–69
  evaluation of, 90–92
  as fundamental life skill, 2
  home language and, 83–84, 94
  importance of, 1
  literacy block schedule, 65
  modeling, 48–50
  opportunities for, 44, 54–57
  setting purpose for, 143
  skill acquisition, 5
  skills involved in, 13
  strategies, 50
  student attitudes toward, 203–4
  writing development and, 23, 33, 55, 156, 166
Reading, Writing, and Learning in ESL: A Resource Book for K–12 Teachers (Peregoy and Boyle), 79
reading comprehension
  assessment of, 189
  learner's stage of development and, 19
  prioritizing, 41
  questioning self, 143
  scaffolding for, 140–46
  strategies, 43, 62
  text analysis, 62
reading conferences, 203, 219
  guidelines for, 212–13
reading logs, 176
reading specialists, 8, 118
reading/writing connection activities, 54, 66–67, 155–83
  advanced supported proficiency level, 176–81
  Author's Chair, 168, 181
  beginning intermediate proficiency level, 161–76
  beginning literacy stage, 54, 158–61
  beginning proficiency level, 161–76
  community-oriented approach, 163–64
  criteria for activities, 157
  dialogue journals, 171–76
  drawing as writing, 166–68
  family-oriented approach, 163–64
  interactive writing, 171–76
  intergenerational connections, 170–71
  intermediate advanced proficiency level, 176–81
  language experience activities, 161–63
  learning how other people write, 178–80
  looking at other people's writing, 178–80
  mimic writing, 158–61
  opportunities for, 156–57
  personal experience writing, 169–70
  storytelling based on photographs and videos, 164–65
  student-made books, 168–69
  students as authors, 166–71
  traits model, 177–78, 182
  using text to master aspects of writing, 180–81
recipes, 67
Reese, L., 4–5, 39, 82
refugee populations, 3
registers, 126
Reiser, L., 115
repetition, 47–48, 128
repetitive text structure
  in picture books, 47–48
  value of, 58
resourcefulness, of ELLs, 9, 29, 63
response to intervention (RTI) programs, 33
retelling, 46, 66, 228
rewriting books, 181
Rey, H. A., 74
Rey, Margaret, 70, 75
Reyes, P., 11
rhymes, 95
  bilingual books, 99
  value of, 57
Riches, C., 22, 29, 30, 39, 44, 50, 52, 82, 125, 142, 180
Rossetti, Christina G., 58
Routman, R., 166
rubrics for writing, 177, 178
Runaway Latkes, The (Kimmelman), 45, 70, 75
Runaway Tortilla, The (Kimmel), 45, 70, 75, 115, 168–69, 182
running records, 215
  benchmark texts for, 91
  for classroom assessment, 201–3, 210
  guidelines for, 202–3, 222
Saint James, Synthia, 70, 75
Samway, K. D., 39, 57, 79
Sanchez-Lopez, C., 11, 31, 32, 33, 221
Saunders, W., 15, 82
scaffolding, 136, 140–46
  cooperative learning, 144–45
  cultural, 11
  graphic organizers, 140–42
  guided reading and writing, 142–44
  learning logs and journals, 146
  promoting literacy growth with, 60
  writing scripts, frames and templates, 144
Schertle, A., 99, 115
Schleppegrell, M. J., 125, 126
Schon, D. A., 4
school libraries
  evaluating, 72
  student-made books in, 166
  tips for multicultural books, 107
Scribner, J. D., 11
scripts, for student writing, 168, 169
second-language literacy development, 14–19, 15–16
  background knowledge and, 15
  complexity of, 15–16
  emergent literacy, 35–73
  engagement and, 15–16
  first-language literacy and, 17
  home language literacy and, 18
  literacy development framework, 24–25
  native-language literacy development and, 17–18
  stages of, 18–19, 35
Segan, P., 114
selective attention, 143
self-assessment, 102, 103
self-editing, 177–78, 225
self-monitoring, 143
semantic cueing systems, 63, 87
semantic feature analysis charts, 138–39
semantic webbing, 138–39
sentence fluency, in traits model, 177–78
sequel books, 169
sequence starters, 169
sequencing events, 13
shallow orthography, 51
Shanahan, T., 15, 18, 22, 39, 41, 50, 52, 60, 125
shared reading, 62–63
Sharp, A., 140
sheltered instruction, 136
Short, D., 121, 125, 127, 193
short stories, 214
Showers, B., 122
Siegel, L. S., 60
sight words, 61
  decoding, 53–54
  teaching in meaningful ways, 50–54
signal words, 142
  graphic organizers for, 141
  guidelines for, 226
6+1 *Traits* model, 177–78
6+1 Trait Writing Assessment in Spanish, 92
Slavin, R. E., 11, 186
Smith, B., 113
Snow, C., 87
Snow, M. A., 121

social language
academic language *vs.*, 117, 125–26
ELL proficiency in, 21, 22
social studies
academic language, 127, 130
classroom assessment, 208
Solorzano, R. W., 190, 191
Some Home Language Literacy (SHL) ELLs
bilingual books for, 102–3
bootstrapping on home language by, 96
defined, 89
evaluating literacy in, 90
student-written bilingual books for, 100
sound-symbol correspondence. *See* letter-sound correspondences
Spada, N., 118, 172
Spandel, V., 177, 182
Spanish Early Intervention Levels, 91
Spanish language
letter-sound correspondences in, 50, 52, 85–86
possession in, 97
professional books for bilingual teachers, 113–14
shallow orthography in, 51
spelling, 92
Spanish-speaking authors, 106
Special Education Considerations for English Language Learners: Delivering a Continuum of Services (Hamayan, Marler, Sanchez-Lopez, and Damico), 221
special education programs, 31, 33
special needs assessment, 31–32
spelling
assessment of, 92
consistency in sound relationships, 51–52
deep (opaque) orthography, 50–51
errors, 63, 85
home languages systems, 85–86
inconsistency of, 50–52
inventive, 63, 85
patterns, 51–52, 85
shallow orthography, 51
Squires, S., 122
standards, state and national, 121
standardized testing, 186
accommodations for ELLs, 193–94
classroom assessment *vs.*, 190–94
district- and state-mandated, 11
ELLs and, 190–94
inadequacy of, 21
instruction planning and, 190
language simplification, 193–94
limitations of, 190–94, 211
scores of ELLs on, 9
uses of, 192–93
Staton, J., 172
Stickler, S., 122
story structure, 213
storytelling, 40
based on photographs and videos, 164–65, 229
choice in, 132
guidelines for, 228
illustrating events, 67
from pictures, 132
retelling, 46, 66, 228
with wordless picture books, 46, 59
wordless picture books for, 101, 104
strategies, reading and writing, 142–143
student achievement data, 11, 186
student-centered classrooms, 26
student-developed definitions, 138
student-made books, 165, 166–71
cookbooks, 169
formats for, 167–68
quality of, 166
text features in, 166
students as authors, 165, 166–71
student-teacher interaction, 44–45
suffixes, 87
summarizing, 143
Sunday (Saint James), 70, 75
Swan, M., 113
synonyms, 61, 181
syntactic cueing systems, 63

Taitague, C., 48
Talking Books Children's Authors Talk About the Craft, Creativity and Process of Writing (Carter), 183
teacher collaboration. *See also* instructional collaboration
for integrated instruction, 121–24
scheduling, 123
teachers
assessment skills of, 204
bilingual, 111
biliteracy and, 81, 110–12
learning about students' home languages, 30, 31, 96, 110–11
planning roles and responsibilities of, 123
responses to dialogue journals by, 172, 173
responsibility for teaching literacy to ELLs, 2
Teachers of English to Speakers of Other Languages (TESOL), 21, 120
Teaching of Reading in Spanish to the Bilingual Student (Carrasquillo and Segan), 114
Teaching Reading and Writing in Spanish in the Bilingual Classroom (Freeman and Freeman), 114
Teaching Reading in Multicultural Classrooms (Freeman and Freeman), 78
Teaching Spanish Literacy in the United States: A Practitioner's Handbook (Beeman and Urow), 113
technical language, 125
technology, 123
templates, 49–50, 144
Templet, C. D., 122
Templeton, S., 77
tense, 125
tests, testing
and decision-making, 186, 192
district- and state-mandated, 196
high-stakes, 190–193
informal, 186
text analysis, 61–62
text features
mathematics, 131
noticing, 63
science, 129
social studies, 130
in student-made books, 166
texts. *See also* books
background knowledge for, 51, 134
for evaluating home language literacy, 90
informational, 134
variety in, 57–59
text sets
curriculum development and, 72
defined, 54
selecting, for content area instruction, 134
using, 54–55
value of, 55
text structure
in academic language, 125
graphic organizers for, 141
text analysis, 62
theme books, 66
themes
bottom-up and top-down processes and, 42
curriculum development and, 72
playing with, 66
T is for Tortilla: A Southwestern Alphabet Book (Alpers), 115
top-down processes, 15, 41
defined, 14
foundational skills and, 42
themes or topics and, 42
Torilleria, Le (Paulsen), 99
Tortilla Factory, The (Paulsen), 155
Tortillas and Lullabies (Reiser), 115
Tortillitas para Mamá and Other Nursery Rhymes (Griego), 95, 115
Tortillería, La (Paulsen), 95, 115
Total Physical Response (TPR) activities, 47–48, 58
Tovani, C., 55
traditional nursery rhymes, 40
traditional sayings, 40
traditional stories, 101
traits model of writing, 177–78, 182
transfer. *See also* bootstrapping
definition, 29–30
from home language, 29, 217
transition words (also in Charts 4.1, 4.2, and 4.3), 128
translated books, 107
translation, 98, 120
Tricou,C., 138

underlying language competencies, 13, 181–82, 201, 203
Understanding Your Refugee and Immigrant Students: An Educational, Cultural, and Linguistic Guide (Flaitz), 34, 93
units of instruction
Pancakes theme, 65–67
producer/consumer unit, 133–40, 149, 150–53
teacher collaboration on, 122
Upshur, J. A., 222
Urow, C., 113, 157

Valdez Pierce, L., 23, 92*n*, 222
Vardell, S. M., 76, 78
Vasquez. L., 85
vocabulary, 41. *See also* words
  in academic language, 125
  cognates, 137–38
  frontloading, 136–40
  learning, 137
  research-based programs, 87–88
  selecting words to teach, 136–37
  semantic/word webs, 138
  student-developed definitions, 138
  text analysis, 61
  wordless picture books and, 46
  in writing, 209
Vocabulary Improvement Program (Lively, August, Carlo, and Snow), 87
Vockley, M., 113
Vogt, M. E., 121
voice, in traits model, 177–78, 214
Vygotsky, L. S., 105

wait time, 196
Walker, B. J., 23
Wein, C. A., 4
Weinstein, G., 170
Wheeler, A., 182
When English Language Learners Write: Connecting Research to Practice, K–8 (Samway), 79
WID, 23
Wise, William, 50, 75
Wolf, M. K., 193
Wood Ray, K., 182
word books, 210
word boxes, 128, 168
word cards, 140
word choice, in traits model, 177–78
word consciousness, 87
word-formation skills, 46
wordless picture books, 6
  for classroom assessment, 200, 201
  parents and, 47, 59
  resources for, 76
  for storytelling, 101, 104
  student-made, 168
  uses of, 46–47
  value of, 46–47
word-level skills, 42
word maps, 140
word play, 50
word roots, 87, 141
word structure, 61
words. *See also* vocabulary
  compound, 61
  concept, 137
  high-frequency, 53–54, 61
  learning, 87, 136
  mimic writing, 158–61
  with multiple meanings, 61
  recognizing, 41
  selecting to teach, 137
  sight, 50–54, 61
  signal, 141, 142, 226
Words Their Way with English Learners (Bear, Helman, Templeton, Invernizzi, and Hohston), 77, 92
word structure, 61
word study, 140, 180, 229
Word Walls, 168, 209
  cognates, 137–38
word webs, 138–39
word work, 65, 66
writers, viewing selves as, 161
writing. *See also* guided writing; reading/writing connection activities
  analysis of, 214–15
  assessment of, 214–16
  as communication, 177, 214–16
  complexity of, 156
  development stages, 57
  displaying student writing, 56–57
  drawings as, 166–68
  editing, 177–78
  effective, 178–80
  engagement in, 55–57
  errors in, 210
  evaluation of, 91–92
  home language literacy and, 83–84, 214
  importance of, 1
  literacy block schedule, 65
  modeling by teachers, 48–50
  modeling with published books, 168–69
  nature of, activities, 179–80
  obtaining student samples, 92
  opportunities for, 44, 54–57, 166
  by others, learning about, 178–80, 225
  personal stories, 69, 169
  reading development and, 23, 33, 55, 156
  rubrics, 177, 178
  scaffolding for, 140–46
  setting purpose for, 143
  short stories, 213
  student attitudes toward, 203–4
  traits model, 177–78, 182
  unique stories of ELLs, 170
  using text to master aspects of, 180–81
  variety in formats, 57–58
  vocabulary in, 214
  voice in, 214
writing conferences, 201, 203, 216,
  guidelines for, 212–13
writing frames/templates, 144, 229
writing paper, 56, 167
writing scripts, 144
  guidelines for, 229
writing strategies
  for common mistakes, 98
  cross-linguistic transfer, 84
  ELL use of, 63
  for texts, 51
writing workshop, 65

Young, T. A., 76, 78

Zehler, A., 148
Zhang, A., 47